SUPERMAN

REG. U. S. PAT. OFF.

FROM THE THIRTIES
TO THE SEVENTIES

INTRODUCTION BY

E. NELSON BRIDWELL,

EDITOR, NATIONAL PERIODICAL COMICS

BONANZA BOOKS • NEW YORK

SPECIAL COVER CREDITS

EXCEPT AS OTHERWISE NOTED ALL COVERS ARE FROM SUPERMAN COMICS.

PAGE	ISSUE	NOTICE	PAGE	ISSUE	NOTICE
18-19	12	© 1941 Superman, Inc. Renewed 1969 by National Periodical Publications, Inc.		161	© 1963 National Periodical Publications, Inc.
	14	© 1941 Superman, Inc. Renewed 1969 by National Periodical Publications, Inc.		169	© 1964 National Periodical Publications, Inc.
	17	© 1942 Superman, Inc. Renewed 1970 by National Periodical Publications, Inc.		171	© 1964 National Periodical Publications, Inc.
	18	© 1942 Superman, Inc. Renewed 1970 by National Periodical Publications, Inc.		173	© 1964 National Periodical Publications, Inc.
	23	© 1943 Superman, Inc. Renewed 1970 by National Periodical Publications, Inc.		174	© 1964 National Periodical Publications, Inc.
	26	© 1943 Superman, Inc. Renewed 1971 by National Periodical Publications, Inc.		175	© 1964 National Periodical Publications, Inc.
	29	© 1944 Superman, Inc.		181	© 1965 National Periodical Publications, Inc.
	32	© 1944 Superman, Inc.		191	© 1966 National Periodical Publications, Inc.
	38	© 1945 Superman, Inc.		198	© 1967 National Periodical Publications, Inc.
	41	© 1946 Superman, Inc.		204	© 1967 National Periodical Publications, Inc.
	45	© 1946 Superman, Inc.		209	© 1968 National Periodical Publications, Inc.
	50	© 1947 National Comics Publications, Inc.	330-331	223	© 1969 National Periodical Publications, Inc.
208-209	60	© 1949 National Comics Publications, Inc.		224	© 1969 National Periodical Publications, Inc.
	66	© 1950 National Comics Publications, Inc.		225	© 1970 National Periodical Publications, Inc.
	71	© 1951 National Comics Publications, Inc.		226	© 1970 National Periodical Publications, Inc.
	76	© 1952 National Comics Publications, Inc.		236	© 1971 National Periodical Publications, Inc.
	87	© 1953 National Comics Publications, Inc.		237	© 1971 National Periodical Publications, Inc.
	101	© 1955 National Comics Publications, Inc.	Action 388		© 1970 National Periodical Publications, Inc.
	103	© 1955 National Comics Publications, Inc.	Action 389		© 1970 National Periodical Publications, Inc.
	110	© 1956 National Comics Publications, Inc.	Action 393		© 1970 National Periodical Publications, Inc.
	123	© 1958 Superman, Inc.	Action 394		© 1970 National Periodical Publications, Inc.
	131	© 1959 Superman, Inc.	Action 399		© 1971 National Periodical Publications, Inc.
	132	© 1959 Superman, Inc.	Action 400		© 1971 National Periodical Publications, Inc.
	133	© 1959 Superman, Inc.			
266-267	160	© 1963 National Periodical Publications, Inc.			

TABLE OF CONTENTS

COLOR SECTIONS

DEDICATION

SUPERMAN! You, who have created not only pleasure for
millions of readers, but a whole new industry for thousands
of my fellow editors, artists, writers, letterers, colorists,
engravers, printers, etc.—we thank you publicly!

Carmine Infantino

Publisher, *Superman Comics*

INTRODUCTION

by
E. Nelson Bridwell

The year was 1938—the ninth year of the Great Depression. It was a time when people were looking for something. Perhaps what they really wanted was a hero.

It was the year Hitler took over Austria; the year Chamberlain met that dictator at Munich and came away predicting "peace in our time." It was a day of tensions, domestic and foreign, when people sought heroes in many places.

In movie theaters, for instance: there was Johnny Weissmuller, mangling the language as the latest screen Tarzan; there were movie serials, with the inevitable cliff-hangers week after week; there were Westerns, which now talked, and, thanks to Gene Autry and his fellow cowboy crooners, sang.

There were the pulps. They bristled with musclemen and masked avengers—*Doc Savage, The Shadow, The Spider,* and all the other adventure aces.

There were comics, too—newspaper strips initially. As the name suggests, they had originally been strictly humor, but the thirties brought the birth of the adventure strip—*Dick Tracy, Buck Rogers, Flash Gordon, Terry and the Pirates, The Phantom*—the list went on and on.

The comic strips had spawned two "children." One, the *Big Little Books,* translated stories from the strips into text, with individual panels, minus dialogue, on facing pages. But it was the other medium that was to prosper most. Comic Books! (Perhaps I should say Comic Magazines, the term preferred by many in the industry.)

Initially, comic books were largely devoted to reprinting newspaper strips. 7

Then, gradually, original material crept in. At last, in 1937, one company dared to put out a comic magazine devoted entirely to new material—*Detective Comics*. So great was its success that today that company, National Periodicals, is popularly known by the intials of that magazine: DC!

A year later they were ready to try another title, and they searched for a lead feature that was different. It was M. C. Gaines, father of William Gaines (the publisher of *Mad*), who suggested a strip that had been rejected by practically every outfit in the business. Still, it was different, and the creators were even then turning out *Slam Bradley* and *Spy* for *Detective*. The publishers decided to take a chance. With *Superman*!

The initial *Superman* story in *Action Comics #1* (June, 1938) had been prepared as a newspaper strip. When it was arranged for this publication, the beginning was omitted—several pages of it—and the story began in the middle of the action. (The full story was published a year later, in *Superman #1*, and is reprinted in this volume.) *Superman* was featured on the cover, but the publishers failed to put him on the covers of many early *Action* issues until sales figures showed that it was Superman who was selling the magazine!

And sell it did! A hero had been found! Countless young people who bought that first issue had an imperishable memory. I am not one of them. I was 6½ years old, and the only comic book I read regularly was *Mickey Mouse Magazine*.

Before I pursue Superman's career further, let me consider his origins. True, his various sides all had antecedents, but the combination into one character was unique.

First, he was superpowerful. One of the oldest stories known is the *Gilgamesh Epic*, of ancient Babylonia. Gilgamesh, part mortal, part god, was the first recorded superhero. Ancient Greece knew countless superbeings, including Herakles (Hercules to the Romans). Indeed, the crew of Jason's ship, the *Argo*, was made up largely of heroes who had most of Superman's powers among them. Besides Herakles, there were Zetes and Kalais, who flew; Euphemos, the super-speedster; Kaineus, who was invulnerable; and even Lynkeus, who, we are told, could see things underground—yes, X-ray vision, in ancient Greece! Possibly, Superman's prototype is to be found in Philip Wylie's *Gladiator*, published in 1930.

Then there was Superman's secret identity. One could go far back and find tales of kings traveling in disguise (even gods had this habit), as well as outlaws such as Robin Hood, who donned disguises. But it was with *The Scarlet Pimpernel* that the modern concept of the hero with a secret identity originated.

Most early double identities were maintained by wealthy young aristocrats, like Sir Percy Blakeney (The Pimpernel) and Don Diego Vega (Zorro). Superman assumed the active role of newspaper reporter Clark Kent.

And Superman had a costume—skintight, with cape and shorts over his leotard. Whence this outfit? From Flash Gordon? From the Phantom? There were resemblances. But where did all these heroes get their costume styles? I have read many suggestions, the psychoanalytic ones being the most amusing—and the most absurd. Yet the answer was always obvious to me.

Perhaps the analysts had never been to a circus, clearly another source of Superman's origin. That's where you'll find people in skintight outfits, somewhat similar to the Man of Steel's, performing amazing acrobatic acts.

(Years later, when Superman's cousin Supergirl debuted in *Action*, she wore an outfit that included a miniskirt and boots, long before these became stylish. They looked suspiciously like the costume of a skater.)

Wherever the various elements did come from, the fact remains that they were clearly a winning combination. Nineteen thirty-nine saw not only the birth of the Man of Steel's own magazine, but his debut in a daily newspaper strip. Then, in 1940, the air waves rang with the now legendary words:

> *Faster than a speeding bullet!*
> *More powerful than a locomotive!*
> *Able to leap tall buildings at a single bound!*
> *Look! Up in the sky!*
> *It's a bird!*
> *It's a plane!*
> *IT'S SUPERMAN!*

Yes, it's Superman, strange visitor from another planet, who came to Earth with powers and abilities far beyond those of mortal men; Superman, who can change the course of mighty rivers, bend steel in his bare hands; and who, disguised as Clark Kent, mild-mannered reporter for a great metro-

politan newspaper, fights a never-ending battle for truth, justice and the American way!

How well I recall those days—listening to the serialized *Adventures of Superman* for fifteen minutes every weekday on the Mutual Network! I have since been informed that, in order to distinguish Clark Kent from his power-packed alter ego, it was intended to have the two sides of the same character played by different actors. However, a fellow named Clayton Collyer proved equal to the necessary voice change, doing Clark as a tenor and Superman as a baritone. He would demonstrate this change to a radio audience dependent on sound by dropping his voice in mid-sentence:

"This is a job

for

SUPERMAN!"

Clayton did other shows, such as *Quick as a Flash*, and later, on TV, *To Tell the Truth,* as Bud Collyer. On the former show there was a dramatization of a detective story using one of the many radio sleuths of the day. With Superman himself emceeing the show, is it any wonder that the Man of Steel was one of them?

By this time, Superman had begun to change. As the origin story from Superman #1 will show, he was conceived as a man who could hurdle skyscrapers and leap an eighth of a mile. Not long afterward, though, he was literally flying. His strength increased, and so did his speed. (Once only able to outrace a train, he finally, in the late forties, began traveling through time by exceeding the speed of light!) And his invulnerability grew, too. "Nothing less than a bursting shell could penetrate his skin" in 1939; by World War II he was shrugging off bursting shells as if they were bursting soap bubbles. At the end of the war, he was surviving atomic blasts!

The early Superman had no supersenses. In one story, suspecting a man he was looking for was in a certain house, he had to crash through the roof to find out. The invention of X-ray vision proved to be a great roof-saver.

Superman, like most heroes of the late thirties, had an extra reason for his double identity. He was wanted by the police for taking the law into his own hands! Before long, however, he stopped dealing out justice himself and began working *with* the police. After all, the world's greatest hero couldn't be an outlaw!

It was partly the multiplicity of media in which Superman appeared that dictated the changes in him. Between 1941 and 1943, Paramount brought out 17 animated cartoons of the Man of Tomorrow, with Bud Collyer doing the voice in the first half-dozen. And in 1942, Superman made his first appearance between hard covers, in a novel by George Lowther, titled (what else?) *Superman.*

The account of Superman's origin depicted him simply as a more advanced Earthling, but this was soon altered and later explained that Earth's size and gravity were far less than that of Krypton; hence, on Earth, a Kryptonian could do fantastic things. He could lift great weights and make incredible leaps. Even after Superman began to fly, this same explanation was given.

It might be added that his parents were originally called Jor-L and Lora. It was in the Lowther novel that their names were changed to Jor-el and Lara, while the future Superman was called Kal-el. Since El is now considered a surname, the names are written as Jor-El and Kal-El.

Lowther also renamed Superman's foster parents; Mrs. Kent had been originally named Mary, and I have heard that somewhere her husband was given the name John. But in the novel, they became Eben and Sarah Kent, and now it was explained that Clark was Sarah's maiden name. (This explanation was kept even after the names were changed again.)

Meanwhile, the name of Clark Kent's paper had been changed. In one issue of *Action Comics,* Clark and Lois Lane were sent by the *Daily Star* to cover a war in Europe. They were still there in the following issue, but now their paper was the *Daily Planet.* Soon after, editor George Taylor mysteriously changed his name to Perry White.

In that war story just mentioned, Superman first encountered a redheaded villain named Luthor. You'll find this early Luthor in the story on page 51; and note that his bald henchman in this one resembles the later Luthor whom you'll find on page 77.

Jimmy, the office boy, who got his first byline in the Archer tale on page 90, was seized upon by the radio writers who wanted a boy their audience could identify with. So Jimmy Olsen, cub reporter, became a feature of the show. Jimmy was featured a good deal more there and in the newspaper strip than in comic books in the early forties.

With the end of the war, things were changing for Superman. Already, in the January–February issue of *More Fun Comics*, a new feature had been born: *Superboy*, the adventures of the youthful Superman. Now his foster parents were rechristened Jonathan and Martha Kent. As the world moved to peacetime, the superheroes—countless imitations of Superman, most of them with circus costumes and secret identities—began to hit the skids. *More Fun*, once devoted to adventure heroes, switched to all-humor, and Superboy moved to *Adventure Comics*.

Curiously, when a tenth anniversary tale of Superman's origin (see page 198) was written, no account was taken of his Superboy career. He was shown beginning his crime-fighting as an adult, in flat contradiction to the stories then appearing in *Adventure*.

Many other elements had been added, including such foes as the Ultra-Humanoid, the Prankster, the Toyman, the Puzzler—and Mr. Mxyztplk, the imp from the fifth dimension. This character first showed up in the newspaper strip, in love with the most beautiful girl in the world. When she rejected him, Mxyztplk caused an accident that scarred her for life. Only one of her countless admirers still loved her after that—and this fellow slugged Mxyztplk and knocked him back into his own world. A different first meeting occured in the *Superman* magazine, as you'll find on page 174.

The radio show came up with many innovations, too, including the first actual team-up of Superman and Batman. And that which most changed the Superman legend—Kryptonite.

Kryptonite was the substance of Superman's home planet, changed by that world's explosion (now explained as an atomic blast) into a radioactive element that could weaken only a native of Krypton. Later, Kryptonite became not only dangerous, but positively deadly—and the only thing (aside from magic) that could kill Superman.

But before Kryptonite reached the comics, Superman had returned to the silver screen in two Columbia serials—*Superman* (1948) and *Atom Man vs. Superman* (1950). This latter picture utilized a villain who had previously lived and died on radio; a man with liquid Kryptonite in his veins. Later came a feature film, *Superman and the Mole Men* (1952).

12 By this time, Kryptonite had hit the magazines—initially it was colored red,

but later it was permanently established as being green. In the story that introduced it, Superman went back into the past to view Krypton while in a sort of ghostly form, and learned for the first time that he was an alien from another world. Before long, with Kryptonite appearing in Superboy's tales, his knowledge of his background was traced back to his early years on Earth.

The decline of the superheroes had continued. Batman had continued to hold his own, with appearances in three magazines. But Superman alone actually expanded his scope during this period. In 1949, Superboy had his own magazine; in 1954, Jimmy Olsen became the star of his own comic book.

Radio was giving way to television, and a new series of *The Adventures of Superman* began on TV, starring George Reeves. Once again, his Superboy career was ignored, and the names of Eben and Sarah Kent were resurrected from the novel. Some scripts gave Superman odd powers which he had nowhere else, including the ability to walk through walls and to split into two Supermen!

For a time in the early fifties, Clark Kent and Lois Lane were married—but only in the newspaper strip. Eventually, the writer ran out of ideas and resorted to an out as old, at least, as *Alice in Wonderland*—he decided the whole marriage had been a dream!

How things changed in the fifties! Superboy got a girl friend who, like Lois Lane, attempted unsuccessfully to penetrate his disguise. This young lady was Lana Lang, who eventually entered the Superman scene as a rival to Lois, after the latter had won her own magazine in 1958. One of her early appearances may be found on page 234. This was one of three "first meetings" between the girls—but it was actually the very first.

Lois began to suspect that Clark was Superman in the tale reprinted on page 125. It may surprise the sophisticate of today that she took so long to penetrate the simple disguise of a pair of glasses. But in a day when people accepted the chestnut about the girl whose attractions are never noticed until she is seen without her glasses, Superman's camouflage worked.

Red Kryptonite came along in the late fifties. It was unlike Green K in that its effects were temporary, but they were also weird and unpredictable. The substance might change Superman into a giant, a madman, or a huge serpent. There was also Brainiac, a space-villain who had shrunk a city of Krypton— **13**

Kandor—and placed it in a bottle before the planet exploded. The bottle-city now resides—with all its millions of microscopic inhabitants—in Superman's Fortress of Solitude.

Which suggests another change. In the forties Superman had had a secret hideaway in the mountains near Metropolis. But in the fifties Luthor discovered the Man of Steel's "Secret Workshop." Thereafter, Superman was shown with a secret Fortress of Solitude in the arctic.

Luthor had changed too. Now he had been Superboy's foe when both were in their teens, and he had a first name, Lex. Mr. Mxyztplk had changed his name, too. Somehow, he had become Mxyzptlk.

Superboy had a superdog now—Krypto. But the greatest addition to the Superman Family in the fifties was Superman's cousin Supergirl. She had been born on a fragment of Krypton which contained a complete city—preserved, it was explained, under a bubble of air (later changed to a plastic dome, so the air could be believably kept in place). When Kryptonite wiped out the inhabitants, Supergirl's parents sent her to Earth.

Bizarro, Superman's imperfect double, was also introduced in the fifties; but in the sixties he changed from a tragic figure to a comedic one. In one story, Bizarro adopted a Clark Kent disguise in his Bizarro World, but didn't fool anyone—mainly because he forgot to take off his medallion which read "Bizarro #1."

The sixties brought a rainbow of Kryptonites—Blue, White, Gold and Jewel —most of which affected something or someone other than Superman. Only Gold K could affect the Man of Might, but it never did—because if that happened, he would lose all his powers, permanently!

Then there was Superman on Broadway. *It's a Bird . . . It's a Plane . . . It's Superman!* was a musical, written by David Newman and Robert Benton, music by Charles Strouse and lyrics by Lee Adams. Not much of the comics' cast appeared in this play; aside from Superman, the only familiar names were Lois Lane and Perry White. But it had its moments, as when Linda Lavin (playing a girl named Sydney) sang "You've Got Possibilities" to Clark Kent. As she sang "Underneath, there's something there," she toyed with his shirt buttons, while Clark (Bob Holiday) nearly panicked at the thought that she might find what was there—his Superman suit!

And Superman returned to TV in a new form—a new series of animated cartoons for the homescreen. Bud Collyer was back doing the voice; thus he had been Superman for radio, movies and TV.

The seventies are now seeing new changes in the Superman magazines. It all began in *Jimmy Olsen,* whose hero, by the way, had finally celebrated his 21st birthday a few years earlier, and who had now been promoted to the status of a full reporter. I had begun my association with these magazines as an assistant editor in 1964, and had written that promotion story. But it was Jack Kirby (a longtime great in the field of comic art) who, as writer-artist, came up with Morgan Edge in the *Olsen* issues. Other editors quickly picked up this villainous character, president of the Galaxy Broadcasting System, who switched Clark Kent from the *Planet* to TV. As I write this, we are planning some fantastic revelations concerning Edge in *Lois Lane* (which, by a strange coincidence, I happen to edit).

For more of what's happening, read the last few tales in this book. Already, the mysterious sand-being has left this world, taking enough of Superman's powers with him to make it easier on the writers to dream up a way to endanger the hero of heroes. So mighty had he become that during the fifties it was decided his origin could no longer be explained by the difference in gravity. So Krypton was moved to another solar system—one with a red sun, and Earth's yellow sun was made the source of at least a portion of the Man of Steel's powers.

What does the future hold for Superman? Now that Lana Lang has given up hoping he'll marry her, leaving the field clear for Lois, will there be a super-wedding? Will Luthor reform? Will Perry White punch Morgan Edge in the mouth? Will I stop asking silly questions? Well, you can look into our magazines to find out—or you can wait a few years till someone decides to publish another hard-cover anthology of Superman stories.

But first, read those in this volume.

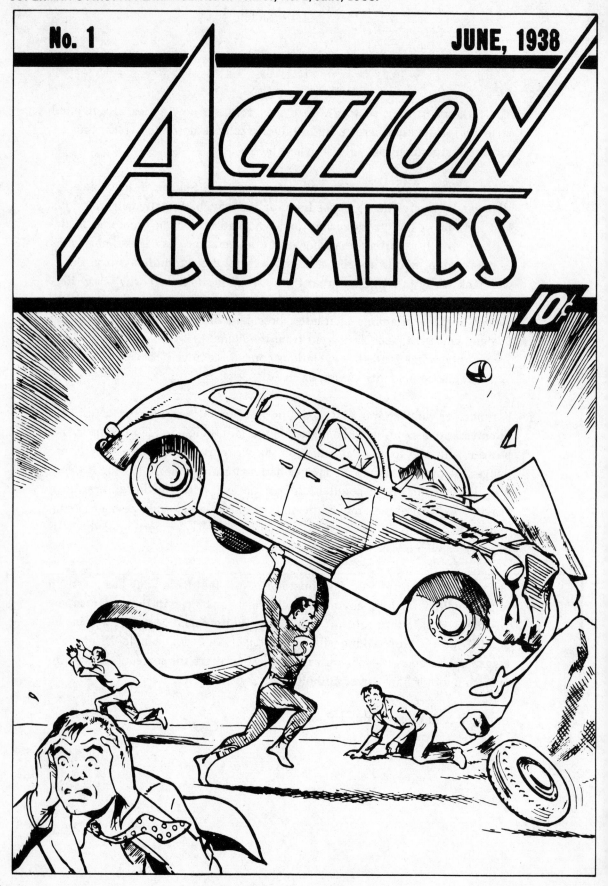

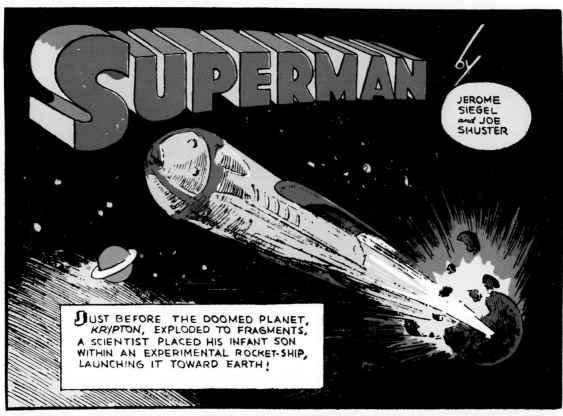

JUST BEFORE THE DOOMED PLANET, *KRYPTON*, EXPLODED TO FRAGMENTS, A SCIENTIST PLACED HIS INFANT SON WITHIN AN EXPERIMENTAL ROCKET-SHIP, LAUNCHING IT TOWARD EARTH!

WHEN THE VESSEL REACHED OUR PLANET, THE CHILD WAS FOUND BY AN ELDERLY COUPLE, THE KENTS.

LOOK, MARY! -- IT'S A CHILD!

THE POOR THING! -- ITS BEEN ABANDONED!

THE INFANT WAS TURNED OVER TO AN ORPHAN ASYLUM, WHERE IT ASTOUNDED THE ATTENDANTS WITH ITS FEATS OF STRENGTH.

WE --- WE COULDN'T GET THAT SWEET CHILD OUT OF OUR MIND.

WE'VE COME TO ADOPT HIM IF YOU'LL PERMIT US.

I BELIEVE IT CAN BE ARRANGED. ("-- WHEW! THANK GOODNESS THEY'RE TAKING HIM AWAY BEFORE HE WRECKS THE ASYLUM!")

THE LOVE AND GUIDANCE OF HIS KINDLY FOSTER-PARENTS WAS TO BECOME AN IMPORTANT FACTOR IN THE SHAPING OF THE BOY'S FUTURE.

NOW LISTEN TO ME, CLARK! THIS GREAT STRENGTH OF YOURS -- YOU'VE GOT TO HIDE IT FROM PEOPLE OR THEY'LL BE SCARED OF YOU!

BUT WHEN THE PROPER TIME COMES, YOU MUST USE IT TO ASSIST HUMANITY.

20

As the lad grew older, he learned to his delight that he could hurdle skyscrapers...

... leap an eighth of a mile...

... raise tremendous weights...

... run faster than a streamline train --

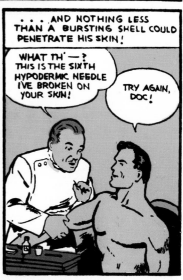

...and nothing less than a bursting shell could penetrate his skin!

WHAT TH'—? THIS IS THE SIXTH HYPODERMIC NEEDLE I'VE BROKEN ON YOUR SKIN!

TRY AGAIN, DOC!

The passing away of his foster-parents greatly grieved Clark Kent. But it strengthened a determination that had been growing in his mind.

Clark decided he must turn his titanic strength into channels that would benefit mankind.

And so was created--

SUPERMAN

CHAMPION OF THE OPPRESSED, THE PHYSICAL MARVEL WHO HAD SWORN TO DEVOTE HIS EXISTENCE TO HELPING THOSE IN NEED!

21

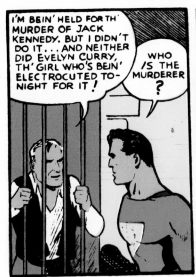

CLARK DROPS IN ON THE HILOW CLUB.

LATER -- WHEN SHE ENTERS HER DRESSING-ROOM...

24

THE *DAILY STAR* OFFICE IS REACHED...

YOU WANTED TO SEE ME?

YES, BE SEATED

34

DID YOU EVER HEAR OF *SUPERMAN*?

WHAT!

EDITOR

35

REPORTS HAVE BEEN STREAMING IN THAT A FELLOW WITH GIGANTIC STRENGTH NAMED *SUPERMAN* ACTUALLY EXISTS. I'M MAKING IT YOUR STEADY ASSIGNMENT TO COVER THESE REPORTS. THINK YOU CAN HANDLE IT, KENT?

LISTEN, CHIEF, IF *I* CAN'T FIND OUT ANYTHING ABOUT THIS *SUPERMAN* *NO ONE CAN!*

36

HURRY, KENT -- A PHONED TIP... WIFE-BEATING AT 211 COURT AVE!

I'M ON MY WAY!

37

AT 211 COURT AVE. -- 39

HOLD IT!

WHAT D'YOU WANT?

DON'T GET TOUGH!

TOUGH IS PUTTING *MILDLY* THE TREATMENT YOUR GOING TO GET!

YOU'RE NOT FIGHTING A WOMAN, NOW!

40

29

YE-EOW

THE OCCUPANTS OF THE CAR ARE SHAKEN OUT--

NEXT, SUPERMAN OVER TAKES BUTCH IN ONE SPRING..

--AND THE CAR, ITSELF, SMASHED TO BITS!

JUST A MINUTE, BUTCH!

DO YOU MIND?

THIS WILL TAKE BUT A FEW SECONDS

34

IN THE CAPITOL CITY, HE ATTENDS A SESSION OF CONGRESS, SITTING IN THE GALLERY

IS THAT SENATOR BARROWS SPEAKING?

YES.

UPON LEAVING THE SENATE CHAMBERS, CLARK SNAPS A PICTURE OF A FURTIVE MAN SPEAKING SWIFTLY TO SENATOR BARROWS

WHEN CAN I SEE YOU?

I TOLD YOU NEVER TO SPEAK TO ME IN PUBLIC!...UH.. MY HOME..TONIGHT AT 8:30

AT THE "MORGUE" OF A LOCAL NEWSPAPER....

WHO'S THE CHAP SPEAKING TO SENATOR BARROWS?

WHY, THAT'S ALEX GREER, THE SLICKEST LOBBYIST IN WASHINGTON. NO ONE KNOWS WHAT INTERESTS BACK HIM.

EIGHT-THIRTY P.M. ! OUTSIDE SENATOR BARROWS' RESIDENCE... AN EAVESDROPPER LISTENS IN ON AN INTERESTING CONVERSATION !

I'VE TOLD YOU TO AVOID ME IN PUBLIC. WHAT WOULD PEOPLE THINK IF THEY KNEW I HAD ANYTHING TO DO WITH YOU?

QUIT SPUTTERING! I HAD TO SEE YOU. TELL ME: DO YOU THINK YOU'LL SUCCEED IN PUSHING THE BILL THRU?

THERE'S NO DOUBT ABOUT IT! THE BILL WILL BE PASSED BEFORE ITS FULL IMPLICATIONS ARE REALIZED. BEFORE ANY REMEDIAL STEPS CAN BE TAKEN, OUR COUNTRY WILL BE EMBROILED WITH EUROPE.

FINE! WE'LL TAKE CARE OF YOU FINAN- CIALLY FOR THIS!

I SUPPOSE YOU'RE GOING TO BE WELL TAKEN CARE OF YOURSELF?

YOU BET HE WILL !

SUPERMAN

by

JEROME SIEGEL and JOE SHUSTER

As THEY TOPPLE LIKE A PLUMMET TO THE STREET BELOW, EIGHTY STORIES DISTANT, GREER SHRIEKS INSANELY THE ENTIRE LENGTH OF THE BUILDING!

1.

AS THEY STRIKE THE SIDEWALK, IT BURSTS INTO FRAGMENTS!

2.

SAY! WASN'T THAT FUN?--LETS DO IT AGAIN!

NO! I'LL TALK!--THE MAN BEHIND THE THREATENING WAR IS EMIL NORVELL, THE MUNITIONS MAGNATE. YOU'LL FIND HIM AT HIS LEXINGTON PARK ESTATE!

3.

HAVING SECURED THE INFORMATION HE DESIRES, SUPERMAN TAKES ABRUPT LEAVE OF GREER, SPRINGS TO THE TOP OF THE WASHINGTON MONUMENT, GETS HIS BEARINGS, THEN BEGINS HIS DASH TOWARD NORVELL'S RESIDENCE

4.

MEANWHILE --

I CAN'T EXPLAIN OVER THE PHONE, NORVELL, BUT YOU'RE ABOUT TO RECEIVE A VISIT FROM THE MOST DANGEROUS MAN ALIVE!

DON'T WORRY, GREER! -- I'LL TAKE CERTAIN PRECAUTIONS TO INSURE HE DOESN'T REMAIN ALIVE LONG!

6.

38

FIVE MINUTES ELAPSE -- THEN... ...SUPERMAN STEPS THRU THE WINDOW OF EMIL NORVELL'S STUDY AND CALMLY CONFRONTS HIM...

WHETHER YOU LIKE IT OR NOT, NORVELL, YOU'RE COMING WITH ME!

SORRY, BUT I HAVE OTHER PLANS!

AS HE SPEAKS, THE MUNITIONS MANUFACTURER SURREPTITIOUSLY REACHES BEHIND HIM TO PRESS A BUTTON ON HIS DESK.

WHAT ARE YOU HOLDING BEHIND YOU? -- GIVE IT TO ME!

ALL RIGHT BOYS! -- HE ASKED FOR IT! LET HIM HAVE IT!!

INSTANTLY SEVERAL PANELS ABOUT THE ROOM SLIDE ASIDE AND OUT STEP A NUMBER OF ARMED GUARDS!

NEXT MOMENT SUPERMAN IS THE CENTER OF A DEAFENING MACHINE-GUN BARRAGE!

UNHARMED BY THE RAIN OF MACHINE-GUN BULLETS, SUPERMAN STREAKS TOWARD HIS WOULD-BE MURDERERS!

GOOD HEAVENS! HE WON'T DIE!

GLAD I CAN'T SAY THE SAME FOR YOU!

A MOMENT LATER A DOZEN BODIES FLY HEADLONG OUT THE WINDOW INTO THE NIGHT, THE MACHINE-GUNS WRAPPED FIRMLY ABOUT THEIR NECKS!

YOU SEE HOW EFFORTLESSLY I CRUSH THIS BAR OF IRON IN MY HAND? -- THAT BAR COULD JUST AS EASILY BE YOUR NECK! ... NOW FOR THE LAST TIME! ARE YOU COMING WITH ME?

YES! YES! IMMEDIATELY!

SEVERAL MINUTES LATER...

YOU SEE THAT STEAMER? IT'S THE BARONTA. TOMORROW, IT LEAVES FOR SAN MONTE. UNLESS I FIND YOU ABOARD IT WHEN IT SAILS, I SWEAR I'LL FOLLOW YOU TO WHATEVER HOLE YOU HIDE IN, AND TEAR OUT YOUR CRUEL HEART WITH MY BARE HANDS!

I-- I'LL BE ON IT!

NEXT DAY AN ODD VARIETY OF PASSENGERS BOARD THE SAN MONTE' BOUND STEAMER BARONTA... CLARK KENT AND LOIS LANE...

LOIS! WHY, WHAT ARE YOU DOING *HERE*?

OUR EDITOR DECIDED TO HAVE ME ACCOMPANY YOU TO THE WAR-ZONE AND SEND BACK DISPATCHES COLORED WITH MY DISTINCTIVE FEMININE TOUCH!

...A GROUP OF SULLEN-FACED TOUGHS WHO POSSIBLY INTEND TO ENLIST WITH ONE OF THE ARMIES AS PAID MERCENARIES...

LOLA CORTEZ, WOMAN OF MYSTERY, AN EXOTIC BEAUTY WHO FAIRLY RADIATES DANGER AND INTRIGUE...

...AND EMIL NORVELL, WHO HURRIES PASTY-FACED UP THE GANG-PLANK AND QUICKLY CONFINES HIMSELF TO HIS CABIN

HALF AN HOUR LATER THE *BARONTA* HOISTS ITS ANCHOR AND SLIPS OUT TO SEA, DESTINED FOR ONE OF THE STRANGEST VOYAGES THE WORLD HAS EVER KNOWN

IT IS THE FIRST NIGHT OUT... AS NORVELL NERVOUSLY PACES HIS CABIN, THERE COMES A KNOCK AT THE DOOR... HE ANSWERS IT....

YOU!

YES -- I THOUGHT I'D DROP BY AND COMPLIMENT YOU ON HAVING HAD SENSE ENOUGH TO SHOW UP!

A MOMENT AFTER *SUPERMAN* DEPARTS....

THAT'S HIM! REMEMBER! -- IF HE DIES, YOUR REWARD WILL BE FABULOUS!

HE'S AS GOOD AS DEAD RIGHT NOW!

AS SUPERMAN STANDS SILENTLY AT THE SHIP'S RAIL, ADMIRING THE MOONLIGHT, HE WHIRLS SUDDENLY AT THE SOUND OF FOOTSTEPS!

ALL TOGETHER, NOW! — GET HIM!

FOR AN INSTANT SUPERMAN BRACES HIMSELF AGAINST THE RAIL -- AND IN THAT SECOND IT GIVES WAY!

HE IS FLUNG, TWISTING AND TURNING, INTO THE OCEAN!

THE THUGS REPORT BACK TO NORVELL

IT WAS SIMPLE! A LITTLE SHOVE AND HE TOPPLED OVERBOARD! -- NOW HOW ABOUT THAT DOUGH YOU PROMISED US!

YOU'LL GET NOTHING! GET OUT OF HERE, YOU TRUSTING FOOLS, AND BE GLAD I DON'T TURN YOU OVER TO THE POLICE!

MEANWHILE -- AT THAT VERY INSTANT SUPERMAN, SWIMMING VIGOROUSLY, HAS CAUGHT UP WITH THE STEAMER . .

. . BUT INSTEAD OF CLIMBING ABOARD, HE CONTINUES ONWARD UNTIL THE BARONTA IS OUT-DISTANCED FAR BEHIND!

SEE YOU LATER!

NEXT EVENING, A FEW MINUTES AFTER THE STEAMER LANDS NORVELL IS ATTACKED BY HIS DOUBLE CROSSED HENCHMEN

41

NORVELL IS SAVED BY THE TIMELY APPEARANCE OF *SUPERMAN*

HOLY CATS -- IT'S **HIM!**

RIGHT! -- AND HERE'S WHERE I EVEN A LITTLE SCORE!

SUPERMAN SUBJECTS THE TOUGHS TO THE SEVEREST THRASHING OF THEIR LIVES!

THE THUGS FLEE BEFORE HIS FURY!

YOU SAVED ME! -- BUT WHY?

BECAUSE THE FATE YOU ESCAPED IS PLEASANT INDEED COMPARED TO THE ONE I HAVE IN STORE FOR YOU!

W-WHAT ARE YOU GOING TO DO TO ME?

NOTHING -- IF YOU JOIN THE SAN MONTE ARMY!

LATER --- IN HIS HOTEL

IF I COULD ONLY DO SOMETHING' -- BUT ITS SUICIDE TO RESIST THAT INHUMAN CREATURE!

I KNOW WHAT I'LL DO! I'LL ENLIST IN THE ARMY -- THEN ESCAPE AT THE FIRST OPPORTUNITY!

AFTER NORVELL ENLISTS --

YOU!

YES, I JOINED TOO -- I COULDN'T BEAR BEING PARTED FROM YOU!

SHORTLY LATER, THE COMPANY PITCHES CAMP.... RETIRES...

SENTRIES ARE PUZZLED BY A DARK SHADOW..

WHAT WAS THAT?

PROBABLY JUST A BIRD!

BUT IN REALITY IT IS SUPERMAN SPEEDING TO A STRANGE RENDEZVOUS

IN THE ENEMY CAMP....

BUT THE QUESTION, GENERAL, IS HOW STRONG ARE OUR LINES?

IMPENETRABLE!

AT THAT INSTANT A FIGURE BURSTS INTO THE TENT.

SMILE, PLEASE! —THANKS!

A FEW MOMENTS LATER --

GONE!— BUT HE WON'T ESCAPE!

GUARDS!

LATER THAT EVENING, CLARK KENT MAILS A PACKAGE...

WHERE TO?

THE EVENING NEWS... CLEVELAND, OHIO

THE EVENING-NEWS PRINTS A PICTURE-SCOOP...

EVENING NEW
AMAZING WAR PICTURES!!

GENERALS CONFER

MEANWHILE, LOIS LANE AND LOLA CORTEZ HAVE REGISTERED AT THE SAME HOTEL

I'M A REPORTER DOWN HERE ON A NEWS ASSIGNMENT. AND YOU?

-- A WEALTHY TRAVELER.

55

AT THAT INSTANT, ARMY OFFICERS ENTERS THE HOTEL --

WHAT'S THE TROUBLE?

OFFICIAL BUSINESS.

56

SUDDENLY PANICKY LOLA DARTS INTO AN ELEVATOR...

57

... AND HIDES A CERTAIN DOCUMENT IN LOIS' ROOM!

58

AN IMPORTANT DOCUMENT HAS BEEN STOLEN. MAY WE SEARCH THE GUESTS' ROOMS?

YOU HAVE MY PERMISSION

59

SORRY, MADAM!

I TOLD YOU THAT YOU WERE WASTING TIME SEARCHING MY ROOM!

60

THE PLANTED DOCUMENT IS DISCOVERED IN LOIS' ROOM!

SORRY. WE MUST PLACE YOU UNDER MILITARY ARREST!

BUT I KNOW NOTHING OF THIS!

61

SENTENCE IS PASSED --

BUT I'M INNOCENT!

IT IS THE JUDGEMENT OF THIS COURT THAT YOU SHALL BE EXECUTED AT DAWN FOR ESPONIAGE!

62

45

KENT, IN HIS DISGUISE AS A SOLDIER, OVERHEARS AN ASTOUNDING BIT OF INFORMATION

HAVE YOU HEARD? LOIS LANE, A SPY, IS TO BE EXECUTED THIS MORNING

YES! AND EXACTLY AT DAWN!

63

AT THAT VERY MOMENT LOIS IS BEING LED OUT TO HER DEATH...

I TELL YOU! YOU'RE GOING TO KILL AN INNOCENT PERSON!

64

ALMOST FASTER THAN THE EYE CAN FOLLOW, A FANTASTIC FIGURE STREAKS PAST MILE AFTER MILE!

65

READY! AIM! FI—

DOWN—DOWN—INTO THE RANGE OF FIRE PLUMMETS SUPERMAN!

67

COVERING LOIS' BODY WITH HIS OWN, HE RECIEVES THE SHOTS MEANT FOR HER!

SHOOT AND BE HANGED!

68

YOU CAN'T DO THIS! —IT'S IMPOSSIBLE!

STOP!

THANKS FOR LETTING ME KNOW!

69

SUPERMAN!

RIGHT! AND STILL PLAYING THE ROLE OF GALLANT RESCUER'—

70

47

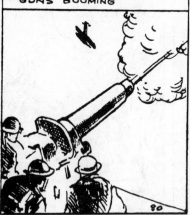

SUPERMAN

by JERRY SIEGEL and JOE SHUSTER

Leaping over skyscrapers, running faster than an express-train, springing great distances and heights, lifting and smashing tremendous weights, possessing an impenetrable skin--these are the amazing attributes which *SUPERMAN*, savior of the helpless and oppressed, avails himself as he battles the forces of evil and injustice!

For the first time in its history, the city of Metropolis is ravaged by a terrible earthquake!

Editorial office of the Daily Planet..

I WANT FIRST-HAND EYE-WITNESS DETAILS OF THE QUAKE!

YOU'LL GET 'EM!

Unobserved, the meek reporter transforms himself into mighty *SUPERMAN*...!

AN EARTHQUAKE IN THIS LOCALITY--IT'S UNHEARD OF!

STORE ROOM

Shortly after--the man of tomorrow's figure streaks down toward the scene of terror!

51

SPRINGING INTO ACTION, **SUPERMAN** SUPPORTS TOTTERING BUILDINGS WHILE TERRIFIED OCCUPANTS DASH TO SAFETY!

HURRY! IT'LL GIVE WAY IN A FEW SECONDS!

HIS AMAZING STRENGTH AND SPEED BRINGING HIM TO WHEREVER THERE IS NEED OF HIS ASSISTANCE!

MY BOY-- PINNED UNDER THAT WRECKAGE!

HE'LL BE FREE IN A MOMENT!

WHEN THE EARTHQUAKE SUBSIDES, **SUPERMAN** LEAPS AWAY WITH THE GRATEFUL CHEER OF THOUSANDS RINGING IN HIS WAKE...!

LATER NICE ARTICLE YOU HANDED IN-- PARTICULARLY THE **SUPERMAN** ANGLE!

I'VE LEARNED THAT THE DISTURBANCE WAS CAUSED BY A NEW WEAPON THE ARMY IS TESTING WHICH ARTIFICIALLY CAUSES EARTHQUAKES. THE MACHINE RAN WILD DURING THE TEST. - I'LL VISIT ITS INVENTOR FOR AN INTERVIEW.

PROFESSOR MARTINSON? I'M CLARK KENT OF THE DAILY PLANET. HOW ABOUT A STORY CONCERNING YOUR NEW DISCOVERY!

I'D BE DELIGHTED!

CLARK SEATS HIMSELF. WHILE HIS BACK IS TURNED--

MEDDLER!

NOT A TICK! HE'S DONE FOR!

WHAT CLARK'S ASSAILANT DOES NOT REALIZE IS THAT KENT POSSESSES THE ABILITY TO TEMPORARILY HALT THE BEATING OF HIS HEART. CLARK IS PLAYING POSSUM TO LEARN WHAT THE SITUATION IS!

OUT YOU GO--TO A MANGLED DEATH!

DOWN HURTLES THE REPORTER'S FIGURE --!

ABRUPTLY--OUT FLASHES ONE OF HIS HANDS, CLUTCHING THE SIDE OF THE SKYSCRAPER IN A STEELY GRIP, HALTING HIS PLUNGE!

TIME OUT!

IT TAKES BUT A FEW SECONDS TO REMOVE HIS OUTER GARMENTS .... THEN HE COMMENCES TO CLIMB SWIFTLY BACK TOWARD THE LABORATORY ---- AS SUPERMAN!

NOW IT'S MY TURN!

WITHIN THE LABORATORY ---

A SNOOPING REPORTER INTERFERED WHILE I WAS GOING THRU THE PROFESSOR'S DESK. BUT I DISPOSED OF HIM!

SPLENDID! BUT IT'S UNFORTUNATE YOU COULDN'T FIND THE PLANS WE SEEK!

AT A DISTANT SPOT...

("-SUPERMAN EAVESDROPPING! I'LL ATTEND TO HIM!-")

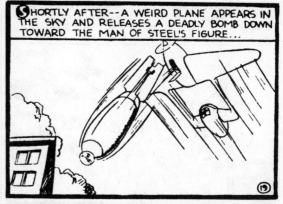

SHORTLY AFTER--A WEIRD PLANE APPEARS IN THE SKY AND RELEASES A DEADLY BOMB DOWN TOWARD THE MAN OF STEEL'S FIGURE...

THIS HAS GOT TO STOP BEFORE BOMBS FALL ON INNOCENT PEOPLE IN THE STREET!

A FLIP OF SUPERMAN'S WRIST, AND THE BOMB HURTLES BACK TO ITS SOURCE, DESTROYING THE PLANE!

53

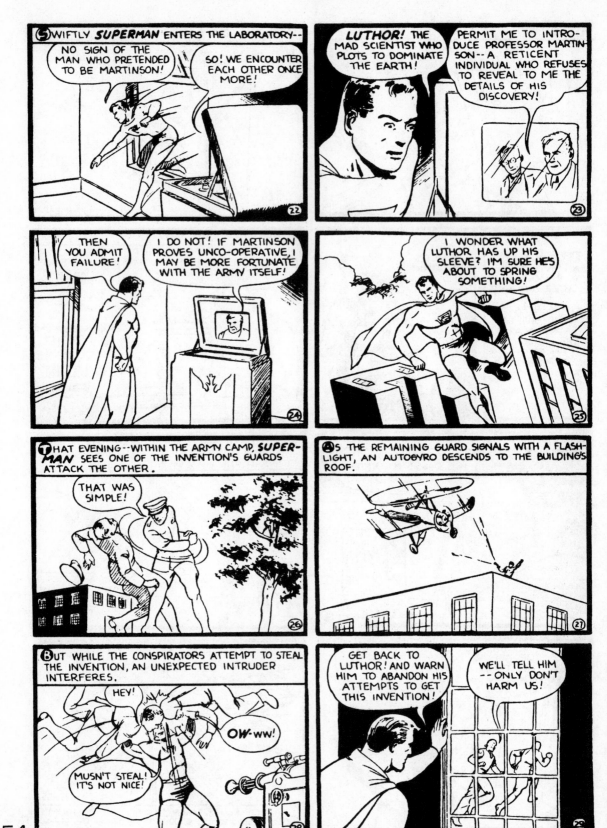

SUPERMAN TRAILS THE AUTOGYRO...

THE WORLD WILL NOT BE SAFE UNTIL LUTHOR NO LONGER EXISTS!

SUPERMAN-- PURSUING MY FUMBLING HIRELINGS!

SORRY TO DISAPPOINT THE MAN OF STEEL, BUT THAT PLANE WILL NEVER REACH HERE!

THE AUTOGYRO-- DESTROYED BY A TERRIFIC EXPLOSION!

A CHALLENGE, SUPERMAN!

WHO SAID THAT?

!! ARE YOU WILLING TO DECLARE A TEMPORARY TRUCE?

THAT ALL DEPENDS--!

HERE IS MY PROPOSITION--AND CHALLENGE! IF YOUR MUSCLES CAN SURPASS MY SCIENTIFIC FEATS, I WILL ADMIT DEFEAT. BUT IF I CAN OUTDO YOU, THEN YOU ARE TO RETIRE AND LEAVE ME A CLEAR PATH!

DO YOU ACCEPT?

DEFINITELY!

SECONDS LATER...TWO WEIRD VESSELS SWOOP DOWN OUT OF THE SKY...

THAT'S WHAT I CALL PROMPT SERVICE!

ONCE AGAIN WE CONFRONT EACH OTHER!

CAN'T SAY THAT IT PARTICULARILY PLEASES ME!

QUIBBLING ASIDE--YOU AGREED TO MATCH ME AT ANY FEAT. WELL, IMPETUOUS ONE, ARE YOU PREPARED TO RACE MY SKY-VESSELS AROUND THE WORLD?

LET'S GO!

THEY'RE OFF--IN THE STRANGEST RACE THE WORLD HAS EVER SEEN-- A *SUPERMAN* VERSUS SUPER-PLANES!

DEFYING TIME, THE WEIRD ADVERSARIES ANNIHILATE ALL SPEED RECORDS IN A THRILLING RACE THAT SPANS CONTINENTS...

...AND OCEANS!

GET A HORSE!

FASTER! FASTER!-- A HUMAN BEING OUTDISTANCE ONE OF MY SUPER-STRATO-LINERS? IMPOSSIBLE!

SORRY--I'M PRESSING THE MOTORS TO THE LIMIT!

LATER-WHEN THEY RETURN TO THE STARTING POINT...

IT APPEARS I AM THE VICTOR!

AND YOU DON'T LOOK THE LEAST BIT TIRED! - INCREDIBLE!

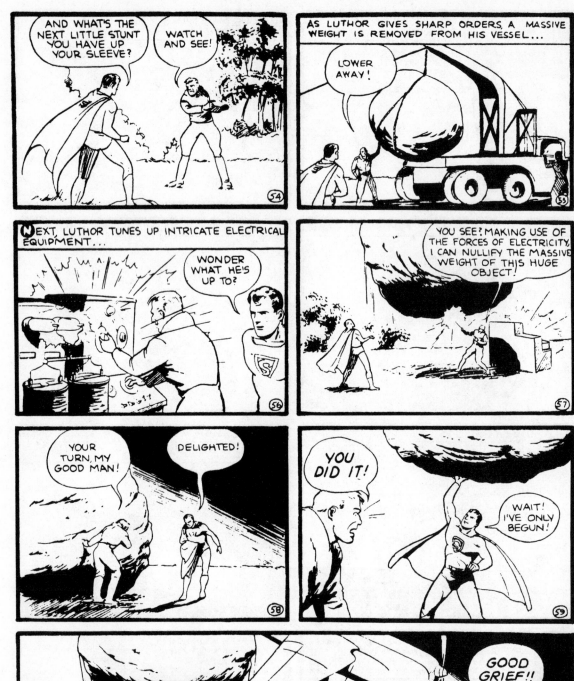

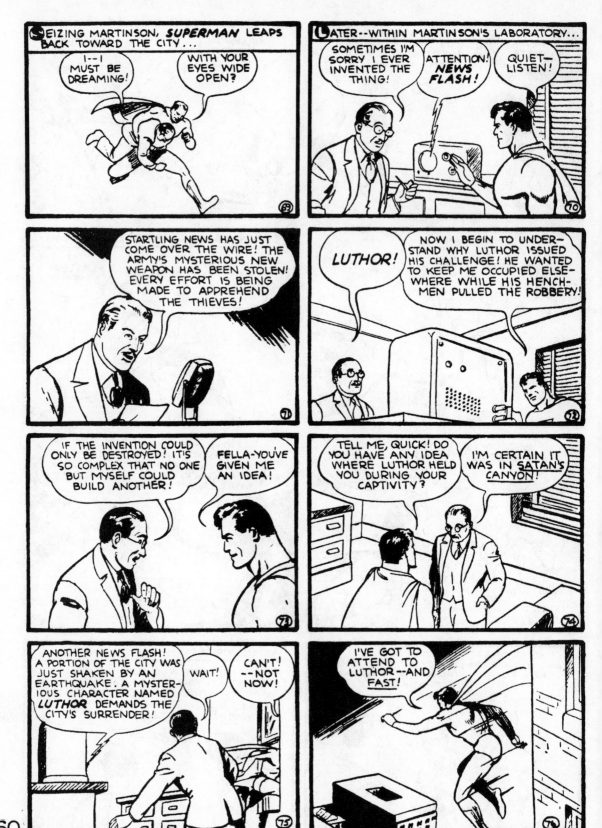

60

BUT LUTHOR IS PREPARED--AND WAITING--

I'VE A CHEERFUL LITTLE SURPRISE PREPARED FOR THE MAN OF STEEL!

SATIN'S CANYON!--NOW IF ONLY MARTINSON'S HUNCH IS CORRECT!

NOW!

DOWN TOWARD SUPERMAN RAINS A MASS OF TORN BOULDERS!

WELL! WELL! THOUGHTFUL OF LUTHOR TO HAVE PREPARED A WARM WELCOME!

BUT AS THE BOULDERS RAIN DOWN, SUPERMAN SMASHES THEM ASIDE IN TURN...

NICE WORKOUT, I MUST SAY!

BUT AS THE MAN OF TOMORROW CONTINUES ON, HE FALLS INTO A GRASS-COVERED PIT!

WHAT--?

THEY DON'T SEEM TO CARE FOR MY COMPANY!

INSTEAD OF FACING A SHRINKING VIOLET, THE WOLVES ARE FLUNG BACK...

DON'T CROWD ME!

I'D LIKE TO REMAIN AND TAME THESE WOLVES, BUT FIRST I'VE GOT TO TAKE CARE OF A HUMAN WOLF -- LUTHOR!

BUT AS *SUPERMAN* EMERGES FROM THE PIT, A POWERFUL NEW GAS IS RELEASED IN HIS FACE .... RENDERING HIM UNCONSCIOUS..

HE'S OUT!

LUTHOR WILL BE PLEASED!

LUTHOR'S HIRELINGS CARRY THE UNCONSCIOUS *SUPERMAN* TO A SPOT NEAR THEIR MASTER'S LABORATORY TOWER!

NOW TO PERMANENTLY REMOVE THIS FOE!

AS THE RAY STRIKES THE EARTH IT TREMBLES IN MIGHTY CONVULSIONS...CREVICES APPEAR IN THE GROUND...

SUPERMAN FALLS INTO ONE OF THEM!

NEXT INSTANT, THE CREVICE CLOSES, *BURYING SUPERMAN ALIVE!*

62

CRUSHED BENEATH TONS OF EARTH, *SUPERMAN* REVIVES --FLAILS ABOUT...

...AND BURROWS HIS WAY TO THE GROUND'S SURFACE!

THE LIGHT OF DAY!

SIGHTING THE RAY EMERGING FROM THE TOWER, *SUPERMAN* ATTACKS THE GREAT STONE EDIFICE---

THE BIGGER THEY ARE...!

...DESTROYING IT!

...THE HARDER THEY FALL!

THAT FINISHES THE EARTHQUAKE-MACHINE --- BUT I'D MUCH RATHER DO THIS TO LUTHOR! NO SIGHT OF HIM!

LATER-- WHEN CLARK KENT GOES TO MARTINSON'S LABORATORY...

SUICIDE!

SO MARTINSON KILLED HIMSELF, EH? HE MUST HAVE REPENTED INVENTING SUCH A TERRIBLE WEAPON!

HIS SECRET DIED WITH HIM! IT WILL NEVER MENACE CIVILIZATION AGAIN!

THE END

From out of nowhere comes the grim figure of the SPECTRE.

Follow his deeds in **MORE FUN COMICS** every Month!

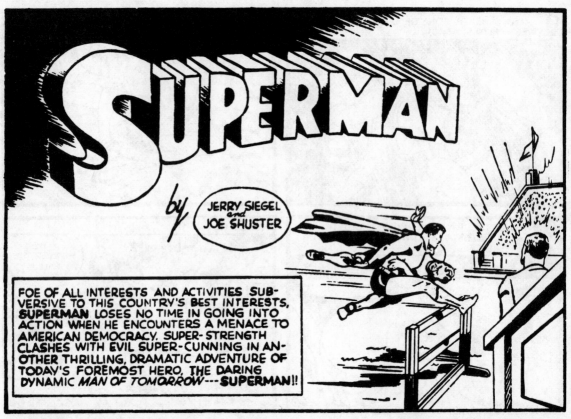

SUPERMAN

by JERRY SIEGEL and JOE SHUSTER

FOE OF ALL INTERESTS AND ACTIVITIES SUBVERSIVE TO THIS COUNTRY'S BEST INTERESTS, **SUPERMAN** LOSES NO TIME IN GOING INTO ACTION WHEN HE ENCOUNTERS A MENACE TO AMERICAN DEMOCRACY. SUPER-STRENGTH CLASHES WITH EVIL SUPER-CUNNING IN ANOTHER THRILLING, DRAMATIC ADVENTURE OF TODAY'S FOREMOST HERO, THE DARING DYNAMIC *MAN OF TOMORROW*---SUPERMAN!!

EDITORIAL OFFICE OF THE *DAILY PLANET*...

WHAT'S ON THE FIRE FOR TODAY, CHIEF?

THE *DUKALIA-AMERICAN SPORTS FESTIVAL* IS BEING HELD TODAY AT THE *MUNICIPAL STADIUM*...I WANT BOTH YOU AND LOIS TO COVER IT...

THAT'S THE KIND OF ASSIGNMENT I LIKE. NOW IF YOU'D ONLY SEND US TO A BALL GAME TOMORROW.

BUT WHEN THE TWO REPORTERS REACH THE STADIUM, THEY DISCOVER TO THEIR DISCOMFITURE...

I DON'T LIKE THIS, CLARK! DUKALIA IS ON UNFRIENDLY TERMS WITH US-- AND THIS LOOKS MORE LIKE AN ANTI-AMERICAN DEMONSTRATION THAN ANYTHING ELSE!

SH-HH! NOT SO LOUD--OR WE MAY GET MORE THAN JUST DIRTY LOOKS!

SEE THAT MAN OVER THERE? IT'S EX-CAPTAIN LANG!

I REMEMBER---HE WAS DISCHARGED FROM THE UNITED STATES NAVY FOR CONDUCT UNBECOMING AN OFFICER.--LET'S GET OUT OF HERE, LOIS. I DON'T LIKE OUR COMPANY. WE'VE SEEN ENOUGH!

BUT SHORTLY AFTER...

WHAT'S THE MATTER NOW?

I MUST HAVE DROPPED MY FOUNTAIN PEN. WAIT HERE!

64

AS SOON AS HE IS OUT OF LOIS' SIGHT, CLARK WHIPS OFF HIS CIVILIAN GARMENTS STANDING REVEALED AS THE MIGHTY SUPERMAN . . . !

I'M CONVINCED THIS SPORTS FESTIVAL IS BUT THE FRONT FOR AN ORGANIZATION FOMENTING UNAMERICAN ACTIVITIES. THE DUKALIAN CONSUL IS ABOUT TO SPEAK—I'LL LEND AN EAR. AND IF I DON'T LIKE WHAT HE SAYS..

DUKALIAN CONSUL KARL WOLFF HOLDS HIS AUDIENCE SPELLBOUND

PRESENT HERE IS THE FLOWER OF DUKALIAN YOUTH! YOU HAVE SEEN THEM PERFORM PHYSICAL FEATS WHICH NO OTHER HUMAN BEINGS CAN. PROOF, I TELL YOU, THAT WE DUKALIANS ARE SUPERIOR TO ANY OTHER RACE OR NATION! PROOF THAT WE ARE ENTITLED TO BE THE MASTERS OF AMERICA!

STREAKING DOWN ONTO THE FIELD, INTERRUPTING THE CONSUL'S SPIEL—SUPERMAN!

LET'S SEE JUST HOW SUPERIOR YOU REALLY ARE!

SO YOU'RE THE SHOT-PUTTER, EH? LET'S SEE IF WE CAN BREAK YOUR RECORD—OR YOUR NECK!

A HEAVE OF THE MAN OF STEEL'S MIGHTY ARM AND THE ATHLETE LANDS A DISTANCE AHEAD OF HIS SHOT-PUT....

NOW YOU CAN SAY YOU BEAT YOUR OWN RECORD-- WITHOUT THE AID OF THE POLE!

②

NEXT, SUPERMAN SNATCHES THE POLE VAULT CHAMP....

SO THAT'S YOUR RECORD HEIGHT, EH?

SEIZING ANOTHER ATHLETE BY THE NECK AND SEAT OF HIS PANTS, SUPERMAN PUSHES HIM BEFORE HIM IN THE FASTEST HUNDRED YARD DASH THAT HAS EVER BEEN RUN!

TWO SECONDS FLAT!

TAKING THE HURDLE CHAMPION UNDER HIS ARM, SUPERMAN CARRIES HIM OVER ALL THE HURDLES IN ONE GREAT LEAP....

HOW'S THAT?

AND NOW-- LET'S SEE WHAT SORT OF A CHAMPION **YOU** ARE!

HELP! HELP ME!

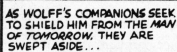

AS WOLFF'S COMPANIONS SEEK TO SHIELD HIM FROM THE *MAN OF TOMORROW*, THEY ARE SWEPT ASIDE...

MAKE ROOM!

AWK! LET GO!

NOT YET. YOU'RE COMING WITH ME!

EEEEEE!

WHY NOT DISPLAY SOME OF THAT DUKALIAN COURAGE YOU DID SO MUCH RAVING ABOUT?

YOU CAN'T LEAVE ME HERE!

DON'T LIKE IT THERE, EH? WELL, YOU'RE FREE TO LET GO ANY TIME YOU WANT!

GET ME DOWN! HURRY!!

RETURNING TO THE SPOT WHERE HE HAD LEFT HIS OUTER GARMENTS, **SUPERMAN** SWIFTLY DONS THEM....

GOT TO HURRY BACK TO LOIS-- BEFORE SHE GETS SUSPICIOUS...

DID YOU FIND THE FOUNTAIN PEN? AND WHAT'S ALL THE TUMULT IN THERE?

A DISTURBANCE IN THERE? I DIDN'T NOTICE ANY!

LANG AT THAT UN-AMERICAN DEMONSTRATION! CLARK, I THINK HE DESERVES INVESTIGATION!

YOU'D JUST BE WASTING YOUR TIME, LOIS! ("-I MUST DISCOURAGE HER. IF LANG IS INVOLVED IN SINISTER ACTIVITIES, IT WOULD BE DANGEROUS FOR LOIS TO INTERFERE-")

("-I MIGHT HAVE EXPECTED HIM TO DISCOURAGE ME. HE WANTS TO HOG THE STORY FOR HIMSELF.-") VERY WELL. IF YOU'RE NOT INTERESTED, GOODBYE!

SEE YOU LATER! ("-OF THAT, THERE CAN BE NO DOUBT!-")

LOIS MAKES A BEE-LINE FOR LIEUTENANT FERGUSON OF THE NAVAL INTELLIGENCE...

YOU KNOW YOU CAN TRUST ME. WHY WAS CAPTAIN LANG DISCHARGED FROM THE NAVY?

HE SHOWED SUSPICIOUSLY UNDUE INTEREST IN BATTLESHIP CONSTRUCTION PLANS.

I REMEMBER HAVING SEEN LANG IN THE LOBBY OF THE CARTWRIGHT HOTEL. THEREFORE-- THAT'S MY NEXT STOP!

YOU'RE CERTAIN THAT LANG IS NOT IN?

I RANG HIS ROOM TWICE. THERE'S NO ANSWER FROM ROOM 221.

LATER-- LOIS RETURNS WITH A SUITCASE....

CAN I HAVE ROOM 219? I FOUND IT VERY QUIET ON MY LAST VISIT.

YOU'RE FORTUNATE. THE ROOM IS UNOCCUPIED.

No SOONER DOES LOIS ENTER ROOM 219 THAN SHE REMOVES A ROPE AND HOOK FROM THE SUITCASE AND SWINGS IT OUT SO THAT IT CATCHES ONTO A LEDGE OUTSIDE ROOM 221....

MADE IT THE FIRST TRY!

STEPPING THRU THE WINDOW, LOIS SWINGS OUT TOWARD HER DESTINATION.

I HOPE THAT HOOK HOLDS!

OOPS!-- ALMOST LOST MY GRIP THAT TIME!

WHAT--! SOMEONE INSERTING A KEY IN THE DOOR!

CAUTIOUSLY ENTERING THE DARKENED ROOM, THE MAN PLACES A PACKAGE IN THE TOP DRAWER OF THE DRESSER

("-IT'S ONE OF THE PRIZE-WINNING ATHLETES WHO ATTENDED THE SPORTS FESTIVAL!--")

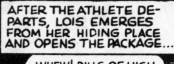

AFTER THE ATHLETE DE-PARTS, LOIS EMERGES FROM HER HIDING PLACE AND OPENS THE PACKAGE...

WHEW! BILLS OF HIGH DENOMINATION-- THEY MUST TOTAL AT LEAST FIFTY THOUS-AND DOLLARS!

ABRUPTLY, STRONG FINGERS ENCIRCLE LOIS' NECK FROM BEHIND....

LOIS KICKS BACK SHARPLY, STRIKING HER ASSAILANT'S KNEE. AS THE GRIP ON HER THROAT QUICKLY RELAXES, SHE TEARS FREE AND DASHES TOWARD THE DOOR...

I'VE GOT TO GET OUT OF HERE!

BUT AS SHE OPENS THE DOOR--!

L-LANG!

WELL...I SEE I'VE COME NOT A MOMENT TOO EARLY!

REMEMBER--THE FIFTY THOUSAND DOLLARS WAS JUST FOR A DEMONSTRATION RIDE ON MY STARTLING INVENTION....

TRUE! AN ADDITIONAL TWO MILLION DOLLARS WILL BE PAID FOR THE INVENTION IF IT MEETS WITH MY COMPLETE SATISFACTION!

IF YOU HAVE MADE A GREAT MILITARY DISCOVERY, DON'T YOU THINK YOUR OWN COUNTRY IS ENTITLED TO IT?

I SWORE THIS COUNTRY WOULD PAY FOR DISMISSING ME FROM THE NAVY! I HAVE WOLFF'S ASSURANCE THAT WHEN DUKALIA CONQUERS AMERICA, I WILL RECEIVE AN IMPORTANT POST!

DUKALIA APPRECIATES GENIUS...AND LOYALTY!

WHEN LOIS HAD DEPARTED, CLARK REMOVED HIS OUTER GARMENTS AND TUCKED THEM BENEATH HIS **SUPERMAN** CLOAK.....

SO LOIS THINKS LANG COULD STAND INVESTIGATING! HM-MM! DOESN'T SOUND LIKE A BAD IDEA, AT THAT!

A GREAT LEAP LAUNCHES THE *MAN OF STEEL* TO A POSITION ATOP THE STADIUM...

LANG BELOW--WHISPERING TO SOMEONE IN THE CROWD.

WHAT **SUPERMAN'S** AMAZING SUPER-SENSITIVE HEARING ENABLES HIM TO OVERHEAR...

I ACCEPT YOUR TERMS!

SPLENDID!

AS EX-CAPTAIN LANG DRIVES OFF, **SUPERMAN** STREAKS DOWN AND SWINGS HIMSELF BENEATH THE CAR.....

GUESS I'LL BE A NON-PAYING PASSENGER!

AS LANG SWIFTLY ROUNDS A CURVE ON A MOUNTAIN ROAD, A HUGE TRUCK UNEXPECTEDLY LOOMS BEFORE HIM...THE DISCHARGED NAVAL OFFICER FRANTICALLY TWISTS THE WHEEL....

A SURE-CRASH!

A COLLISION IS NARROWLY AVOIDED! BUT--THE CAR'S WHEELS SLIP OFF THE ROAD!

THE AUTO COMMENCES TIPPING OVER, PREPARATORY TO BEGINNING THE TERRIBLE DOWNWARD PLUNGE!

BRACING HIS HAND AGAINST THE SIDE OF THE CLIFF, SUPERMAN SWERVES THE CAR BACK TO AN UPRIGHT POSITION ON THE ROAD. . . .

WHEW! I'VE NEVER COME CLOSER TO DEATH! I CAN THANK MY LUCKY STARS!

NO, LANG, YOU CAN THANK SUPERMAN!

LATER--PARKING NEAR THE WATERFRONT, LANG CAUTIOUSLY OPENS A HIGH GATE, THEN LOCKS IT AFTER HIMSELF. . . .

AN INSTANT LATER, THE MAN OF STEEL EASILY VAULTS OVER THE BARRIER . . . . .

THEY'LL HAVE TO BUILD THIS MUCH HIGHER IF THEY HOPE TO KEEP ME OUT!

TAKE IT OUT FOR A TRIAL SPIN!

AS YOU DIRECT, SIR!

SLOWLY, THE CRAFT MOVES SEAWARD, THEN COMMENCES TO SUBMERGE. . . .

PROVIDING YOU DELIVER THE MONEY AS PROMISED, I'M READY TO TAKE YOU ON A DEMONSTRATION VOYAGE AT ONCE!

NO NAME HAS BEEN MENTIONED BUT I COULD RECOGNIZE THAT VOICE ANYWHERE! LANG IS SPEAKING TO WOLFF!

AN INSTANT LATER, SUPERMAN IS AMAZED TO DISCOVER THAT THO HE MAKES USE OF HIS TELESCOPIC VISION. . . .

THAT STRANGE VESSEL--COMPLETELY DISAPPEARED-- NO LONGER TO BE SEEN!

71

THIS CALLS FOR A MORE THOROUGH SEARCH!

BUT THO SUPERMAN RAPIDLY SWIMS UNDERWATER, EXPLORING THE VICINITY, HE FINDS...

--NOT A TRACE OF IT!

ON LAND ONCE AGAIN, SUPERMAN STREAKS OFF THRU THE NIGHT....

THIS GROWS MORE MYSTERIOUS--AND SINISTER--EVERY MOMENT! WOLFF IS THE MAN I WANT TO SEE RIGHT NOW!

SUPERMAN FINDS THE WINDOWS OF THE DUKALIAN CONSULATE BARRED, BUT...

THAT'S NO OBSTACLE TO ME!

AS HE ENTERS THE ROOM....

GAS!--DEADLY HYDROCYANIC GAS!

DUE TO HIS GREAT POWERS OF RESISTANCE, THE MAN OF TOMORROW IS UNHARMED. AS POWERFUL VENTILATORS CLEAR THE ROOM OF THE GAS, ARMED MEN WEARING GAS-MASKS ENTER.

WHAT--I HE'S--UNINJURED!

WELL, HE WON'T BE FOR LONG --SHOOT HIM DOWN!

THAT'S FINE!

YOU SEE, I COLLECT BULLETS! A SORT OF HOBBY!

D-DO YOU SEE WHAT I SEE??

KEEP FIRING!

I THINK YOU'VE WASTED ENOUGH AMMUNITION FOR TODAY!

YII--III!

HELP!!

I CAN TAKE MY LEAVE, NOW! IF MY HUNCH IS TRUE, I'LL SOON HAVE COMPANY!

WH-WHAT HAS HAPPENED? WHERE IS THE INTRUDER?

WE WERE POWERLESS TO PREVENT HIS ESCAPE!

IT WAS THAT INCREDIBLY STRONG MAN WHO MADE FOOLS OF US AT THE STADIUM. HIS STRENGTH IS BEYOND ALL BELIEF!

JUST AS I HAD HOPED! WOLFF IS LOSING NO TIME MAKING A BEE-LINE FOR THAT WHARF!

AS WOLFF NOTES SUPERMAN'S SHADOW ON THE ROAD....

THAT HUGE SHADOW-- WHAT CAN CAUSE IT? --MUST BE A BIRD!

WOLFF JOINS LANG....

LOIS AMONG THEM--A CAPTIVE! I'VE GOT TO DO SOMETHING...!

SWIFTLY, SUPERMAN DONS HIS OUTER GARMENTS WHICH HE HAS CARRIED BENEATH HIS CLOAK....

ENTER CLARK KENT!

CLARK DELIBERATELY PERMITS HIMSELF TO BE CAPTURED...

GOT YOU!

UH-HHH!

CLARK! HOW-- HOW DID YOU GET HERE?

YOU'RE NOT THE ONLY ENTERPRISING REPORTER ON THE STAFF!

ANOTHER REPORTER, EH? I SUGGEST WE DISPOSE OF BOTH OF THEM IMMEDIATELY!

NO WE'LL TAKE THEM ALONG AS PRISONERS.-- PLENTY OF TIME TO ATTEND TO THEM LATER!

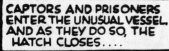

CAPTORS AND PRISONERS ENTER THE UNUSUAL VESSEL, AND AS THEY DO SO, THE HATCH CLOSES....

THE SIDES --MADE OF A TRANSPARENT PLASTIC! WE SEEM TO BE MOVING AT TERRIFIC SPEED!

YOU ARE VERY OBSERVANT... TOO MUCH SO FOR YOUR OWN GOOD!

YOU THINK THAT ASTONISHING? WATCH THIS!

AS LANG PULLS THE LEVER, THE VESSEL SLANTS SHARPLY UP INTO THE AIR!

THEN--AS IT DIVES BENEATH THE WATER'S SURFACE ONCE AGAIN

YOU SEE... MY SHIP CAN TRAVEL *ABOVE* WATER AS WELL AS *BENEATH* IT! -- QUITE AN IMPORTANT DISCOVERY FOR MODERN WARFARE, EH? AND ANYONE CAN OPERATE IT WITH THIS SIMPLE LEVER!

THAT'S ALL I WANT TO KNOW! HEAD FOR THE PANAMA CANAL-- AND FORGET ABOUT THE TWO MILLION... YOU'LL NEVER LIVE TO SEE IT!

YOU CAN PUT DOWN THAT GUN! THIS SIGNAL SUMMONS MY MEN!

AH--BUT I'VE ANTICIPATED YOU. HALL HAS ALREADY ATTENDED TO THEM ...*SPY!* YOU CAN DROP THE POSE. I HAPPEN TO HAVE KNOWN ALL ALONG YOU STILL SERVE THE U.S. NAVY AND HAVE USED THIS NEW INVENTION TO SNARE FOREIGN SPIES!

YOU MUST BE COMPLETELY MAD! THIS CRAFT HASN'T THE SLIGHTEST CHANCE OF PENETRATING THE PANAMA CANAL DEFENSES!

YOU UNDERESTIMATE MY INGENUITY!

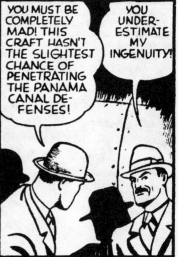

AS WOLFF HAD PRE-ARRANGED, THE SKY-SUB IS MANEUVERED SO THAT IT IS ATTACHED TO A HOOK BENEATH A LARGE FREIGHTER...

WITH THE AID OF SPECIAL APPARATUS, TORPEDOES AND BOMBS ARE TRANSFERED FROM THE FREIGHTER TO THE SUB ...

WHEN THE FREIGHTER APPROACHES THE PANAMA CANAL, IT WILL BE INSPECTED AND PASSED. NO ONE WILL KNOW THAT HIDDEN BENEATH IT IS A CRAFT THAT WILL BE RELEASED AT A VITAL SPOT TO BLOW UP THE CANAL!

YOU WON'T GET AWAY WITH IT!

BUT IT APPEARS HE IS!

AT THE CONSUL'S ORDERS, CLARK IS PLACED WITHIN AN EMPTY TORPEDO-TUBE....

PLEASE DON'T! THIS IS MURDER!

YOU'LL ONLY BE IN THE WAY NOW. YOU FIRST--THEN... THE OTHERS SHARE YOUR FATE!

--YOU BUTCHER!

BUT DESPITE LOIS' PLEAS, THE TORPEDO BEARING CLARK IS SHOT INTO THE WATER...

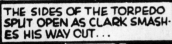

THE SIDES OF THE TORPEDO SPLIT OPEN AS CLARK SMASHES HIS WAY OUT...

HERE'S WHERE' EXIT!

SWIFTLY CHANGING HIS GARMENTS, **SUPERMAN** HIDES HIS CIVILIAN GARMENTS BENEATH HIS CLOAK...

GOT TO GET BACK --BEFORE HE HARMS LOIS--!

SO HERE GOES!

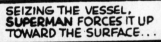

SEIZING THE VESSEL, **SUPERMAN** FORCES IT UP TOWARD THE SURFACE...

GET MOVING!

LET THE GIRL AND LANG ALONE OPEN THE HATCH WHEN WE REACH THE SURFACE AND SEE WHAT THE TROUBLE IS!

WHAT CAN IT BE?

IT'S THAT INFERNALLY STRONG MEDDLER --GET HIM!

THIS BOMB OUGHT TO TAKE CARE OF HIM!

SUPERMAN

REG. U. S PAT. OFF.

by JERRY SIEGEL and JOE SHUSTER

THE UNITY OF THE NATION IS THREATENED BY THE MACHINATIONS OF A CUNNING BEING KNOWN AS "THE LIGHT". **SUPERMAN,** *DEFENDER OF DEMOCRACY,* SWINGS INTO ACTION TO COMBAT A DARK MENACE THAT THREATENS TO ENGULF AND ENSLAVE A CONTINENT!

EDITORIAL OFFICE OF THE *DAILY PLANET*....

SENATOR BILLINGSLEY IS TO SPEAK AT *NATIONAL HALL.* I WANT BOTH OF YOU TO COVER THE EVENT.

A POLITICAL SPEECH!

WHY NOT ASSIGN US SOMETHING MORE INTERESTING?

I'VE BEEN INFORMED ON THE QUIET THAT SOMEONE NAMED "THE LIGHT" HAS ISSUED A WARNING THAT BILLINGSLEY WILL NEVER SPEAK AT THAT MEETING. ANYTHING MAY HAPPEN!

THAT'S *DIFFERENT!*

COME ON, CLARK!

LATER...

HE'S ALREADY LATE-- DO YOU THINK...?

I DON'T KNOW WHAT TO THINK! EXCUSE ME, LOIS. I'D LIKE TO MAKE A TELEPHONE CALL.

BUT INSTEAD OF APPROACHING THE TELEPHONE BOOTH, CLARK STEPS INTO AN EMPTY OFFICE AND REMOVES HIS OUTER GARMENTS...

"THE LIGHT" MAY NOT BE A CRANK AFTER ALL-- I'D BETTER LOOK INTO THIS-- AS **SUPERMAN**...!

77

MOMENTS LATER--THE COLOR-FUL COSTUMED FIGURE OF THE MIGHTY *MAN OF TOMORROW* STREAKS THRU THE FLEECY CLOUDS AT BREATH-TAKING SPEED....

THE SENATOR'S CAR SHOULD BE COMING ALONG THE *CARROLL HIGHWAY.* IT'S ENTIRELY POSSIBLE THAT I'M BEING UNDULY APPREHENSIVE, BUT...

THAT INSTANT--WITHIN SENATOR TOM BILLINGSLEY'S AUTO....

"THE LIGHT" MAY BE A JOKE TO YOU, SENATOR--BUT WE'RE NOT TAKING ANY CHANCES!

NONSENSE! "THE LIGHT" IS A HARM-LESS POISON PEN WRITER.

TOWARD THE SENATOR'S CAR DRIVES A SEDAN.--UNUSUAL? DEFINITELY *NOT!* THAT IS, *UNTIL*...

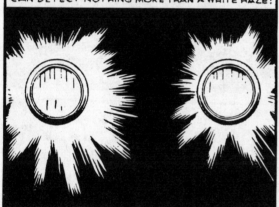

THE HEADLIGHTS OF THE NEARING CAR UN-EXPECTEDLY FLASH ON! FROM THEM EMERGES A BRILLIANCE OF SUCH STARK, BLINDING QUALITIES THAT THE HUMAN EYE INSTANTLY CAN DETECT NOTHING MORE THAN A WHITE HAZE!

THOSE HEAD-LIGHTS--! I--I CAN'T SEE!

WHAT --!!

NEITHER CAN I!

BLINDED, THE DRIVER OF THE SENATOR'S AUTO INSTINCTIVELY JAMS ON HIS BRAKES! THERE IS THE SOUND OF APPROACHING FOOTSTEPS--THEN SILENCE, EXCEPT FOR THE SHOUTS OF THE CONFUSED BODYGUARDS...

ABRUPTLY--THE GLARE IS GONE! IT TAKES SOME TIME FOR THEM TO ACCUSTOM THEIR EYES AGAIN TO NORMAL LIGHT, BUT WHEN THEY DO, THE GUARDS DISCOVER...

HE'S GONE--! THE SENATOR IS **GONE!**

KID-NAPPED!

AT THAT MOMENT, THE *MAN OF STEEL* ALIGHTS BESIDE THE SENATOR'S CAR....

WHAT HAPPENED?

IT'S **SUPERMAN!**

HE MUST BE TO BLAME! GET HIM!

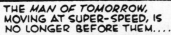

DOWN IN THE VERY PATH OF THE ONRUSHING AUTO PLUMMETS **SUPERMAN**....!

WHOA, THERE!

THE CAR *INCREASES* SPEED! ON FLASH THE HEADLIGHTS, BOMBARDING THE *MAN OF STEEL* WITH BLINDING BEAMS...

WANT TO FIGHT, EH?

FULL INTO THE FIGURE OF **SUPERMAN** CRASHES THE MYSTERY-AUTO! UP INTO THE AIR HIS BODY IS WHIRLED...!

BUT--SOMERSAULTING--THE *MAN OF TOMORROW* ALIGHTS UPON THE AUTOMOBILE'S REAR BUMPER...!

CAN'T GET RID OF ME *THAT* EASILY!

ONE SWIFT MOVEMENT AND **SUPERMAN** RIPS OPEN THE BACK OF THE CAR....

I'VE BEEN MIGHTY PATIENT UP TO NOW, BUT DON'T GET ME *SORE!*

FRANTICALLY, THE SENATOR'S CAPTORS DISCHARGE BOLTS OF BLAZING BRILLIANCE TOWARD **SUPERMAN** FROM THEIR TINY RODS.... BUT TO NO AVAIL....

HERE'S SOME OF THE PUNISHMENT YOU'VE BEEN BEGGING FOR!

OUT OF CONTROL, THE AUTO PLUNGES TOWARD A RAVINE. BUT SEIZING THE LIMB OF A PROJECTING TREE, **SUPERMAN** HALTS THE MACHINE AT THE VERY EDGE OF THE SHARP INCLINE....

THAT'S FAR ENOUGH!

MOMENTS LATER--DOWN OUT OF THE SKY PLUMMETS THE AMAZING *MAN OF STEEL.* DEPOSITING THE CAR BEFORE THE ASTOUNDED GUARDS, HE SPRINGS OFF....

YOU'LL FIND THE SENATOR AND THE MEN WHO CAPTURED HIM IN THERE--CONFISCATE THEIR LIGHT-RODS!

FIRST YOU KIDNAP THE SENATOR, THEN RETURN HIM! I DON'T GET IT!

RETURNING TO *NATIONAL HALL,* **SUPERMAN** DONS HIS OUTER GARMENTS, ONCE AGAIN ASSUMING HIS IDENTITY OF THE MEEK *DAILY PLANET* REPORTER....

BETTER HURRY BACK TO LOIS BEFORE SHE BEGINS TO WONDER WHETHER I'M DICTATING A NOVEL OVER THE TELEPHONE!

IT CERTAINLY TOOK YOU LONG ENOUGH!

I MIGHT SAY THE SAME FOR THE SENATOR.

SHORTLY AFTER, SENATOR BILLINGSLEY ENTERS THE AUDITORIUM--HE LOSES NO TIME IN MAKING A SPECIAL ANNOUNCEMENT....

A FANATIC NAMED *"THE LIGHT"* PROPHECIED I WOULD NOT SPEAK TO YOU TODAY. HE TRIED TO MAKE THAT THREAT COME TRUE.-- FORTUNATELY, HE FAILED!

LATER--AS THE SENATOR MAKES THE ANNOUNCED ADDRESS, CLARK, KEEPING KEEN WATCH, OBSERVES A SUSPICIOUS INDIVIDUAL ENTER...

("-HE DELIBERATELY DROPPED A SMALL PILL BEHIND THAT VASE!")

MOMENTS LATER--THERE IS A SUDDEN BLINDING FLASH--AN EYE-SCORCHING BLAZE OF LIGHT. THEN....

WHAT --!!

SHIELD YOUR EYES!

A MESSAGE IS TO BE SEEN ON THE WALL, WRITTEN IN LETTERS OF BLAZING *LIGHT!*

YOU MAY HAVE ESCAPED THIS TIME, SENATOR, BUT THERE WILL BE OTHER ATTEMPTS, AND THEY MAY NOT FAIL

--*"THE LIGHT"*

⑤

IN THE CONFUSION THAT FOLLOWS, CLARK ATTEMPTS TO FOLLOW THE SUSPICIOUS CHARACTER HE HAD OBSERVED, BUT LOIS BLOCKS HIS PATH....

LET GO, LOIS!

FORGET YOUR PANIC! GO TO THE PHONE AND CALL THE NEWSPAPER OFFICE!

THAT YOU, CLARK? GET BACK TO THE OFFICE AT ONCE! PROMINENT MEN ARE VANISHING BY THE DOZEN--KIDNAPPED BY *"THE LIGHT"*!

I'LL BE RIGHT THERE, WHITE!

⑤

AND TO THINK WE BELIEVED "THE LIGHT" MIGHT BE A HARMLESS CRANK!

THAT'S ALL CHANGED NOW!

("-I'D LIKE TO HAVE TRAILED THAT SUSPICIOUS CHAP, BUT THAT PLEASURE WILL HAVE TO BE INDEFINITELY POSTPONED.-")

UNKNOWN TO CLARK AND LOIS, THEY ARE PURSUED BY A SLEEK SEDAN....

WITHIN THE TRAILING CAR....

BUT WHY WASTE OUR TIME ON THESE TWO REPORTERS?

"THE LIGHT" CONSIDERS THEM DANGEROUS, AND THAT'S ENOUGH FOR ME.

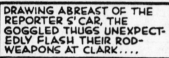

DRAWING ABREAST OF THE REPORTERS' CAR, THE GOGGLED THUGS UNEXPECTEDLY FLASH THEIR ROD-WEAPONS AT CLARK....

("-I'LL PRETEND TO BE BLINDED.-")

I--I--CAN'T SEE!

MY-- EYES--!

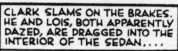

CLARK SLAMS ON THE BRAKES. HE AND LOIS, BOTH APPARENTLY DAZED, ARE DRAGGED INTO THE INTERIOR OF THE SEDAN....

WH-WHAT --??

NOT A PEEP OUTA EITHER OF YA-- GET IN THERE!

MINUTES LATER....

I SEE THE EFFECTS OF "THE LIGHT" HAVE WORN OFF!

I SEE, NOW! YOU'RE AGENTS OF "THE LIGHT"!

BRIGHT GIRL!

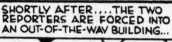

SHORTLY AFTER....THE TWO REPORTERS ARE FORCED INTO AN OUT-OF-THE-WAY BUILDING...

IN THERE!

WHAT-- WHAT ARE YOU GOING TO DO TO US?

THAT'S WHAT WE'D LIKE TO KNOW.

THE BOSS SAYS TO RUB 'EM OUT!

THERE'S YOUR ANSWER, LADY!

NO!

("-WHAT A PREDICAMENT!--I CAN'T PERMIT THESE THUGS TO GET AWAY WITH MURDER, YET--IF I ACT AS SUPERMAN I'LL BE FORCED TO REVEAL MY TRUE IDENTITY!-")

82

NOW?

SURE, WHY NOT?

LET'S GET IT OVER WITH!

THE THUGS WHIRL AT THE SOUND OF AN UNEXPECTED VOICE BEHIND THEM....

DROP THOSE GUNS!

WHA---!!

I DON'T SEE ANYONE!

BUT I HEARD A VOICE!

SO DID I!

ACTING AT TERRIFIC SPEED, SUPERMAN REMOVES HIS OUTER GARMENTS....

HOPE THIS LITTLE BIT OF VENTRILOQUISM DOES THE TRICK...!

OUT THRU THE DOOR HE SPEEDS FASTER THAN A GUST OF WIND...

...AROUND THE SIDE OF THE BUILDING....

THIS CALLS FOR SPEED...AND I MEAN SPEED PLUS!!

CRASHING IN THRU A WINDOW, SUPERMAN BANGS THE THUGS TOGETHER....

SURPRISE!

HEY! OUCH!

UH-HHH!

HUH!

...THEN, BACK AROUND THE HOUSE SPEEDS SUPERMAN RETRACING HIS STEPS....

ALL I HOPE IS THAT LOIS HASN'T YET HAD TIME TO GLANCE BACK TOWARD ME!

⑦

...SWIFTLY SUPERMAN DIVES INTO HIS OUTER GARMENTS AS LOIS COMMENCES TO TURN....

("-SECONDS... TO MAKE IT...!-")

CLARK-- DID YOU SEE THAT? SUPERMAN!

GOOD THING FOR US HE SHOWED UP!

("-AND A GOOD THING FOR ME LOIS DIDN'T TURN A SECOND SOONER!-")

83

CASEY? HURRY DOWN TO THE FOLLOWING ADDRESS--WE'VE GOT SOME OF *"THE LIGHT"*'S THUGS HERE--AND I'M NOT KIDDING!

WE'D BETTER GET THEM TIED BEFORE THEY REVIVE!

LATER....

SO YOU WEREN'T FOOLING, AFTER ALL! HOW DID YOU EVER CAPTURE ALL THOSE MEN SINGLE-HANDED, CLARK?

THE TRUTH IS THAT CLARK WAS STANDING BESIDE ME, WHILE **SUPERMAN** CLEANED UP THOSE CRIMINALS.

WHO IS *"THE LIGHT"*?

YOU'LL LEARN NOTHIN' FROM US, COPPER!

PERHAPS YOU'LL HAVE BETTER LUCK WITH THEM AT HEAD-QUARTERS, SERGEANT!

LATER--AT THE *DAILY PLANET*...

PROMINENT MEN THROUGHOUT THE COUNTRY ARE DISAPPEARING BY THE SCORE!

BUT WHAT CAN BE *"THE LIGHT"*'S MOTIVE--RANSOM?

I'M AFRAID IT MAY BE SOMETHING EVEN MORE SINISTER.

NEWS FLASH! GOVERNOR BENSON HAS JUST RECEIVED A THREAT FROM THE NOTORIOUS CRIMINAL KNOWN AS "THE LIGHT"!

COVER THAT STORY!

BUT AS LOIS AND CLARK EMERGE FROM THE *PLANET* BUILDING,....

WHERE'S CLARK?-- WELL, I CAN'T WASTE ANY TIME WAITING FOR THAT SLOW-POKE!

LOIS WOULD HAVE BEEN VERY SURPRISED TO KNOW THAT THE "SLOWPOKE" HAS NEARLY REACHED THE GOVERNOR'S RESIDENCE BY THIS TIME....

I'LL KEEP AN EYE ON THE GOVERNOR'S MANSION.

NO SOONER DOES THE MIGHTY *MAN OF STEEL* ALIGHT UPON A TREE LIMB HIGH ABOVE THE GOVERNOR'S ESTATE WHEN,....

SO WE MEET AGAIN...

84

SUPERMAN'S TELESCOPIC VISION HAS REVEALED TO HIM THAT ONE OF THE GUARDS PATROLLING THE ESTATE IS THE SUSPICIOUS CHARACTER HE HAD SEEN AT *NATIONAL HALL*....

AS THE GUARD WALKS UNDER THE TREE, A HAND SUDDENLY JERKS HIM UP INTO THE FOLIAGE

ULP--!

THEN--TWO FIGURES HURTLE HIGH UP INTO THE SKY LIKE AN UNLEASHED BOLT....

LET GO! WHAT'S THE IDEA--?

DON'T PLAY INNOCENT! I KNOW YOU WERE PLANTED THERE BY *"THE LIGHT"*! WHAT ARE HIS PLANS?

PLANS? I DON'T KNOW WHAT YOU'RE TALKING ABOUT!

WOULDN'T IT BE A PITY IF I WERE TO LOSE MY GRIP?

A MOMENT LATER--AS THE *MAN OF STEEL* RELEASES HIS HOLD, DOWN PLUNGES THE SCREAMING GUARD....

YEEE-EEEE!

AS HE DROPS, A VOICE BOOMS OUT OF THE CLOUDS NEAR HIM...

WHERE ARE YOU?

HERE I AM! CATCH ME! CATCH ME!

STRANGE--BUT UNLESS YOU'RE WILLING TO TALK, I'M AFRAID I WON'T BE *ABLE* TO FIND YOU!

I'LL TALK! I'LL TALK!

THAT'S BETTER!

I'LL TELL YOU ANYTHING YOU WANT TO KNOW-- ANYTHING!

⑨

GRADUALLY, THE BEAM CHANGES COLORS.- BLUE, RED, ORANGE, GREEN, YELLOW, PURPLE-- "THE LIGHT" WHISPERS HYPNOTICALLY TO HIS CAPTIVE....

THOSE LIGHTS--BEATING INTO YOUR BRAIN--ROBBING YOU OF ALL INITIATIVE.

THE LIGHTS-- THE PRETTY COLORED LIGHTS...

NOW-- FREE HIM!

MOMENTS LATER, THE CAPTIVE RISES AT "THE LIGHT"'S COMMAND.

NOW WILL YOU OBEY ME?

YOU ARE MY MASTER, I SHALL DO AS YOU DIRECT...

YOU SEE HOW HE IS NOW AN INSTRUMENT OF MY WILL? SO SHALL IT BE WITH ALL OF YOU! YOU ARE ALL PROMINENT MEN IN YOUR LINES--WITH YOUR HELP, VICTORY IS ASSURED!

SOMEONE IS COMING!

SUPERMAN! I MIGHT HAVE EXPECTED HIS APPEARANCE--AND SO I AM PREPARED!

PLUNGING STRAIGHT AT BARROWS' RIDGE, SUPERMAN CLEARS A WAY FOR HIMSELF THRU THE SOLID ROCK....

HERE'S WHERE I PUT OUT "THE LIGHT"!

INTO THE VILLAINOUS SCIENTIST'S LABORATORY CRASHES THE MAN OF TOMORROW....

WE MEET AT LAST!

A MOMENT I HAVE LONG AWAITED!

THE MECHANISM BLASTING FORTH VARI-COLORED BEAMS OF LIGHT STRIKES AT THE MAN OF STEEL...

CAN'T-- MOVE!

HE'S HELP-LESS! AND NOW--I HAVE PLANS FOR SUPERMAN!

MY INSTRUCTIONS ARE AS FOLLOWS--COMPLETELY DESTROY ANY MILITARY MATERIALS THAT MAY BE USED AGAINST ME! GO!

I-- OBEY!

SHORTLY AFTER...THE *MAN OF STEEL* PLUNGES DOWN OUT OF THE SKY BEFORE A GOVERNMENT ARMORY....

CRUSH-- DESTROY --!!

DRIVING BY, LOIS HALTS HER AUTO AS SHE SIGHTS THE *MAN OF TOMORROW*....

IT'S-- SUPERMAN!

WHAT'S HAPPENED TO YOU-- YOUR EYES...

"THE LIGHT" HAS COMMANDED ME TO CAUSE WHOLE-SALE DESTRUCT-ION--AND I MUST OBEY!

BUT YOU MUSTN'T-- YOU CAN'T--YOU'VE ALWAYS FOUGHT EVIL... NEVER CHAMPIONED IT!

FOUGHT EVIL... FOUGHT IT...!

AIDED BY LOIS' APPEAL, SUPER-MAN'S MIND CLEARS OF *"THE LIGHT"'S* INFLUENCE....

I--I'M ALL RIGHT NOW. YOU'LL NEVER KNOW HOW CLOSE I CAME TO...

I KNOW. BUT HADN'T YOU BETTER HURRY AND STOP *"THE LIGHT"* BEFORE IT'S TOO LATE?

MEANWHILE...

NOW TO MAKE ALL OF YOU MY SLAVES!

ABRUPTLY--IN THRU THE WALL CRASHES...

SUPERMAN! BUT I THOUGHT--

THAT I'D BE BUSY SPREADING DESTRUCTION? GUESS AGAIN!

AND AS FOR YOUR HYP-NOTIZING THESE MEN TO DO YOUR WILL... THAT'S *OUT!*

YOU'VE DESTROYED THE CONTROL-BOARD...BUT I'VE AN ACE UP MY SLEEVE!

MY FOOT RESTS ON A PLUNGER... ONE MOVE TOWARD ME AND I BLOW US ALL TO KINGDOM COME!

YOU THINK OF EVERYTHING, DON'T YOU?

HERE'S ANOTHER SURPRISE FOR YOU, MAN OF STEEL!

LUTHOR!

SUPERMAN TAKES A GREAT LEAP FORWARD....

I THREATENED TO BLOW US UP--AND I WILL!

YOU MEAN YOU'LL TRY TO!

THE MAN OF STEEL SUCCEEDS IN WEDGING HIS POWERFUL FINGERS BETWEEN THE SMALL PLUNGER AND THE FLOOR...

LUTHOR ATTEMPTS FLIGHT...

NO YOU DON'T!

GET HIM!

AS LUTHOR'S HIRELINGS CLOSE IN, SUPERMAN SENDS THEM FLYING IN ALL DIRECTIONS....

WANT TO FIGHT, EH?

BUT WHEN HE TURNS BACK TO SEIZE HIS CAPTIVE....

GONE! HE MADE GOOD HIS ESCAPE WHILE MY BACK WAS TURNED!

LATER, AT THE DAILY PLANET, AFTER SUPERMAN HAS RETURNED THE PROMINENT MEN TO SAFETY.

SO LUTHOR WAS AT THE BOTTOM OF THIS MESS! WE MIGHT HAVE SUSPECTED IT!

WHEN I THINK HOW CLOSE SUPERMAN CAME TO BECOMING A DESTRUCTIVE FORCE, I SHUDDER. IT'S A LUCKY THING HE'S ON THE SIDE OF LAW AND ORDER!

⑬

THE END

SUPERMAN

by JERRY SIEGEL and JOE SHUSTER

SUPERMAN MEETS A STRANGE FOE IN THE MYSTERIOUS BEING KNOWN ONLY AS *"THE ARCHER"*. VICTIMS ARE GIVEN THE CHOICE OF PAYING A HEAVY FEE OR PERISHING BEFORE THE UNIQUE CRIMINAL'S DEADLY ACCURACY WITH THE BOW AND ARROW!

LIMOUSINE AFTER LIMOUSINE PULLS UP BEFORE THE *GAYFORD MANSION*....

THE REASON: WEALTHY THOMAS GAYFORD IS HOLDING ONE OF HIS INTERNATIONALLY FAMOUS PARTIES....

HAVE FUN, FOLKS! I'M FOOTING THE BILLS!

LATER--AS THE GUESTS LINE UP AROUND A BANQUET TABLE....

YOU'LL NEVER KNOW JUST HOW GLAD I AM TO HAVE ALL OF YOU HERE. YOU SEE, I HAVE HERE AN ANONYMOUS NOTE, SIGNED *"THE ARCHER"*. IT IT PROPHESIES THAT SINCE I HAVE FAILED TO PAY A DEMANDED RANSOM, I SHALL DIE TONIGHT.

WHAT?

SURELY YOU'RE JOKING!

NOT AT ALL. BUT THE JOKE'S ON *"THE ARCHER"*! I'VE POSTED GUARDS ABOUT THE PLACE. IT WILL BE IMPOSSIBLE FOR HIM TO ENTER!

BUT UNKNOWN TO GAYFORD --AT THAT VERY MOMENT ONE OF THE GUARDS LIES STILL IN DEATH...!

90

A GREEN-CLAD FIGURE LAUNCHES ITSELF FROM THE LIMB OF A HIGH TREE TO A BALCONY ON THE SIDE OF THE MANSION....

A TOAST, FRIENDS-- TO 'THE ARCHER'-- WHO MISSED HIS MARK!

LOOK!

UP THERE!

AAAGH HHH!!

GET "THE ARCHER"!

HE'S GONE!

CALL THE POLICE!!

EDITORIAL OFFICE OF THE DAILY PLANET....

WHERE IN BLAZES ARE LOIS LANE AND CLARK KENT?

THEY'RE NOT TO BE FOUND ANYWHERE, MR WHITE!

FINE THING! JUST WHEN THE BIGGEST NEWS STORY OF THE YEAR IS BREAKING, THEY HAVE TO PLAY HIDE-AND-SEEK!

ER-- MR. WH-WHITE...

YES?

I'LL BE GLAD TO COVER THE STORY FOR YOU!

91

YOU'LL COVER IT?

I--I'D LIKE TO BECOME A REAL REPORTER-- LIKE CLARK KENT, AND IF YOU'D ONLY GIVE ME A CHANCE...

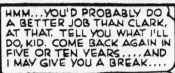

HMM...YOU'D PROBABLY DO A BETTER JOB THAN CLARK, AT THAT. TELL YOU WHAT I'LL DO, KID. COME BACK AGAIN IN FIVE OR TEN YEARS.....AND I MAY GIVE YOU A BREAK....

T-TEN YEARS? --THAT'S A LONG TIME!

CLARK AND LOIS RETURN TO THE NEWSPAPER OFFICE....

SO HERE YOU ARE! WHERE HAVE YOU TWO BEEN?

OUT LOOKING FOR MATERIAL --BUT NOT A THING IS STIRRING!

NOTHING, EH? GET DOWN TO THE GAYFORD MANSION! --THOMAS GAYFORD HAS BEEN SLAIN BY A MYSTERIOUS PERSON NAMED "THE ARCHER". HE REFUSED TO PAY THE AMOUNT DEMANDED!

WHAT --?!

"THE ARCHER"! SOUNDS MELO-DRAMATIC!

--AND EXCITING

YOU, EH? IT DOESN'T TAKE YOU LONG TO SHOW UP WHEREVER NEWS IS BEING MADE!

THAT'S OUR BUSINESS!

HAVE YOU ANY IDEA WHO THIS "ARCHER" MAY BE, CASEY?

NONE AT ALL--YET, BUT WE HAVE SOME INTERESTING CLUES.

WHY DON'T YOU COOK UP A NEW COME-BACK?

THAT ONE'S A LITTLE SHOP-WORN!

QUIET, YOU TWO--OR I'LL HAVE YOU RUN OFF THE PLACE!

③

AT THAT MOMENT----

A NOTE-- PINNED TO THE WALL BY THE ARROW!

WHAT DOES IT SAY?

KEEP BACK. THIS IS CONFIDENTIAL POLICE BUSINESS!

WELL --??

NO HARM IN LETTING YOU KNOW. *"THE ARCHER"* SAYS HE KILLED GAYFORD TO SHOW THAT HE MEANS BUSINESS WHEN HE MAKES HIS DEMANDS!

QUICK, A TELEPHONE!

AS THEY DRIVE OFF, CLARK'S QUICK EYES NOTE....

("-AN ARROW-- STREAKING DOWN TOWARD US!-")

SWIFTLY, CLARK RAISES HIS HAND SO THAT THE ARROW BOUNCES OFF BEFORE IT REACHES LOIS....

WHAT WAS THAT NOISE?

I DIDN'T HEAR ANYTHING!

BUT THEN-- AS THEY SPEED DOWN AN INCLINE... CLARK MAKES ANOTHER STARTLING DISCOVERY....

("-THE BRAKES --THEY DON'T WORK--!-")

CLARK'S X-RAY VISION REVEALS TO HIM THAT THE BRAKES OF HIS CAR HAVE BEEN TAMPERED WITH....

("-COMING AROUND THAT CURVE AHEAD-- A TRUCK! THERE'S SURE TO BE A COLLISION--UNLESS...!-")

CAREFUL, CLARK!

93

SWIFTLY CLARK FOCUSES HIS EYES HYPNOTICALLY UPON LOIS LANE SO THAT SHE IS SWIFTLY AND PAINLESSLY RENDERED UNCONSCIOUS....

SHE'S OUT!

NO TIME TO CHANGE TO MY SUPERMAN COSTUME!

AS THE TRUCK HURTLES TOWARD HIM, KENT HEAVES HIS ROADSTER UP...!

HOPE THE TRUCK DRIVER DOESN'T GET A GOOD LOOK AT ME!

...AND VAULTS OVER THE ONCOMING TRUCK, ROADSTER AND ALL...!

THAT DOES IT!

THERE! THE BRAKE'S ARE OKAY AGAIN! BUT NOW TO START DRIVING AGAIN!

I--I MUST HAVE FALLEN ASLEEP!

YOU CERTAINLY DON'T FIND MY COMPANY VERY INTERESTING!

GOODNIGHT, LOIS.-- PLEASANT DREAMS!

I DOUBT IF I'LL SLEEP A WINK--NOT WITH "THE ARCHER" LOOSE...!

ONE THING I KNOW DEFINITELY--"THE ARCHER" DISLIKES INQUISITIVE REPORTERS!

WHEN CLARK REACHES HIS APARTMENT....

THIS DEMANDS FURTHER INVESTIGATION--FROM SUPERMAN!

SHORTLY AFTER THE COLORFUL MAN OF TOMORROW HURTLES THRU THE DARK SKY...

TRACKING DOWN SOMEONE AS COLD AND CRUEL AS "THE ARCHER" WILL BE NO CINCH!

AND LATER--HE ALIGHTS ATOP THE BALCONY OUTSIDE THE GAYFORD MANSION....

ONE CLUE HE'S SURE TO HAVE LEFT BEHIND!

HIS FOOTPRINTS! MY MICROSCOPIC VISION MAKE THEM APPEAR AS CLEAR AS SIGN POSTS!

SUPERMAN LEAPS DOWN TO THE ROAD BELOW AND FAILS TO SIGHT SHADOWS CREEPING TOWARD HIM...

AND HERE'S WHERE HE STOOD WHEN HE TAMPERED WITH MY CAR'S BRAKES!

SUDDENLY, SEVERAL POLICEMEN SPRING AT THE MAN OF STEEL..

IT'S SUPERMAN!

GRAB HIM!

A MOMENT BEFORE THE POLICE REACH HIM, SUPERMAN DIVES AT THE GROUND AND BURROWS OUT OF VIEW...!

I'D BETTER EXIT!

STOP HIM!

6

AN INSTANT LATER HE POPS OUT OF THE GROUND BEHIND THE OFFICERS...

WERE YOU GENTLEMEN PAGING ME?

THERE HE IS!

DON'T LET HIM GET AWAY!

BUT OFF RACES SUPERMAN SO SWIFTLY THAT HE IS OUT OF VIEW IN MOMENTS...!

IT WOULD BE USELESS TO ATTEMPT TO REASON WITH THEM!

THIS--"THE ARCHER"? --I WONDER...

I HEARD A RADIO NEWS FLASH AND HURRIED OVER TO DEMONSTRATE MY SKILL WITH THE BOW AND ARROW!

LATER--AT HEADQUARTERS....

REMEMBER TO MENTION IN THE PAPER THAT IT WAS ME WHO CAPTURED THIS DANGEROUS CRIMINAL.

IF YOU ASK ME, I THINK THIS FELLOW IS A HARMLESS NUT WHO IMAGINES HIMSELF TO BE THE REAL "ARCHER"!

AMOS KENDRICK, THE JEWELER, CALLED.--HE CLAIMS TO HAVE RECEIVED A THREAT FROM "THE ARCHER"!

PAY NO ATTENTION TO HIM. HE'S GOT NOTHING TO WORRY ABOUT NOW THAT "THE ARCHER" IS BEHIND BARS.

("--I'D BETTER EXIT!--")

FAR FROM THE POSSIBILITY OF SCRUTINY, CLARK REMOVES HIS OUTER GARMENTS....

IT'S MY PERSONAL OPINION THAT KENDRICK MAY BE VERY MUCH IN DANGER!

SHORTLY AFTER...THE MAN OF TOMORROW ALIGHTS ATOP THE ROOF OF KENDRICK'S RESIDENCE...

NOW TO MAKE USE OF MY X-RAY VISION!

WHAT THE MAN OF STEEL SIGHTS...

WHY DON'T THE POLICE ARRIVE? THIS SUSPENSE IS DRIVING ME MAD!

⑧

SUDDENLY-- IN THRU THE WINDOW SPEEDS A DEADLY SHAFT...!

IN A TWINKLING, SUPERMAN RIPS AN OPENING IN THE ROOF....

NO TIME TO SEARCH FOR ANOTHER ENTRANCE!

97

SOMETIME LATER....

I MESSED UP A BEAUTIFUL OPPORTUNITY TO SNARE *"THE ARCHER"*, MIGHT AS WELL CHANGE NOW.

THIS NOTE CAME FOR MR. KENT, THE MESSENGER SAID IT WAS ABOUT *"THE ARCHER"*.

THANKS, I'LL TAKE IT, JIMMY.

HM-MM! IT SAYS FOR CLARK TO COME TO BINSTON AND ANNEX AVENUES IF HE WANTS TO KNOW WHO *"THE ARCHER"* IS! WHAT A BREAK FOR *ME!*

CLARK ENTERS THE *DAILY PLANET* EDITORIAL OFFICE TWO MINUTES LATER....

CONGRAT-ULATIONS, CLARK! THIS IS YOUR LUCKY DAY!

YES?

A TIP HAS COME IN THAT THERE'S A BIG STORY BREWING AT 1411 WINGATE ROAD! I'D COVER IT MYSELF, ONLY IT'S TOO SENSATIONAL.

THANKS, LOIS, I CERTAINLY APPRECIATE YOUR GENEROSITY.

BUT AS CLARK CHANGES TO HIS IDENTITY AS *SUPERMAN*...

THIS UNSELFISHNESS ON LOIS' PART IS ALMOST TOO MUCH FOR ME, IT'S RATHER UNUSUAL FOR A REPORTER TO PASS UP A GOOD STORY!

WAIT TILL CLARK FINDS OUT WHAT *I'VE* UNCOVERED WHILE HE'S ON A WILD-GOOSE CHASE!

UNKNOWN TO LOIS, JIMMY THE OFFICE BOY, CONCEALS HIMSELF IN THE TRUNK AT THE REAR OF HER CAR....

IF I WAITED FOR A CHANCE TO BE *HANDED* TO ME, IT MAY *NEVER* COME! I'VE GOT TO BE LIKE LOIS-- *MAKE MY OPPORTUNITIES!*

10

MEANWHILE....
THIS IS 1411 WINGATE ROAD, ALL RIGHT. --BUT THERE'S NOTHING HERE EXCEPT AN EMPTY LOT! IF THIS IS LOIS' IDEA OF A JOKE...!

SUPERMAN RETURNS TO THE DAILY PLANET IN HIS IDENTITY AS CLARK KENT....

THIS NOTE ON LOIS' DESK EXPLAINS EVERYTHING! SHE SENT ME OUT TO NO-MAN'S-LAND SO SHE'D HAVE AN OPPORTUNITY TO INVESTIGATE THAT TIP ABOUT "THE ARCHER" WITHOUT INTERFERENCE FROM ME!

ONCE AGAIN AS SUPERMAN, CLARK SPEEDS TOWARD BINSTON AND ANNEX AVENUES....

FOOLISH GIRL! SHE MAY BE GETTING INTO TERRIBLE DANGER!

HE ALMOST GOT ME --AGAIN!

BENEATH THAT LEDGE-- A PERFECT HIDING PLACE!

LOIS AND JIMMY HUDDLE IN SILENT TERROR BENEATH THE LEDGE, UNAWARE THAT "THE ARCHER" APPEARS ATOP THE LEDGE BEHIND THEM AND TAKES CAREFUL AIM....

DOWN FLASHES AN ARROW TOWARD LOIS' UNPROTECTED BACK...!

BUT FROM A GREAT HEIGHT, SUPERMAN SIGHTS LOIS' DANGER

GOT TO OVERTAKE THAT ARROW!

101

NECK AND NECK!

THE *MAN OF TOMORROW* SWOOPS DOWN BEHIND LOIS, RECEIVING THE ARROW UPON HIS OWN SUPER-TOUGH SKIN....

SUPER-MAN!

WHAT A GENIUS YOU ARE, LOIS-- FOR GETTING INTO TROUBLE!

OFF RACES *"THE ARCHER"* IN FRANTIC FLIGHT....

IF I CAN ONLY REACH MY CAR...!

UP WITH YOU!

FLUNG BY THE *MAN OF STEEL'S* TREMENDOUSLY POWERFUL MUSCLES, THE HUGE BOULDER SMASHES THE CRIMINAL'S AUTO TO BITS!

LET GO!

THAT MASK IS COMING OFF!

IT'S QUIGLEY --THE FAMOUS BIG-GAME HUNTER!

I--I THOUGHT HUNTING HUMAN BEINGS WOULD PROVE MORE PROFITABLE!

ANY KID COULD TELL YOU THAT CRIME DOESN'T PAY, MR. QUIGLEY.

I'LL BIND HIM FOR YOU-- THEN SEE TO IT THAT POLICE GET HERE PROMPTLY!

⑬

LATER--AT THE *DAILY PLANET*...

TELL ME, JIMMY-- HOW DOES IT FEEL TO GET YOUR FIRST BY-LINE?

SWELL. AND I OWE IT TO BOTH OF YOU!

LET SOME OF THE CREDIT GO TO *SUPERMAN*, JIMMY.

THE END

WHAT CLARK SEES... A LOOSE PLATE AT THE BATTLESHIP'S BOTTOM...

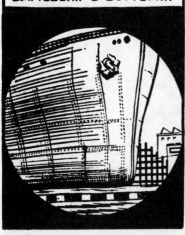

SWIFTLY, NOISELESSLY, CLARK SLIPS AWAY FROM LOIS' SIDE...

("-I'VE GOT TO GET AWAY!-")

AWAY FROM ANY CHANCE OF OBSERVATION, THE DAILY PLANET REPORTER REMOVES HIS OUTER GARMENTS, TRANSFORMING HIMSELF TO DYNAMIC SUPERMAN!

UNLESS I ACT SWIFTLY, SEVERAL MILLION DOLLARS WORTH OF BATTLESHIP WILL GO TO WASTE!

RACING SO QUICKLY HE CANNOT BE SEEN, THE MAN OF TOMORROW SPEEDS DIRECTLY THROUGH THE CROWD'S CENTER AS THE CHRISTENING CEREMONY DRAWS TO A CLOSE..!

INTO THE OCEAN HE DIVES...

SECONDS TO ACT!

...AS THE Y-92 SLIDES DOWN THE WAYS AND INTO THE WATER!

BUT BENEATH THE SEA, SUPERMAN POUNDS THE PLATE BACK INTO PLACE WITH HIS BARE FISTS...

THERE! IT'S ALL RIGHT NOW!

MY GOOD DEED FOR THE DAY!

RACING BACK TO THE ALLEY, THE MAN OF TOMORROW RESUMES HIS IDENTITY AS CLARK KENT...

NOW TO HURRY BACK TO LOIS!

WHERE WERE YOU? I'VE BEEN LOOKING ALL OVER FOR YOU.

AND I'VE BEEN DOING THE SAME, I GUESS WE GOT SEPARATED IN THE CROWD.

LATER...IN THE PRIVACY OF HIS APARTMENT, CLARK CHANGES TO SUPERMAN ONCE AGAIN...

TIME TO GO CALLING!

OVER THE CITY OF METROPOLIS STREAKS THE MAN OF STEEL AT BREATHTAKING SPEED...

THE SECRETARY OF THE NAVY OUGHT TO KNOW ABOUT THIS!

SHORTLY AFTER...THE MAN OF TOMORROW PLUMMETS DOWN OUT OF THE CLOUDS TOWARD SECRETARY HANK FOX'S HOME...

HE'S IN HIS STUDY. GOOD!

③

SUPERMAN!

SORRY I COULDN'T HAVE WAITED FOR AN INVITATION, MR. FOX--BUT I'M CALLING ON AN URGENT MATTER!

MEETING YOU IS A DISTINCT PLEASURE... I'VE READ SO MUCH ABOUT YOUR BATTLE AGAINST INJUSTICES, BUT WHY HAVE I THE HONOR OF A PERSONAL CALL?

THE Y-92, JUST LAUNCHED TODAY, WAS OBVIOUSLY A VICTIM OF SABOTAGE. I FOUND A PLATE HAD BEEN LOOSENED IN ITS BOTTOM, AND REPAIRED IT IN TIME.

YOU'VE DONE YOUR COUNTRY A SPLENDID SERVICE.—SABOTAGE. OUR DEFENSE EFFORT IS BEING CONSTANTLY PLAGUED BY IT. AND THE WORST PART OF IT IS WE STRONGLY SUSPECT WHO IS REALLY RESPONSIBLE, BUT CAN DO LITTLE ABOUT IT.

WHOM DO YOU SUSPECT?

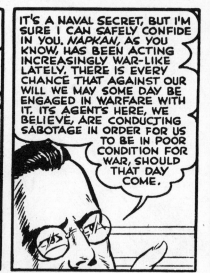

IT'S A NAVAL SECRET, BUT I'M SURE I CAN SAFELY CONFIDE IN YOU. NAPKAN, AS YOU KNOW, HAS BEEN ACTING INCREASINGLY WAR-LIKE LATELY. THERE IS EVERY CHANCE THAT AGAINST OUR WILL WE MAY SOME DAY BE ENGAGED IN WARFARE WITH IT. ITS AGENTS HERE, WE BELIEVE, ARE CONDUCTING SABOTAGE IN ORDER FOR US TO BE IN POOR CONDITION FOR WAR, SHOULD THAT DAY COME.

THANKS FOR THE INFORMATION. YOU CAN BE SURE I'LL PUT IT TO GOOD USE!

GOOD LUCK!

HOW FORTUNATE WE ARE HERE IN AMERICA TO HAVE SOMEONE OF SUPERMAN'S CALIBRE TO AID US! IN MY OPINION, HE'S WORTH SEVERAL ARMIES AND NAVIES!

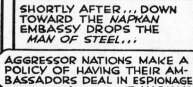

SHORTLY AFTER... DOWN TOWARD THE NAPKAN EMBASSY DROPS THE MAN OF STEEL...

AGGRESSOR NATIONS MAKE A POLICY OF HAVING THEIR AMBASSADORS DEAL IN ESPIONAGE. IF NAPKAN REALLY IS BEHIND THIS WAVE OF SABOTAGE, I'LL KNOW SOON ENOUGH!

HOKOPOKO, NAPKAN AMBASSADOR IN METROPOLIS, IS INTERVIEWING A VISITOR AT THAT MOMENT...

I COME ALL THE WAY FROM EQUARU IN SOUTH AMERICA WITH NEWS OF IMPENDING VICTORY IN OUR CAMPAIGN THERE.

LET ME HAVE THE DETAILS, UTSUM!

IT APPEARS I'VE COME JUST IN TIME! MY SUPER-SENSITIVE HEARING SHOULD SERVE ME WELL, NOW!

④

I SUCCEEDED IN FORMING A PRO-*NAPKAN* PARTY THERE WHICH WILL ATTEMPT TO OVERTHROW THE *EQUARUIAN* GOVERNMENT TODAY! IF THEY SUCCEED, IT WILL BE BUT THE BEGINNING. WE WILL PERFORM SIMILAR COUPS IN THE OTHER LATIN AMERICAN NATIONS, UNTIL SOUTH AMERICA IS ALL ANTI-AMERICAN. AFTER THAT, ATTACKING THE UNITED STATES WILL BE A SIMPLE MATTER.

YOU HAVE DONE WELL. YOU MAY EVEN GET A MEDAL FOR THIS!

AND WHAT PROGRESS ARE YOU MAKING HERE IN THE U.S. IN YOUR WORK?

OUR SABOTAGE EFFORTS ARE INCREASING WITH MOST SATISFACTORY EFFECT. BUT SOON WE WILL STRIKE A GREAT BLOW THAT WILL MAKE ALL THE OTHERS LOOK PUNY BY COMPARISON!—AND NOW, GOOD DAY!

AT THAT MOMENT—SIGHTING THE *MAN OF STEEL* EAVESDROPPING, A GUARD RUSHES HIM...

GOING TO TRY TO GIVE ME THE OFFICIAL BOUNCE, EH?

YOU WILL GET A DEMONSTRATION OF JIU JITSU YOU WILL NEVER FORGET!

BUT AS THE GUARD SEIZES SUPERMAN...

I--I CAN'T EVEN BUDGE YOU!

IN THAT EVENT, I'LL SHOW YOU A LITTLE TRICK!

THIS ISN'T AS FANCY AS JIU JITSU... BUT EVEN MORE EFFECTIVE!

YII-II! HELP! HELP!

AS OTHER GUARDS DASH UP...

PLEASE DON'T THINK I'M RUNNING AWAY FROM A FIGHT, I'LL BE BACK...BUT FIRST THERE'S ANOTHER ERRAND I'VE GOT TO ATTEND TO!

⑤

107

ACROSS THE CONTINENT SPEEDS THE *MAN OF STEEL* AT INCREDIBLE SPEED...

SOUTH AMERICA... HERE I COME!

AND SHORTLY AFTER, HE IS STREAKING DOWN TOWARD THE CAPITAL OF *EQUARU*...

THE *NAPKAN* EMBASSY IN *EQUARU*... BELOW!

ATOP THE EMBASSY BUILDING, **SUPERMAN** LISTENS INTENTLY....

UTSUM WASN'T LYING!

WITHIN THE EMBASSY...

THE PRO-*NAPKAN* BLACK CIRCLE *SOCIETY* WILL TAKE OVER THE GOVERNMENT BUILDING AT THE APPOINTED TIME.

IN OTHER WORDS— TWO MINUTES!

THAT DOESN'T GIVE ME VERY LONG TO ACT!

AT THAT MOMENT, THE REVOLUTIONISTS ADVANCE ON THE GOVERNMENT.. BUILDING....

DOWN WITH THE GOVERNMENT!

HOORAY FOR NAPKAN!

THE *BLACK CIRCLE* MUST RULE!

TAKEN OFF GUARD, THE SMALL NUMBER OF DEFENDERS STAND THUNDERSTRUCK AT SIGHT OF THE CHARGING REVOLUTIONISTS...

WE'RE OUTNUMBERED! WE HAVEN'T A CHANCE!

WE MAY AS WELL SURRENDER!

NOT IF I CAN HELP IT!!

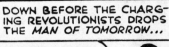

DOWN BEFORE THE CHARGING REVOLUTIONISTS DROPS THE *MAN OF TOMORROW*...

GOING TO AID *NAPKAN* IN ENCROACHING ON THE WESTERN HEMISPHERE, EH?

STREAKING IN AND OUT AMONG THE ARMED RIOTERS WITH SUPER-SPEED, *SUPERMAN* SNATCHES AWAY THEIR WEAPONS...

I'M AFRAID I CAN'T PERMIT **THAT!**

...SO THAT A MOMENT LATER THE REVOLUTIONISTS' GUNS ARE NEATLY PILED BEHIND THE GOVERNMENT BUILDING'S DEFENDERS!

YOU WON'T FIND THEM SO BELLIGERENT WITHOUT THEIR WEAPONS!

A MIRACLE!

ARREST THOSE TRAITORS!

MINUTES LATER...THE REVOLUTION HAS BEEN SQUELCHED...

WAIT! LET US THANK YOU!

MY JOB ISN'T FINISHED --YET!

THE ATTEMPT FAILED!

THAT MEANS WE'D BETTER HURRY OFF BEFORE SOME OF THE *BLACK CIRCLE* MEMBERS TALK!

BUT AS THE TWO CONSPIRATORS ARE ABOUT TO DRIVE OFF, **SUPERMAN** STREAKS DOWN AND RAISES THEIR CAR OVERHEAD...

GOING SOMEPLACE?

YOU'RE GOING WHERE YOU BELONG!

JOIN YOUR FRIENDS!

THE HEAD OF THE *BLACK CIRCLE* SOCIETY AND THE *NAPKAN* COUNSEL!

WHAT A CATCH THIS IS!

BACK TO THE *UNITED STATES* RACES THE AMAZING *MAN OF TOMORROW*...

TO THINK THAT IN A FEW MINUTES I CHANGED THE FATE OF SOUTH AMERICA!

AND LATER...AT THE *DAILY PLANET*...

NICE STORY YOU HANDED IN, CLARK, BUT HOW DID YOU CHECK THE FACTS?

I HAVE RELIABLE SOURCES OF INFORMATION.

AND AT THE *NAPKAN* EMBASSY...THE EMBASSADOR HAS SIMILAR THOUGHTS...

THIS REPORTER, CLARK KENT-- HIS FACTS HERE ARE SO ACCURATE, IT'S UNBELIEVABLE. HE'S A DEFINITE MENACE TO *NAPKAN'S* ASPIRATIONS FOR WORLD EXPANSION!

MAY I SUGGEST, THEREFORE, THAT THIS PRESUMPTUOUS MR. KENT BE-- ER-- ATTENDED TO?

THAT EVENING...AS CLARK RETIRES...

I HAVEN'T DONE BADLY AT ALL... BUT THERE'S STILL THE GREAT WAVE OF SABOTAGE IN THE U.S. TO BE ATTENDED TO!

LATER...SHADOWY INVADERS ENTER THE DARKENED ROOM...

AND STILL LATER...

HE HAS CEASED STRUGGLING!

THE CHLOROFORM HAS TAKEN EFFECT!

OFF INTO THE NIGHT SPEEDS THE AUTO WITH THE APPARENTLY UNCONSCIOUS REPORTER...

("-WHAT A BREAK! SINCE THEY'VE COME TO *ME*, THAT SAVES ME THE TROUBLE OF GOING TO *THEM!*-")

⑧

SWIFTER SPEEDS THE AUTO, 80-90-100 MILES PER HOUR... CLARK IS HURLED OUT BODILY...

GUNFIRE FROM THE HURTLING AUTO SPRAYS THE FALLING FIGURE WITH BULLETS...

DOWN A STEEP SLOPE IT ROLLS... OVER AND OVER...

BUT AS THE AUTO SPEEDS OUT OF SIGHT, THE REPORTER'S FIGURE SOMERSAULTS AND SNAPS ERECT!

ALL CLEAR!

SWIFTLY HE REMOVES HIS PAJAMAS, TRANSFORMING HIMSELF TO **SUPERMAN**!

THEY MAY HAVE RID THEMSELVES OF CLARK KENT, BUT THERE'S STILL **SUPERMAN** TO BE RECKONED WITH!

UP THE PERPENDICULAR SIDE OF THE CLIFF RACES THE *MAN OF STEEL*...

I'M ON MY WAY!

IT TAKES HIM BUT SECONDS TO CATCH SIGHT OF THE FLEEING AUTO...

THERE THEY GO!

9

LATER... THEY'RE ENTERING THE *NAPKAN EMBASSY*-- AS I EXPECTED THEY WOULD!

HAVE YOU ATTENDED TO THE REPORTER?

HE WILL TROUBLE US NO LONGER!

GOOD, SPLENDID!

IT IS A FINE OMEN. IT BODES WELL FOR THE SUCCESS OF OUR MASTER STROKE OF SABOTAGE.

CAN YOU TELL US NOW WHAT THAT STROKE IS TO BE?

A FEW MINUTES FROM NOW, THE *NAPKAN* LINER, *SUNYAT,* WILL ENTER THE PANAMA CANAL WITH A SUICIDE CREW ON BOARD. AT THE PROPER MOMENT THERE WILL BE A DEVASTATING EXPLOSION... THOSE ON BOARD WILL BE KILLED IN THE "UNFORTUNATE ACCIDENT"... BUT AT THE SAME TIME WE WILL HAVE ACCOMPLISHED OUR PURPOSE...

THE DESTRUCTION OF THE PANAMA CANAL! WHAT A BLOW TO THE DEFENSE OF THE *UNITED STATES!* SUPERB!

GOT IT ALL FIGURED OUT, EH?

SUPERMAN!

STOP HIM!! HE OVERHEARD OUR PLANS!

BUT THE CHARGING HIRELINGS ARE NO MATCH FOR THE SUPER-STRONG *MAN OF TOMORROW...*

YOU DON'T FARE SO WELL WHEN YOU FIGHT IN THE OPEN!

GET THIS! UNLESS YOU AND YOUR BLOODTHIRSTY CREW CLEAR OUT OF HERE IN RECORD TIME YOU'LL BE ANCIENT HISTORY WHEN I FINISH WITH YOU!

I--I'LL GET OUT!

W-WITH ALACRITY!

OFF RACES THE *MAN OF TOMORROW* ON HIS TREMENDOUSLY IMPORTANT MISSION...

THE FATE OF THE PANAMA CANAL IN THE BALANCE!

ACROSS THE OCEAN SWIMS THE MIGHTY *MAN OF TOMORROW* AT SO GREAT A SPEED THE OCEAN APPEARS SPLIT IN TWAIN....

SPEED... SPEED... AND *MORE* SPEED...!!!

MEANWHILE--THE *SUNYAT* BEGINS TO ENTER THE *PANAMA CANAL*....

THE SUICIDE CREW STANDS AT ITS POSTS, FACES SET IN EXPRESSIONLESS MASKS-- HIDING THE TERROR IN THEIR HEARTS...

FOR EACH ONE OF THE DOOMED SAILORS KNOWS THAT IN THE HOLD OF THE VESSEL A TIME-BOMB HAS BEEN SET INTO OPER- ATION THAT WILL DESTROY THEM ALL...

FOR THE GLORY OF *NAPKAN!*

...AND THE *DESTRUCTION* OF THE *UNITED STATES!*

11

SIGHTING THE *NAPKAN* LINER ENTERING THE CANAL, THE *MAN OF STEEL* HURTLES DESPERATELY AFTER IT...

PERHAPS I'M STILL NOT TOO LATE!

A TERRIFIC BURST OF STRENGTH AND HE LIFTS THE MIGHTY LINER UP-- UP OUT OF THE WATER...!

UP YOU GO!!

113

ATOP A GREAT LOCK CLAMBERS THE *MAN OF TOMORROW* WITH HIS MASSIVE BURDEN...

WE'VE GOT TO GET **AWAY** FROM HERE!

AS HE SPRINGS OCEAN-WARD, THE CREW MEMBERS FIRE DOWN FRANTICALLY AT HIM...

SHOOT HIM! DESTROY HIM!

NO USE! THE BULLETS **BOUNCE** OFF!

IT'S ABOUT **TIME** YOU MADE THAT DISCOVERY!

OUT INTO THE SEA SWIMS *SUPERMAN* SWIFTLY, SHOVING THE *SUNYAT* BEFORE HIM AT GREAT SPEED...

I WANT TO PUT AS MUCH SPACE BETWEEN THE CANAL AND US AS POSSIBLE!

A GIGANTIC EXPLOSION...!

BUT THE DYNAMIC *MAN OF STEEL* SURVIVES...

THE END OF THE *NAPKAN* PLOT!

ON BOARD THE CLIPPER BOUND FOR ANOTHER HEMISPHERE...

HAVE YOU HEARD? THE *SUNYAT* FAILED IN ITS MISSION!

I HEARD, AND I FEAR IT MEANS THAT OUR SUPERIORS WILL DEMAND **OUR** DESTRUCTION!

IN HANK FOX'S STUDY...

"SABOTAGE ATTEMPT ON PANAMA CANAL FAILS!" "NAPKAN AMBASSADOR RETURNS TO NATIVE LAND"-- IT'S OBVIOUS TO ME, AT LEAST, THAT THE MAN BEHIND THESE HEADLINES IS **SUPERMAN**! WHAT A DEBT HIS COUNTRY OWES HIM!

EDITORIAL OFFICE OF THE *DAILY PLANET*...

NICE ARTICLE, CLARK!

AND I'D SAY NICE WORK ON THE PART OF **SUPERMAN**!

WITH THE WORK OF SAB-OTEURS GREATLY DECREASED DEFENSE PRODUCTION SHOULD SPEED UP! AND YOU KNOW HOW NECESSARY **THAT** IS!

THE END

114 ⑫

SUPERBOY

The ADVENTURES *of* SUPERMAN WHEN HE WAS A BOY!

TAKE A GOOD LOOK AT THE YOUNG GIRL SHAKING HANDS WITH YOUNG CLARK KENT! RECOGNIZE HER? IT'S **LOIS LANE!** THE SAME LOIS WHO KEEPS **SUPERMAN** BUSY RESCUING HER! BUT THIS IS LOIS AS A YOUNG GIRL... AND YOUNG CLARK HAS TO GO THROUGH A ROUTINE HE WILL REPEAT AS A MAN! HERE, AT LAST, IS THE STORY OF HOW THE CLARK KENT-LOIS LANE-**SUPERMAN** TRIANGLE BEGAN. READ ALL ABOUT IT IN — *"How Clark Kent Met Lois Lane!"*

FOR SOME TIME NOW, YOUNG CLARK KENT HAS BEEN A CRACK REPORTER ON HIS SCHOOL NEWSPAPER...

"...AND TOM OBERS TOOK FIRST PLACE WITH A PERFECT JACK-KNIFE DIVE..."

THEN ONE DAY COMES HIS REWARD IN THE FORM OF A LETTER FROM THE NEARBY CITY OF METROPOLIS...

DAILY PLANET
METROPOLIS

Clark Kent
??? Main St...

Congratulations!
You are one of the two winners of our annual contest to honor the best school newspaper reporters. Your prize is a free trip to Metropolis, where you will be allowed to work as cub reporter for one week on Metropolis' greatest newspaper—
THE DAILY PLANET

SO IT IS THAT THE SMALL-TOWN BOY ARRIVES IN THE BIG CITY...

WELCOME TO METROPOLIS, MY BOY! I'M EDITOR MORTON! FIRST, I WANT YOU TO MEET THE OTHER WINNER...

AND HERE SHE IS! MEET LOIS LANE!

YES, HERE IS A HISTORIC MOMENT...THE FIRST MEETING OF LOIS AND CLARK... A MEETING THAT WILL BE REPEATED SOME DAY WHEN SUPERBOY GROWS UP TO BE SUPERMAN!

GOLLY! SHE'S SO PRETTY!

GOLLY! HE'S SO UNEXCITING!

I HEAR YOU LIVE IN THE SAME TOWN SUPERBOY DOES! DO YOU KNOW HIM...PERSONALLY? WOULD YOU INTRODUCE ME TO HIM? HE'S WONDERFUL!

HUH! ALL SHE TALKS ABOUT IS SUPERBOY...AND NOT ONE WORD ABOUT ME!

BETTER GET USED TO THAT, CLARK! IT WILL BE JUST THE SAME WHEN YOU BECOME SUPERMAN!

NOW, KIDS, HOW ABOUT A LITTLE COMPETITION? THE ONE WHO BRINGS IN THE BEST STORY OF THE DAY GETS IT ON THE FRONT PAGE...WITH A BYLINE!

GEE!

I'LL WIN...NATURALLY! ANY GIRL IS SUPERIOR TO A BOY...THAT IS, ANY BOY BUT SUPERBOY... AND YOU'RE NO SUPERBOY!

IF YOU ONLY KNEW!

HOW ABOUT A LITTLE PRIVATE BET? THE LOSER TREATS THE WINNER TO AN ICE CREAM SUNDAE?

I NEVER BET... BUT I'LL MAKE AN EXCEPTION IN YOUR CASE!

LATER...AS THE TWO WALK THE BUSY STREETS, A STREET-WATERING TRUCK RUMBLES NEAR...

SUDDENLY...THE NOZZLES SPRAY ...NOT WATER...BUT SLEEPING GAS!

GAS!

OHHH!

UHHH!

③

AS THE GAS DOES ITS WORK, BANDITS EMERGE FROM THE TRUCK AND SWIFTLY ENTER A FASHIONABLE JEWELLERS SHOP...

OKAY, BOYS! ANY COP THAT ISN'T SLEEPING BY NOW IS TOO BUSY OUTSIDE!

WHILE **SUPERBOY** RESTORES THE BILLBOARD, THE BANDITS MAKE THEIR GETAWAY!

OH-OH! LOIS IS RETURNING! GOT TO SWITCH BACK FAST!

FOAMY SOAP

BUT LOIS HAS ALREADY REACHED THE ALLEY, AND...

SO YOU'RE AWAKE NOW? BUT WHY IS YOUR JACKET OFF?

I...I...

I...I'M USING IT AS A FAN TO BLOW THE GAS AWAY FROM YOU!

HMMPH! THANKS... BUT **SUPERBOY** BEAT YOU TO IT... AND YOU SHOULD'VE SEEN THE FAN **HE** USED!

I WAS CONSCIOUS ALL THE TIME AND HAVE I GOT A **SCOOP!** TOO BAD **YOU** WERE SLEEPING AND DIDN'T SEE IT!

BACK AT THE *DAILY PLANET*...

IT LOOKS LIKE LOIS IS GOING TO GET THAT ICE CREAM, CLARK! SHE CERTAINLY SCOOPED YOU!

AW...THE DAY ISN'T OVER YET!

SILLY! DO YOU THINK YOU CAN GET A MORE EXCITING STORY THAN ONE ABOUT **SUPERBOY**?

FINE THING! LOIS GETS A SCOOP AND I DON'T... AND ALL BECAUSE I CAN'T REVEAL MY **SUPER-IDENTITY!** HOW LONG CAN I KEEP THIS UP?

FOR A LONG, LONG TIME, CLARK! AFTER ALL, YOU'RE ONLY A **BOY** NOW! IT WILL GET WORSE WHEN YOU'RE A **MAN**!

5

121

123

WITH HIS BARE HANDS, SUPERBOY TWISTS THE CRANE'S STEEL GIRDERS... FORMING A MAKESHIFT JAIL-CELL!

THERE, KORY... LET'S SEE YOU ENGINEER AN ESCAPE!

SUPERBOY! WAIT FOR ME!

SHE'S AFTER ME AGAIN! I WISH SHE WAS AS EAGER FOR CLARK KENT!

LATER... LOIS DELIVERS HER STORY...

WHAT A SCOOP! CLARK, WHY CAN'T YOU GET STORIES LIKE THIS?

SO... CLARK PAYS OFF HIS DEBT!

HOW MANY SCOOPS?

TWO!

SCOOPED AGAIN!

A WEEK PASSES QUICKLY...AND SUDDENLY IT'S TIME FOR PARTING...

'BYE! GIVE MY REGARDS TO SUPERBOY WHEN YOU SEE HIM!

SHE'S GOING! I WONDER IF I'LL EVER SEE HER AGAIN? I WONDER IF WE'LL MEET SOME DAY... WHEN I'M SUPERMAN?!?

THE END

124

10

SORRY I CAN'T DRIVE YOU HOME AS USUAL TODAY, LOIS-- BUT I'M TAKING THE TIRE-RATIONING CRISIS SERIOUSLY.

EVERY ONE SHOULD-- IT'S THE PATRIOTIC THING TO DO!

BUT AS CLARK STRUGGLES TOWARD THE TRAIN WITH LOIS, HIS X-RAY VISION BRINGS TO HIM A START-LING SCENE...

HURRY, CLARK-- BEFORE THE DOOR CLOSES!

(PUFF!) RIGHT WITH YOU!

("-WHAT'S THAT?-")

WHAT CLARK'S AMAZING VISION REVEALS TO HIM... A SECTION OF THE SUBWAY TRACK-- MISSING...!

AS LOIS IS CROWDED INTO THE PACKED CAR, THE DOOR SLIDES SHUT AND SHE DISCOVERS...

CLARK DIDN'T MAKE IT! HE'S STILL ON THE PLATFORM!

BUT AT THAT MOMENT THE **DAILY PLANET** REPORTER IS STREAKING THRU THE MOB ON THE SUBWAY PLATFORM AT SO GREAT A SPEED THAT NO ONE CAN OBSERVE HIM-- AND AS HE RACES, HE SWITCHES TO HIS WORLD-FAMOUS ACTION-COSTUME ...

IMPOLITE OF ME TO DASH AWAY FROM LOIS LIKE THIS-- BUT SUPERMAN HAS WORK TO DO!

DOWN ONTO THE TRACKS LEAPS THE **MAN OF TOMORROW**, AND AS THE SUBWAY TRAIN BEGINS TO MOVE HE FLASHES AHEAD OF IT AT FULL SPEED...

ALMOST AT THE SPOT WHERE THE RAIL IS MISSING-- NO ROOM HERE FOR HALF-MEASURES!

BAY

②

WHIRLING, **SUPERMAN** PITS HIS STRENGTH AGAINST THE SPEEDING SUBWAY TRAIN ..

NOT ANOTHER INCH DO I BUDGE!!

THE COLORFULLY-CLAD FIGURE SUCCEEDS IN HALTING THE TRAIN'S FORWARD PLUNGE BARELY IN TIME...

ANOTHER FOOT OR SO-- AND THERE'D HAVE BEEN... DISASTER!

WHAT HAPPENED?

I HEARD SOMEONE SAY SUPERMAN STOPPED THE TRAIN!

SUPERMAN! HERE!!

HERE IT IS-- THE PART OF THE RAIL THAT'S MISSING!

SO POWERFUL IS SUPERMAN'S STRENGTH THAT HE MOLDS THE RAIL SECTION BACK INTO PLACE AS THO THE STEEL WERE PUTTY...

THERE! AN EMERGENCY JOB-- BUT IT SHOULD BE SATISFACTORY!

SECONDS LATER, THE MAN OF TOMORROW VAULTS ONTO THE PLATFORM OF THE NEXT STATION AND WHIPS BACK INTO HIS CIVILIAN GARMENTS...

NOW TO PHONE IN THE STORY TO WHITE.

3

THAT'S RIGHT. SUPERMAN AVERTED A SUBWAY TRAIN WRECK!

BUT AS CLARK LEAVES THE PHONE BOOTH....

ULP!

CLARK! HOW DID YOU GET HERE? I LEFT YOU BACK ON THE PLATFORM AT THAT OTHER STATION!

127

("-IT'S GOING TO TAKE SOME **FAST THINKING** TO GET OUT OF **THIS** SPOT! LOIS KNOWS I WAS LEFT BEHIND ON THAT OTHER SUBWAY PLATFORM. WHAT SORT OF FAIRLY LOGICAL EXPLANATION **CAN** I OFFER HER WITHOUT REVEALING MY **SUPERMAN** IDENTITY?-")

WELL--YOU SEE--I--I--ER...I TOOK AN EXPRESS TRAIN AND GOT HERE FIRST! YES, THAT'S IT!

YOU DID, EH? WELL LET ME AT THAT TELEPHONE! I'VE A GREAT YARN TO TELEPHONE IN. **SUPERMAN** JUST HALTED A SUBWAY WRECK!

BUT, LOIS...

QUIET! CAN'T YOU SEE I'M TRYING TO TALK INTO THE TELEPHONE!

WHAT'S THAT? YOU SAY-- CLARK **ALREADY** REPORTED THE STORY??!

HOW DID YOU MANAGE TO TELEPHONE THAT STORY IN FIRST? **HOW** DID YOU EVER KNOW MY TRAIN WAS INVOLVED IN AN ENCOUNTER WITH **SUPERMAN!**

I--I--ER... ("-NOW I'M IN AN EVEN **WORSE** SPOT!-")

UH--UH--...NEWS LIKE THAT TRAVELS FAST. IF I WERE TO LET YOU IN ON ALL MY METHODS, YOU'D FOREVER BE SCOOPING ME. HEH! HEH! ("-I'M AFRAID THAT FELL KINDA FLAT.-")

THERE'S SOMETHING SUSPICIOUS HERE.

LATER...OUTSIDE LOIS' APARTMENT...

COME TO THINK OF IT, **SUPERMAN** HIMSELF COULDN'T HAVE ACTED ANY FASTER!

YOU'RE JUST MAKING IT APPEAR MORE MYSTERIOUS THAN IT REALLY WAS.

④

WHEW! THAT WAS THE CLOSEST I'VE EVER COME TO HAVING MY IDENTITY DISCOVERED. THANK GOODNESS LOIS WILL FORGET THE INCIDENT!

BUT WILL LOIS FORGET?

I'M **STILL** NOT COMPLETELY CONVINCED BY CLARK'S EXPLANATION. HE LOOKED VERY AGITATED--AS THO HE WERE TRYING TO CONCEAL SOMETHING...

COME TO THINK OF IT, IT'S MIGHTY PECULIAR THAT CLARK IS NEVER PRESENT WHEN **SUPERMAN** GOES INTO ACTION, AND ON MORE THAN ONE OCCASION I'VE NOTED A FAINT RESEMBLANCE BETWEEN THE FEATURES OF CLARK KENT AND **SUPERMAN**!

CLARK KENT REALLY **SUPERMAN**? THE VERY THOUGHT SEEMS ABSURD. AND YET-- I THINK I'LL GLANCE THRU MY SCRAP BOOK,

"--I'LL NEVER FORGET THE FIRST TIME I ENCOUNTERED **SUPERMAN**. MY, HOW HE MAN-HANDLED THOSE THUGS..."

"--IT WASN'T SO LONG AFTER THAT THAT A CRIMINAL TOSSED ME OUT OF AN **AIRPLANE**. IT CERTAINLY WAS A RELIEF WHEN **SUPERMAN** CAUGHT ME IN MID-AIR!--"

"--WILL I EVER FORGET THE TIME **SUPERMAN** RACED A BULLET TO ITS TARGET AND CAUGHT IT? I WILL **NOT**! FOR I WAS THAT TARGET!--"

5

129

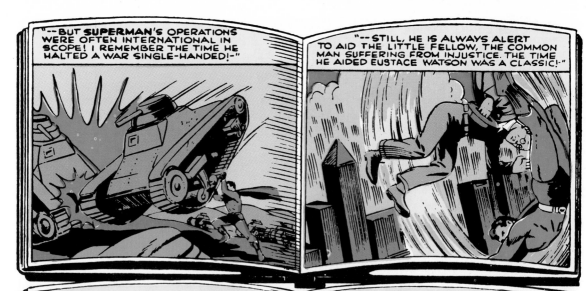

"--BUT SUPERMAN'S OPERATIONS WERE OFTEN INTERNATIONAL IN SCOPE! I REMEMBER THE TIME HE HALTED A WAR SINGLE-HANDED!--"

"--STILL, HE IS ALWAYS ALERT TO AID THE LITTLE FELLOW, THE COMMON MAN SUFFERING FROM INJUSTICE. THE TIME HE AIDED EUSTACE WATSON WAS A CLASSIC!--"

"--HE ENCOUNTERED AND BESTED SOME OF THE WORST SCOUNDRELS THE WORLD HAS EVER SEEN. THERE WAS ULTRA, WHO TRIED HIS BEST TO ERASE THE MAN OF TOMORROW, BUT HIS BEST WASN'T GOOD ENOUGH!--"

"--AND, OF COURSE, I'M NOT FORGETTING LUTHOR WHO SIMPLY REFUSES TO RECOGNIZE THAT SUPERMAN IS THE BETTER MAN!--"

"--HE IS ALWAYS QUICK TO AID ANY GOOD CAUSE: KIDTOWN, SLUM ELIMINATION, CHARITY DRIVES, ETC.--"

"--SUPERMAN WAS THE DOWNFALL OF MANY A POLITICAL GRAFTER!--"

HOW COULD I HAVE IMAGINED THAT MEEK, SHRINKING CLARK KENT COULD BE DYNAMIC **SUPERMAN**? A SILLY THOUGHT. AND THE SOONER I FORGET IT, THE BETTER!

AFTER LOIS RETIRES THAT EVENING, CLARK FINDS THAT A PERSISTENT THOUGHT PREVENTS SLEEP. HE CHANGES TO **SUPERMAN**.

THAT SUBWAY RAIL WASN'T MISPLACED BY ACCIDENT! THERE'S SOMETHING WRONG GOING ON IN THE LABYRINTHS OF THE SUBWAY SYSTEM AND I'M GOING TO TRACK IT DOWN!

SHORTLY AFTERWARD, AS THE **MAN OF TOMORROW** RACES ALONG A SUBWAY TUNNEL, HIS SUPER-SENSITIVE HEARING DETECTS...

MASSIVE DYNAMOS—!

AVAILING HIMSELF OF HIS X-RAY VISION AND SUPER-HEARING, HE DETECTS A STARTLING SIGHT IN A NEARBY BUILDING....

THE WIRES HAVE BEEN CONNECTED TO THE SUBWAY TRACKS....AFTER I FLING THIS SWITCH, THE TREMENDOUS ELECTRICITY GENERATED BY THESE DYNAMOS WILL SURGE INTO THE TRACKS...THE PASSENGERS ABOARD TRAINS PASSING THIS SECTION, WILL BE **ELECTROCUTED**...!

WE KNOW ALL THAT! THROW THE SWITCH!

THE TALON DOESN'T LIKE DELAYS!

THRU THE EARTH BURROWS THE **MAN OF TOMORROW** AT DESPERATE SPEED...!

GOT TO PREVENT A MASS EXECUTION!

SUPERMAN!

AND NOT TOO LATE, I HOPE!

THROW THE SWITCH!

8

OUT OF MY WAY!

YOU'RE TOO LATE!!

THE SUBWAY TRACKS CRACKLE WITH ELECTRICAL ENERGY--AND A SHORT DISTANCE OFF A TRAIN HURTLES TOWARD THE WAITING DOOM,....!!

SMASHING INTO THE DYNAMOS, **SUPERMAN** RIPS THEM APART WITH HIS BARE HANDS--AND AS HE DOES, A TERRIFIC BARRAGE OF ELECTRICAL FORCE IS UNLEASHED IN THE ROOM...

THE THREAT'S BANISHED--BUT THE TALON'S HIRELINGS WERE SLAIN BY THEIR OWN ELECTRICAL APPARATUS! ONLY MY SUPER-PHYSIQUE SAVED ME!

EARLY MORNING--LOIS IS ROUSED BY THE SHOUTING OF NEWSBOYS...

WHA--?

EXTRA! DAILY PLANET EXTRA! SUPERMAN SMASHES SABOTEURS!!

DRESSING HASTILY, LOIS PURCHASES A COPY...

ANOTHER SCOOP BY CLARK KENT! THAT SETTLES IT! I'M GOING TO FIND OUT ONCE AND FOR ALL IF CLARK IS **SUPERMAN** OR NOT!

LATER...

THIS ARTICLE OF MINE STATES THAT I KNOW ALL ABOUT **THE TALON** AND HIS WORKING METHODS. IF ANYTHING WILL MAKE **THE TALON** BETRAY HIS HAND, THIS OUGHT TO!

BUT IT'S A DANGEROUS TRICK, LOIS!

DON'T LET HER DO IT!

BUT CLARK'S PROTESTS ARE OF NO AVAIL...WHIRLING PRESSES PRINT LOIS' ARTICLE IN GREAT QUANTITIES--THE NEWSPAPER'S LATEST EDITION IS DISTRIBUTED THROUGHOUT THE CITY....

AND IN THE TALON'S HIDEAWAY...

GET-- THAT-- GIRL!!

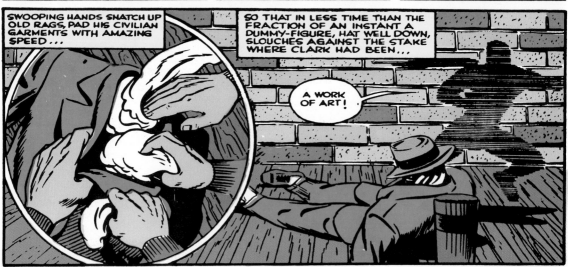

WHILE LOIS TURNS TOWARD THE STAKE, **SUPERMAN** WHIPS PAST HER AT SUPER-SPEED...

("-GOT TO MAKE IT BEFORE SHE COMPLETELY TURNS!-")

SWISH!

EMPTYING THE RAGS, HE DONS HIS OUTER GARMENTS AND ADJUSTS THE ROPES IN PLACE...

("-SHE'S ALMOST GOT HER EYES ON ME!-")

COME TO, CLARK! **SUPERMAN** SAVED US! WE'VE GOT TO GET TO THE SUBWAY SYSTEM HEADQUARTERS AND WARN THEM OF **THE TALON'S** THREAT!

I--I WANT TO KEEP AS FAR AWAY FROM **THE TALON** AS I CAN!

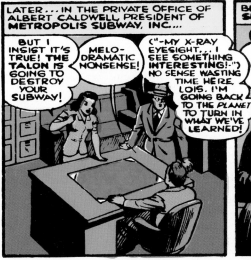

LATER... IN THE PRIVATE OFFICE OF ALBERT CALDWELL PRESIDENT OF METROPOLIS SUBWAY, INC...

BUT I INSIST IT'S TRUE! **THE TALON** IS GOING TO DESTROY YOUR SUBWAY!

MELO-DRAMATIC NONSENSE!

("-MY X-RAY EYESIGHT... I SEE SOMETHING INTERESTING!-") NO SENSE WASTING TIME HERE, LOIS. I'M GOING BACK TO THE **PLANET** TO TURN IN WHAT WE'VE LEARNED!

BUT ONCE HE IS OUTSIDE THE OFFICE, CLARK CHANGES TO **SUPERMAN** AND RACES BACK IN....

SUPERMAN! STRANGE HOW YOU SHOWED UP SO SOON AFTER CLARK'S DEPARTURE!

WHAT DOES THIS INTERRUPTION MEAN?

I WAS WONDERING, CALDWELL, IF YOU DABBLE IN AMATEUR THEATRICALS?

OF COURSE NOT!

THEN THERE'S ONLY ONE OTHER EXPLANATION FOR THE TRACES OF YELLOW PIGMENT AND GREASE PAINT I CAN STILL DETECT ON YOUR SKIN, TALON!

MR. CALDWELL— THE TALON!

HE'S MAD!

I'M BETTING HE'S THE BIRD WE'RE AFTER!

OBOY! IT'S OFF FOR THE DAILY PLANET FOR ME!

IF I'M FAST ENOUGH I MAY BE ABLE TO SCOOP CLARK!

12

SUPERMAN STUNTS DIZZILY, BUT WITH NO APPARENT RESULT...

READY TO TELL ME WHERE THE FORCES OF DESTRUCTION ARE TO BE UNLEASHED?

I KNOW NOTHING, I TELL YOU-- NOTHING!

DID I GET YOU HERE FAST ENOUGH, LADY?

FAST ENOUGH TO EARN ME A FRONT PAGE BY-LINE... I HOPE!

RUNNING INTO THE SUBWAY TUNNEL, SUPERMAN RACES BACK AND FORTH THRU THE ENTIRE SUBWAY SYSTEM AT SUPER-SPEED, DODGING IN AND OUT, ABOVE AND BELOW THE TRAINS.

AT THE SPEED I'M GOING WE'RE SURE TO BE ON THE SCENE OF THE DISASTER WHEREVER IT HAPPENS! WILL YOU TALK?

YES-- IN THE TUBE BENEATH THE CHANNEL RIVER! A TIME BOMB!

SPEEDING TO THE SCENE OF THE IMPENDING DISASTER, SUPERMAN HURTLES TOWARD THE BOMB -- AND AS HE DOES... IT EXPLODES....

YOU'RE UNHARMED! AND SO IS THE TUNNEL!

YES, MY BODY ABSORBED MOST OF THE EXPLOSION'S FORCE. YOU'RE HEADED FOR A CELL!

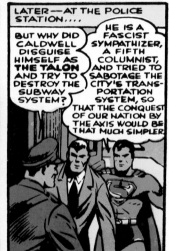

LATER -- AT THE POLICE STATION....

BUT WHY DID CALDWELL DISGUISE HIMSELF AS THE TALON AND TRY TO DESTROY THE SUBWAY SYSTEM?

HE IS A FASCIST SYMPATHIZER, A FIFTH COLUMNIST, AND TRIED TO SABOTAGE THE CITY'S TRANSPORTATION SYSTEM, SO THAT THE CONQUEST OF OUR NATION BY THE AXIS WOULD BE THAT MUCH SIMPLER!

SEVERAL MOMENTS LATER....

KENT AROUND? NO. I HAVEN'T SEEN HIM. WHY DO YOU ASK?

SWELL! THIS ONE TIME I SCOOPED HIM!

DID SOMEONE MENTION MY NAME?

YOU HERE? ER--I--I GUESS I WAS MISTAKEN.

HERE'S A FULL EXPOSE OF THE TALON, WHITE.

BUT ARE LOIS' SUSPICIONS OF CLARK'S TRUE IDENTITY COMPLETELY ALLAYED? ONLY FUTURE RELEASES OF YOUR FAVORITE STRIP WILL TELL! DON'T MISS A SINGLE ADVENTURE OF -- SUPERMAN!

THE END

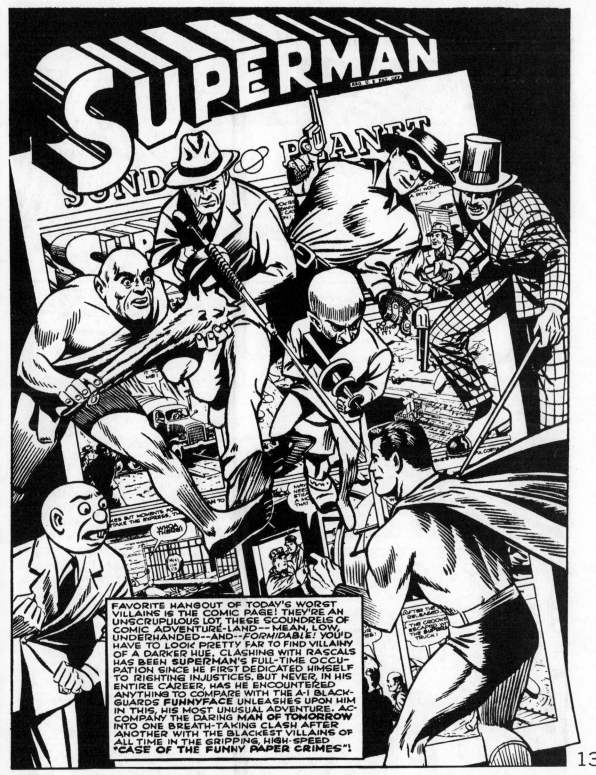

FAVORITE HANGOUT OF TODAY'S WORST VILLAINS IS THE COMIC PAGE! THEY'RE AN UNSCRUPULOUS LOT, THESE SCOUNDRELS OF COMIC ADVENTURE-LAND—MEAN, LOW, UNDERHANDED—AND—FORMIDABLE! YOU'D HAVE TO LOOK PRETTY FAR TO FIND VILLAINY OF A DARKER HUE. CLASHING WITH RASCALS HAS BEEN SUPERMAN'S FULL-TIME OCCUPATION SINCE HE FIRST DEDICATED HIMSELF TO RIGHTING INJUSTICES. BUT NEVER, IN HIS ENTIRE CAREER, HAS HE ENCOUNTERED ANYTHING TO COMPARE WITH THE A-1 BLACK-GUARDS FUNNYFACE UNLEASHES UPON HIM IN THIS, HIS MOST UNUSUAL ADVENTURE. ACCOMPANY THE DARING MAN OF TOMORROW INTO ONE BREATH-TAKING CLASH AFTER ANOTHER WITH THE BLACKEST VILLAINS OF ALL TIME IN THE GRIPPING, HIGH-SPEED "CASE OF THE FUNNY PAPER CRIMES"!

137

138

141

BUT TO SUPERMAN'S AMAZEMENT...

WHIZZED RIGHT THRU!

BUT NEXT TIME...!

THEY'RE-- GONE...!

YES, YOU POOR, HELPLESS AND BEWILDERED EX-SUPERMAN ...GONE!

AND WHO IN BLAZES ARE YOU?

NOW WOULDN'T YOU LIKE TO KNOW!

TELL ME...OR I'LL SOCK THAT SILLY GRIN CLEAR DOWN TO YOUR TOES!

YOU MAY CALL ME FUNNY-FACE!

BUT BEFORE HE CAN REACH THE APPARITION--IT VANISHES...

FIRST A GIANT OUT OF A COMIC STRIP... NEXT A PREHISTORIC MONSTER... THEN A SILLY-FACED GALOOT NAMED FUNNYFACE... AND THEY ALL VANISHED!

I'M NOT KIDDING, CHIEF! THAT BANK ROBBERY WAS PULLED BY NONE OTHER THAN TORGO, THE FUNNY PAPER MENACE IN PRINCE PERIL!

IMPOSSIBLE-- ABSURD! I SUPPOSE NEXT YOU'LL BE TELLING ME THAT DETECTIVE CRAIG'S FOE, MACHINE-GUN MIKE IS RUNNING WILD.

CALLING ALL CARS! MACHINE-GUN MIKE ROBBING MINTON MUSEUM!

HUH?!

ONLY ONE EXPLAN- ATION, BOSS! YOU'RE PSYCHIC!

142

143

144

QUICK! LET'S BEAT IT WHILE WE CAN!

TRYING TO RUN OUT, EH?

I PROMISED YOU'D GO TO A CELL-- AND I KEEP MY PROMISES!

GOOD WORK, SUPERMAN! IF YOU ONLY COULD HAVE CAPTURED MACHINE-GUN MIKE, TOO...!

YOU CAN'T HAVE EVERYTHING, SERGEANT CASEY!

IN A NEARBY ALLEY, SUPERMAN CHANGES TO CLARK KENT...

IT MIGHT BE A GOOD IDEA IF I WERE SEEN HEREABOUTS IN MY IDENTITY AS CLARK KENT..., SO THE QUESTION WON'T ARISE AS TO HOW I GOT MY FACTS...

CLARK! SO HERE YOU ARE!

BEEN LOOKING FOR ME, LOIS?

I'LL SAY I HAVE! WHAT'S THE IDEA OF RUNNING OFF AND COVERING THIS STORY YOURSELF?

SORRY, LOIS-- BUT THIS CASE FASCINATED ME SO... IT'S ALMOST AS THO SOMEONE WERE USING THE COMIC PAGE AS A CHART FOR CRIME...

CHART FOR CRIME...! HM-MM. MAYBE YOU'VE GOT SOMETHING THERE, CLARK. IF THAT WERE TRUE, THE NEXT VILLAIN TO POP UP WOULD BE THE BLACK RAIDER FROM THE SOLITARY RIDER COMIC.

IF IT WERE TRUE! BUT UNDOUBTEDLY IT ISN'T. FORGET THE IDEA, LOIS. IT'S SILLY.

("SILLY, EH? I WONDER? HM-MM. THE MOST LOGICAL PLACE FOR THE BLACK RAIDER TO STRIKE IN METROPOLIS WOULD BE THE STOCKYARDS. THEREFORE, THAT'S MY NEXT STOP!-")

145

SHORTLY AFTER--WHEN LOIS REACHES THE ADMINISTRATIVE BUILDING OF METROPOLIS' HUGE STOCKYARDS....

BUT I'M ALMOST POSITIVE OF IT!

WHAT UTTER NONSENSE! THE BLACK RAIDER ROB US? PREPOSTEROUS!

UP WITH YOUR HANDS --THIS IS A HOLDUP!

WHO IS RESPONSIBLE FOR THIS OUTRAGE?

LOOK OUT THE WINDOW-- AND YOU'LL SEE!

THE BLACK RAIDER!

I TOLD YOU SO!

STOP THAT GIRL! SHE DUCKED INTO THE NEXT ROOM!

I'LL WARN-- BLACK RAIDER!

SLAM!

CLARK--I'M CALLING FROM THE STOCKYARDS! THE BLACK RAIDER HAS--EEE-EEEEE!!

LOIS-- LOIS... WHAT IS IT??! --THE LINE WENT DEAD!

LET'S GO, MEN!

LET ME GO-- YOU BIG STIFF!

CHANGING TO HIS SUPERMAN COSTUME, THE MAN OF TOMORROW STREAKS TO THE STOCK-YARD TO SIGHT AN AMAZING SCENE...

A CARAVAN OF CATTLE-LOADED TRUCKS!

STOCKYARDS

HIT THE ROAD! I'M TAKING OVER THOSE TRUCKS!

AT THE TERRIFIC SPEED OF WHICH ONLY HE IS CAPABLE, SUPERMAN SPEEDS BACK AND FORTH, RETURNING THE TRUCKS TO THE STOCKYARD WITH THEIR STOLEN CARGO...

HERE YOU ARE! THE LAST OF THEM!

STOP BLACK RAIDER! HE'S SPED OFF WITH A GIRL REPORTER!

GIRL REPORTER! ...THAT SOUNDED LIKE A DESCRIPTION OF LOIS, AND SURE ENOUGH-- IT IS. I'LL SOON FREE HER!

I BEG TO DIFFER!

HEY! STOP IT!!

HO! HO! CAN'T TAKE IT, EH?

THEN...

GONE-- FUNNYFACE --BLACK RAIDER-- LOIS...BUT WAIT... WHAT'S THAT UP IN THE SKY?

HOVERING OVER A TRAIN LOADING A GOLD CARGO, A SPACE-VESSEL LOWERS A ROD THAT SUCKS THE GOLD INTO THE VESSEL'S INTERIOR...

IT'S-- GOOLA-- THE MARTIAN VILLAIN IN STREAK DUGAN!

BUT AS HE SEEKS TO ENGAGE HIS FOE IN COMBAT--AGAIN... FUNNYFACE!

WHAT IS THIS--A BALLOON BARRAGE?

THEN ONCE AGAIN FUNNYFACE IS GONE--AND SO IS GOOLA...

WE'RE BEING BOMBARDED BY VILLAINS OUT OF THE COMIC PAGE! THAT LEAVES ONLY VIPER, THE VILLAIN OF THE HAPPY DAZE STRIP. I RECALL THAT IN THE COMIC VIPER IS ATTEMPTING TO ROB THE OLD FOLKS HOME OF ITS CAMPAIGN FUND.

LATER...

PERHAPS MY FEAR IS BASE-LESS, BUT I THOUGHT I OUGHT TO WARN YOU AGAINST THE CHARACTER NAMED VIPER.

YOUR WARNING WAS UN-NECESSARY.

BECAUSE I AM VIPER!

AND SO YOU ARE!

OLD FOLKS HOME

BLAST YOU! THIS IS YOUR FAULT! I'LL FIX YOU FOR IT!

NO! LET GO!

HA-HA! MY RAY CAN ALSO REVERSE THE PROCESS! YOU'LL BE PUNISHED BY BEING TRANSFERRED TO A DRAWING ON A PIECE OF PAPER! HA, HA, HA!

FREE THAT GIRL!

I WON'T DO IT!

LET US ATTEND TO HIM!

ENOUGH! I'VE HAD ENOUGH!

THERE-- I'VE BROUGHT HER BACK TO NORMAL AGAIN.

WHAT A RELIEF!

I SUPPOSE ALL OF YOU ARE ANXIOUS TO GET BACK INTO YOUR MAKE-BELIEVE WORLD!

BY ALL MEANS!

AND SO THE FUNNY PAPER CHARACTERS ARE TRANSFERRED PERMANENTLY BACK TO THEIR COMIC PAGE EXISTENCE...THEREUPON, SUPERMAN SMASHES THE WEIRD MACHINE FOR ALL TIME...

NEXT--TO UNMASK YOU!

NO!

AND WHO ARE YOU? YOU LOOK UNFAMILIAR!

THAT WAS THE WHOLE TROUBLE! NOBODY KNOWS ME! I WANTED TO BE A CELEBRITY-- THE CREATOR OF A FAMOUS COMIC STRIP. BUT NO ONE WOULD BUY MY STRIPS. MY DIMENSIONAL EXPERIMENTATION ENABLED ME TO BRING COMIC CHARACTERS TO LIFE--AND I PUT THE STRIP VILLAINS TO WORK FOR ME TO GATHER ILLEGAL PROFITS!

LATER....

EVERY TIME I LOOK AT A COMIC PAGE I STILL CAN'T BELIEVE MY INCREDIBLE ADVENTURES WITH THE STRIP VILLAINS EVER HAPPENED!

IT'S FUNNY-- BUT IT'S TRUE!

THE END

149

152

153

155

157

159

161

CAMP TOWNE, TRAINING BASE FOR THE FINEST FIGHTING MEN ON EARTH, IS AGOG WITH EXCITEMENT TODAY!

JUST THINK-- SUPERMAN IS COMING HERE IN PERSON!

I CAN HARDLY WAIT TO SEE HIM IN ACTION!

THE MEN ARE CERTAINLY KEYED UP OVER THE SUPERMAN PROGRAM THE U.S.O. HAS ARRANGED, COLONEL!

CONFIDENTIALLY, CAPTAIN-- SO AM I!

AT THE MAIN GATE...

HALT! WHO GOES THERE?

LOIS LANE AND CLARK KENT OF THE DAILY PLANET! WE'RE GOING TO WRITE UP SUPERMAN'S VISIT!

HERE'S OUR PASS...

LUCKY YOU! I'M DYING TO SEE SUPERMAN-- BUT I'VE GOT TO STAY AT MY POST!

THAT'S TOO BAD!... COME ON, CLARK!

UH--I DON'T FEEL SO WELL! ...("GOT TO FIND AN EXCUSE TO SLIP AWAY, OR THERE WON'T BE ANY SHOW!-")

BUT LOIS HAS NO INTENTION OF LETTING HER FELLOW-REPORTER OUT OF HER SIGHT...

NONE OF YOUR THREAD-BARE EXCUSES! THIS IS ONE TIME YOU'RE NOT GOING TO DISAPPEAR IN THE MIDDLE OF AN ASSIGNMENT AND LEAVE ME TO DO ALL THE WORK!

("-I'M AFRAID SHE'S GOING TO BE DIFFICULT, AND I CAN'T RISK DOING ANYTHING THAT WOULD REVEAL THAT I REALLY AM SUPERMAN!-")

THOUSANDS OF MEN LINED UP ON THE PARADE GROUND TO RECEIVE SUPERMAN WITH SUPER-MILITARY HONORS!

AND HE SHOULD BE THERE NOW! I--I THINK I'LL GET A DRINK OF WATER!

THAT WON'T WORK, EITHER! THERE'S A DRINKING FOUNTAIN-- AND THERE'S COLONEL MCNAB WAITING FOR US!

IT SEEMS YOU'RE RIGHT ON ALL THREE COUNTS!

SLOW MINUTES DRAG BY WHILE EAGER SOLDIERS WAIT IMPATIENTLY FOR THEIR FIRST GLIMPSE OF THE MAN OF TOMORROW...

HE'S LATE...IT WOULD BE A TERRIBLE LET-DOWN FOR THE MEN IF SUPERMAN DIDN'T SHOW UP AT ALL!

HE'LL BE HERE, COLONEL, IF HE HAS TO MOVE MOUNTAINS TO MAKE IT! HE'D NEVER DISAPPOINT OUR FIGHTERS!

("-MOVING MOUNTAINS WOULD BE COMPARATIVE-LY EASY!-")

2

SO WITH ALL THE IMPRESSIVE TRAPPINGS OF REAL WAR, BEGINS A VAST, GRIM GAME OF MEN AND MACHINES -- A FULL-DRESS REHEARSAL OF THE TIDAL WAVE OF RETRIBUTION THAT HAS ALREADY BEGUN TO SWEEP OVER HALF THE WORLD, BLOTTING OUT FLAMES OF DESTRUCTION SET BY MAD CRIMINALS AT THE HEAD OF MISLED NATIONS!

YOU SEE, MY STRATEGY IS TO FIND THE REDS' MAIN FORCE AND STRIKE WITH OUR MOBILE WEAPONS BEFORE THEY CAN GET THEIR PLANES AND TANKS INTO LARGE-SCALE ACTION!

GENERAL ARMOR, IT'S DECENT OF YOU TO EXPLAIN THESE THINGS TO ME -- A RAW ROOKIE!

PRESENTLY...

THIS IS SERIOUS! ACCORDING TO THE REFEREES, RED PLANES "BOMBED" THE BRIDGE AN HOUR AGO, AND WE'LL HAVE TO BUILD A NEW ONE! IT WOULD TAKE ALL DAY!

("ONLY ONE THING TO DO...")

THAT'S WHAT I SAID! THE BRIDGE ISN'T THERE! THE ENEMY BLEW IT UP!

BUT, SARGE -- ALL YA GOTTA DO IS LOOK, AN' SEE HOW WRONG YA ARE!

MAYBE I CAN SAVE YOU SOME TIME, GENERAL!

GREAT SCOTT! I MUST BE DREAMING!

HUH?

AND YOUR WHOLE CAMPAIGN DEPENDS ON SPEED, EH?

ALMOST FASTER THAN THE EYE CAN FOLLOW, THE MAN OF STEEL PERFORMS A MILITARY MIRACLE!

FIRST THEY SAY THERE AIN'T NO BRIDGE -- WHICH IS CRAZY, BECAUSE THERE IS -- AN' THEN SUPERMAN CARRIES THE ARMY ACROSS, WHICH IS CRAZIER, BECAUSE IT AIN'T POSSIBLE!

YOU'RE THE LAST, GENERAL! NOW YOU CAN GET ON WITH THE ATTACK!

SUPERMAN, IT'S TOO BAD THEY DON'T GIVE MEDALS FOR DISTINGUISHED SERVICE IN MANEUVERS!

LUCKILY FOR THE BLUES, THERE'S NOTHING IN THE RULE BOOK AGAINST IT!

5

A THREAT OF NEW TROUBLE APPEARS IN THE HEAVENS...

A RED OBSERVATION PLANE, SIR! IT'S SIGHTED US!

THEY'LL RADIO THEIR AIR BASE TO "BOMB" US! IF ONLY WE KNEW WHERE THEIR AIR ARM WAS LOCATED, WE COULD SEND OUR OWN PLANES TO INTERCEPT THEM--PERHAPS EVEN "DESTROY" THEM ON THE GROUND!

WITH YOUR PERMISSION, SIR, I'LL TAKE A LOOK AROUND!

SUPERMAN'S TELESCOPIC X-RAY VISION STABS THROUGH MOUNTAINS AS IF THEY WERE CRYSTAL LENSES, AND SPIES--

"--THERE'S THE AIRPORT-- AND JUDGING BY THE ACTIVITY, THE BOMBERS ARE GETTING READY TO TAKE OFF!--"

I HATE TO GO A.W.O.L.-- BUT THIS IS NO TIME FOR EXPLANATIONS!

CRASHING THROUGH THE UPPER BRANCHES OF A TALL PINE TREE, SUPERMAN GATHERS A HARVEST OF PINE CONES...

WHA--? WHERE--? HOW--?

A FELLOW CAN'T "DIVE BOMB" AN AIRPORT WITHOUT BOMBS --OR AT LEAST, IMITATION GRENADES!

PILOTS, BOMBARDIERS AND MECHANICS STAND PARALYZED WITH ASTONISHMENT AS A VIVID FIGURE ROCKETS DOWN UPON THE RED AIRPORT.

JUST IN TIME! THE PLANES ARE WARMING UP! ...AND SINCE THEY'RE THE BEST SHIPS IN THE WORLD, I'M GLAD THESE AREN'T REAL GRENADES!

WHERE'S HIS PARACHUTE?

SUPERMAN, OR I'M A GOGGLE-EYED BABOON!

ONCE AGAIN THE STAFF OFFICERS WHO REFEREE MOCK WARFARE CREDIT A BRILLIANT VICTORY TO THE SUPERFIGHTER OF THE BLUE FORCES!

WELL, GENERAL, I'M AFRAID SUPERMAN HAS "DESTROYED" YOUR AIR FORCE WITH HIS "GRENADES!"

AND I'D COUNTED ON THAT AIR RAID AS THE OPENING BLOW IN A SURPRISE ATTACK THAT WOULD HAVE WIPED THEM OUT!

ISN'T HE WONDERFUL-- EVEN IF HE ISN'T ON OUR SIDE?

AS SUPERMAN FLASHES UPWARD, ANTI-AIRCRAFT BATTERIES OPEN FIRE BELATEDLY...

GETTING TOUGH AFTER THE DAMAGE IS DONE IS LIKE LOCKING THE BARN DOOR AFTER THE HORSE HAS BEEN STOLEN!

6

BUT THIS TIME, THE DECISION OF THE REFEREES IS HOTLY DISPUTED!

THEY COULDN'T MISS AT THAT RANGE! WE'LL CONSIDER **SUPERMAN** DEAD--TECHNICALLY SPEAKING!

YOU CAN'T DO THAT! **SUPERMAN** IS INDESTRUCTIBLE!

NOW OCCURS ONE OF THOSE RARE ACCIDENTS THAT SOMEHOW DO MANAGE TO HAPPEN, EVERY NOW AND THEN, DESPITE THE MOST ELABORATE PRECAUTIONS...

BLINDED BY SMOKE, A YOUTHFUL GUNNER UNINTENTIONALLY LOADS HIS CANNON, NOT WITH A BLANK SHELL, BUT WITH A LIVE ONE FROM AN EMERGENCY SUPPLY!

JUST MY LUCK! **SUPERMAN** COMES AROUND-- MY FAVORITE HERO --AND SMOKE GETS IN MY EYES!

NONSENSE, MISS LANE! IF THOSE SHELLS WERE REAL, INSTEAD OF BLANKS, THEY'D RIP A FLYING FORTRESS TO BITS!

AND A SLAMMING BLAST OF STEEL AND TNT FINDS ITS TARGET!

THE NEXT MOMENT...

I DON'T MIND IF YOU WANT TO WASTE AMMUNITION -- BUT LOOK OUT FOR FALLING SHRAPNEL!

WHAT DID I TELL YOU? IS HE ALIVE, OR ISN'T HE?

GREAT GUNS-- STARRETT MIGHT AS WELL SURRENDER RIGHT NOW!

RECONNOITERING, **SUPERMAN** SIGHTS THE MAIN FORCE OF THE "ENEMY" AND SOMETHING ELSE...

THAT MUST BE THE MAIN FORCE OF THE REDS -- AND THERE'S A TANK COLUMN, SNEAKING AROUND THE MOUNTAIN TO CATCH GENERAL ARMOR'S OUTFIT OFF GUARD!

POOR LITTLE CREEPING THINGS-- IT SEEMS ALMOST A SHAME TO TAKE ADVANTAGE OF THEM! BUT NO DOUBT MY COMMANDING GENERAL WOULDN'T LOOK AT IT THAT WAY!

169

AT THE RED ARMY HEADQUARTERS...

HOW DOES IT LOOK, GENERAL STARRETT?

PRETTY BAD FOR US, I'M AFRAID! BUT OUR SCOUTS ARE WATCHING THE ROAD, WHICH IS THE ONLY WAY THE BLUES COULD GET TO US!

IF WE CAN HOLD THEM ON THE ROAD, WE'LL HAVE A CHANCE TO SOLIDIFY OUR POSITION-- UNLESS SUPERMAN HAS SOME MORE SURPRISES UP HIS SLEEVE!

ABRUPTLY...

I DO HOPE I'M NOT BUTTING IN!

WHAT!?!

WHAT CHANCE HAS A POOR GENERAL GOT IN A CASE LIKE THIS?

BUT THEY CAN'T DEPEND ON SUPERMAN TO WIN SINGLE-HANDED, CAN THEY?

ON THE HEELS OF THE MAN OF TOMORROW COME THUNDERING TANKS AND PICKED SHOCK TROOPS!

QUICK! SEND THE EMERGENCY CALL TO ALL STATIONS!

DON'T LOOK AT ME AS IF I NEEDED RESCUING! FOR ONCE, I DON'T!

YOU WOULD, IF THIS WERE REALLY WAR!

STUNNED BY THE SUDDENNESS OF THE ATTACK FROM AN UNEXPECTED DIRECTION, THE REDS ARE CONFUSED AND DISORGANIZED...

BRING UP THE ANTI-TANK GUNS! DIG FOXHOLES WHERE YOU CAN!

NOT FIGHTING, SUPERMAN? HAVE YOU RETIRED?

IT LOOKS AS IF MY SIDE HAS ALL THE HELP IT NEEDS!

AND THE REFEREES, SWIFTLY WEIGHING THE ODDS, REACH A PROMPT DECISION...

WHAT! AMERICAN SOLDIERS SURRENDER WHEN THEY'VE HARDLY BEGUN TO FIGHT?

I'M AFRAID YOU'VE LOST, GENERAL! ARE YOU READY TO SURRENDER?

("-SHE'S RIGHT! WE'VE STILL GOT A CHANCE!")

170

⑨

172

173

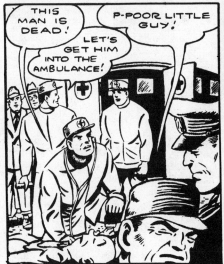

175

177

178

179

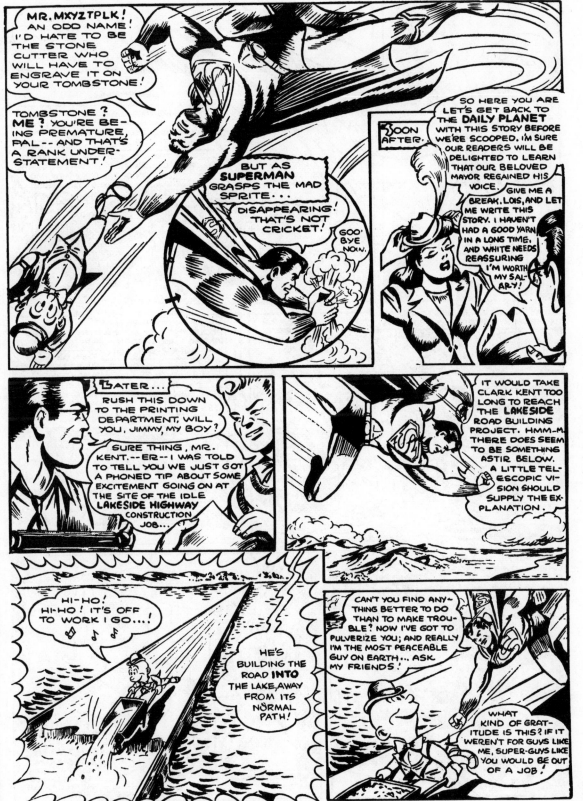

HIT THE ROAD, PEST!

THAT'S FUNNY! YOU LOSE YOUR TEMPER, AND I GET "SOAR"!

THIS REQUIRES A MAJOR SURGICAL OPERATION!

SWINGING TO THE SHORE WITH HIS MASSIVE BURDEN, SUPERMAN LOWERS THE COMPLETED ROAD INTO ITS CORRECT PLACE...

ONE BRIGHT SIDE TO THIS...THE CITY WILL HAVE ITS LAKESIDE HIGHWAY AT A FRACTION OF THE COST THAT HAD BEEN ESTIMATED!

BUT AS SUPERMAN BEGINS TO RETURN TOWARD THE NEWSPAPER BUILDING...

WHAT'S THIS?

SCRAPS OF PAPER EVERYWHERE! I GIVE UP!

RACING ABOUT THE CITY, SUPERMAN GATHERS UP THE THOUSANDS OF PAPER SCRAPS AT SUPER-SPEED...

WHEN I GROW UP, I WANTA BE LIKE HIM!

THEN BE SURE TO EAT EVERYTHING YOUR MOTHER TELLS YOU, AND GET LOTS OF REFRESHING SLEEP!

CLEAN-LINESS IS NEXT TO GODLINESS!

I'VE WORKED LIKE A TROJAN... BUT ALL MY LABOR WILL BE IN VAIN UNLESS I LEARN THE SOURCE OF THIS PAPER DELUGE...AND BRING IT TO A HALT!

OH-HO! I MIGHT HAVE EXPECTED TO FIND YOU INVOLVED IN THIS AFFAIR!

GENERAL WASTE PAPER CORP.

I THOUGHT IT WOULD BE FUN TO SABOTAGE THE CITY'S CLEAN-UP WEEK CAMPAIGN! AREN'T I JUST AS MEAN AS MEAN CAN BE. HEE HEE!

183

185

AFTER LOIS FINISHES HER STORY...

ER-UH – VERY INTERESTING STORY, LOIS.' A WAVE OF A MAGIC WAND AND YOU'RE JUST LIKE **SUPERMAN.'** ER-EXCUSE ME A MINUTE...

THEN, LOIS FINDS SHE DOESN'T KNOW HER OWN STRENGTH.'

JUST A SECOND, CHIEF.' I'M NOT CRAZY– I CAN PROVE IT. LOOK! I CAN LIFT YOU!

HEY! LET ME DOWN!

ER-UH-C-CALL UP NEW ROSES HOSPITAL.' T-TELL THEM I WANT THEIR BEST PADDED CELL!

RELAX, CHIEF, WHILE I ANSWER THIS!

WHAT ? YOU'RE **SURE?** ALL THREE OF THEM ? WHERE ? YES–YES.' FINE.' THANKS!

HUH? WHAT IS IT?

SOME WAITRESS SAYS SHE OVERHEARD THE **BBB** GANG PLANNING A HOLD-UP! I'LL PROVE I'M **REALLY** AS GOOD AS **SUPERMAN** BY BRINGING IN THAT TRIC SINGLE-HANDED!

NOW–MEET THE **BBB** GANG, WHOSE VICIOUS CRIMES BLOT THE POLICE LEDGERS OF 16 STATES.' COLD, VIOLENT, INHUMAN, **THESE** ARE THE BRUTES LOIS SINGLE-HANDEDLY CHALLENGES.'

WANTED
EWARD
BRUTE
BUZZARD
BEAR

⑦

194

198

THE WHOLE WORLD KNOWS OF **SUPERMAN'S** TITANIC STRENGTH...

YOU'RE SAFE NOW!

...OF HIS IMPENETRABLE SKIN, WHICH NOT EVEN A CANNON SHELL CAN PIERCE...

...AND OF HIS AMAZING X-RAY VISION, WHICH CAN SEE THROUGH STEEL AND BRICK...

STOP! NITRO KALE IS WAITING FOR YOU BEHIND THAT BUILDING!

SUPERMAN HAS DEDICATED HIS MIRACULOUS POWERS TO CONSTANT WAR AGAINST THE EVIL MECHANISMS OF SUCH CRIMINALS AS THE **PRANKSTER, TOYMAN** AND **LUTHOR**...

YOUR ROBOT IS FINISHED, **LUTHOR!**

...AND, MORE OFTEN, HE HAS USED HIS WONDERFUL POWERS TO AID WORTHY CAUSES...

I'LL REBUILD THIS AREA SO PEOPLE WON'T HAVE TO LIVE IN SLUMS!

BUT WHO IS **SUPERMAN**? HOW DID **THE MAN OF STEEL** ACQUIRE HIS INVINCIBILITY? MILLIONS HAVE ASKED THESE QUESTIONS!

NOW WE GIVE YOU THE ANSWERS!...

②

199

ONCE, IN THE OUTER REACHES OF TRACKLESS SPACE, THERE EXISTED THE GREAT PLANET **KRYPTON**!

THERE WAS LIFE ON **KRYPTON**... HUMANS OF HIGH INTELLIGENCE AND MAGNIFICENT PHYSICAL PERFECTION...

I'M WORRIED! JUNIOR HAS REACHED THE THIRD GRADE AND DOES NOT YET KNOW HIS CALCULUS.

HE IS A TRIFLE BACK-WARD, BUT NEXT YEAR HE'LL BE FIVE YEARS OLD AND HE'LL KNOW IT BY THEN.

THE FORCE OF GRAVITY ON **KRYPTON** WAS FAR GREATER THAN THAT ON EARTH...

IF OUR ASTRO-CALCULATIONS ARE CORRECT, A KRYPTONIAN, ON PLANET **EARTH**, COULD TAKE A NORMAL STEP AND LEAP OVER ITS TALLEST BUILDING!

HE COULD ALMOST DEFY ITS WEAK GRAVITY ENTIRELY.

THEN ONE FATEFUL DAY ON KRYPTON, UNEASY MUTTERINGS WERE HEARD...

YOU FEEL IT? THE GROUND IS SHAKING AGAIN.

LAST NIGHT, THERE WERE DEEP RUMBLES BENEATH THE SURFACE!

AND IN THE HALL OF WISDOM, THE COUNCIL OF FIVE AWAITED THE ARRIVAL OF JOR-EL, KRYPTON'S GREATEST SCIENTIST...

WHAT IS THIS IMPORTANT MESSAGE JOR-EL HAS FOR US?

HERE HE COMES NOW! HE'S ABOUT TO SPEAK!

GENTLEMEN... KRYPTON IS DOOMED!

JOR-EL LEFT, A TRAGIC, BEATEN FIGURE... WHILE KRYPTON'S RUMBLINGS AND QUAKINGS INCREASED...

FOOLS... BLIND FOOLS! THEY ARE ALL DOOMED! I PRAY I MAY YET HAVE TIME TO SAVE MY WIFE... AND THE BABY!

AT HOME, JOR-EL'S BRAVE WIFE LOOKED AT HIM AND UNDERSTOOD...

I SEE IT IN YOUR FACE! THEY REFUSED TO BELIEVE YOU!

I TRIED, LARA ...BELIEVE ME, I TRIED.'

SUDDENLY, BUILDINGS ROCKED VIOLENTLY... GREAT FISSURES OPENED IN THE GROUND...

IT HAS COME!

JUST AS JOR-EL PREDICTED!

QUICKLY, LARA— THE SPACE SHIP! THERE IS JUST ROOM IN IT FOR YOU AND THE BABY!

NO, MY HUSBAND... MY PLACE IS HERE WITH YOU! BUT OUR SON... LET HIM HAVE HIS CHANCE FOR LIFE!

LARA... MY DEAR... MY DEAR...

THE HELPLESS INFANT WAS PLACED INTO THE SPACE-SHIP—AND MOMENTS LATER THE TINY CRAFT ROCKETED INTO THE VOID!

FAREWELL, MY SON!

GOOD LUCK!

202

⑤

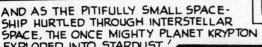

205

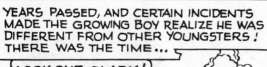

YEARS PASSED, AND CERTAIN INCIDENTS MADE THE GROWING BOY REALIZE HE WAS DIFFERENT FROM OTHER YOUNGSTERS! THERE WAS THE TIME...

LOOK OUT, CLARK! THAT TRACTOR! OHHH!

GOOD GOSH! YOU'RE NOT EVEN HURT!

BUT LOOK AT THE TRACTOR!

ONCE, WHEN HE WAS LATE FOR SUPPER AND STARTED TO HURRY HOME...

GOLLY! I'M GOING FASTER THAN THE EXPRESS TRAIN!

ANOTHER TIME, WHEN HE WANTED TO HURDLE A FENCE, AND INSTEAD...

HUH? I'M GOING OVER THE HOUSE, TOO!

... AND THERE WAS THIS INCIDENT...

NOW WHERE DID I PUT MY SPECTACLES?

THEY'VE FALLEN BEHIND THE CABINET, MOTHER!

WHY, SO THEY ARE! HOW EVER DID YOU KNOW, SON?

I... I DON'T UNDERSTAND! IT'S AS IF I HAD X-RAY EYES!

HMMM!

⑨

ON AN ANCIENT ROOFTOP, STEEL RINGS AGAINST STEEL AS TWO SWORDSMEN FIGHT A DUEL TO THE DEATH...

SUDDENLY, A FATAL THRUST, AND ONE OF THE COMBATANTS PLUNGES FROM THE PARAPET...

AND AS THE DEFEATED SWORDSMAN LIES IMMOBILE ON THE GROUND, ABRUPTLY A VOICE SHOUTS THE COMMAND—"CUT!"

CUT!!

YES, "CUT!" FOR THIS IS A MOVIE SET IN THE HEART OF THE ALPS, THE LAST SCENE OF THE HISTORICAL PICTURE, "BLACK MAGIC", STARRING ORSON WELLES AS THE SINISTER MAGICIAN, CAGLIOSTRO, HAS JUST BEEN PUT ON FILM.

AND DON'T FORGET THE FANCY DRESS BALL TONIGHT. AS YOU KNOW, ALL OF YOU ARE GOING IN YOUR "BLACK MAGIC" COSTUMES!

LATER, AS WELLES, AND ACTRESS NANCY GUILD DRIVE UP A STEEP MOUNTAIN ROAD, HEADED FOR THE TOWN WHERE THE COSTUME BALL IS TO BE HELD...

I'LL BE QUITE SORRY TO TAKE OFF THIS COSTUME—I ENJOYED PLAYING THE VILLAINOUS CAGLIOSTRO!

AND I ENJOYED PLAYING MARIE ANTOINETTE!

SUDDENLY...

LOOK! WHAT'S THAT?

IT LOOKS LIKE A ROCKET SHIP! LET'S STOP—I WANT TO GET UP CLOSE TO IT!

THIS BABY LOOKS POWERFUL ENOUGH TO REACH ANOTHER PLANET!

ORSON WELLES IS RIGHT, THOUGH HE DOESN'T KNOW IT YET. FOR ON THE OTHER SIDE OF THE HILL IS GATHERED A VAST CONCOURSE OF PEOPLE BREATHLESSLY AWAITING THE LAUNCHING OF THE FIRST ROCKET SHIP TO MARS!

...AND THIS SPACE SHIP, THE RESULT OF COOPERATION AMONG ROCKET SOCIETIES OF THE WORLD, MARKS A MILESTONE IN SCIENCE...

MEANWHILE, CURIOUS ABOUT THE STRANGE PROJECTILE ORSON WELLES ENTERS ITS INTERIOR THROUGH AN OPEN PORTHOLE..

NO DOUBT THE PAPERS HAVE CARRIED THE NEWS OF THE SHIP, BUT I'VE BEEN CUT OFF FROM CIVILIZATION SINCE WORKING ON THE PICTURE!

AS ORSON EXAMINES THE SHIP'S CONTROLS, THROUGH AN OPEN PORTHOLE FLOAT THE WORDS OF THE DIRECTOR OF THE INTERNATIONAL ROCKET SOCIETY..

I AM PRESSING THE BUTTON. IN TEN SECONDS, THE PORTHOLES WILL CLOSE AND THE FIRST PILOTLESS ROCKET WILL TAKE OFF FOR MARS!

"PILOTLESS ROCKET... TEN SECONDS...CLOSED PORTHOLES"— I'VE GOT TO GET OUT OF HERE!!

THE PORTHOLES WILL NOT OPEN AGAIN UNTIL THE SPACE-SHIP REACHES MARS, WHEN THE ROBOT INSTRUMENTS WILL BROADCAST BACK, BY RADAR, INFORMATION ABOUT THE PLANET...

FRANTIC, ORSON DASHES TO THE PORTHOLE, BUT THE THICK GLASS CLOSES IN HIS FACE!

I'M TRAPPED-- IN A MARTIAN ROCKET SHIP!

VOLCANO-LIKE BLASTS ERUPT FROM THE JETS OF THE ROCKET SHIP, PROPELLING IT AWAY FROM EARTH AT INCREDIBLE VELOCITY...

AND, AS THE ROCKET SHIP PLUNGES INTO THE BLACK ABYSS OF OUTER SPACE, ORSON WELLES TAKES A LAST LOOK AT HIS OWN PLANET!

WHEN I FOOLED THE WORLD WITH MY MARTIAN INVASION BROADCAST-- I NEVER DREAMED I WOULD INVADE MARS MYSELF!

INSIDE THE ROCKET SHIP'S CABIN, ORSON WELLES FLOATS LIKE A FEATHER, FOR THERE IS NO GRAVITY TO HOLD HIM TO THE FLOOR!

I'VE READ AND WRITTEN ABOUT THIS IN SCIENCE FICTION STORIES, BUT I NEVER THOUGHT IT WOULD ACTUALLY HAPPEN TO ME!

TWO HOURS LATER, THE SPACE SHIP ARRIVES WITHIN THE GRAVITATIONAL PULL OF MARS. REVERSING ITSELF, IT FALLS BASE DOWNWARDS WITH THE ROCKET'S BLAST NOW ACTING AS A BRAKE. THE STRANGE RED PLANET APPROACHES FAST.

SOON, THE ROCKET SHIP LANDS. THE PORTHOLES OPEN AUTOMATICALLY. AND ORSON STEPS OUT...ONTO THE SOIL OF ANOTHER WORLD!

213

214

SECONDS LATER, IT'S "UP, UP, AND AWAY!" AS **SUPERMAN** BRIDGES THE ASTRONOMICAL DISTANCE BETWEEN EARTH AND MARS, AT COMET SPEED!

THAT HOAX OF ORSON'S, YEARS AGO, ABOUT A MARTIAN INVASION, SURE BACKFIRED! NOW, EVEN THOUGH HE'S TELLING THE TRUTH, NO ONE WILL BELIEVE HIM!

MEANWHILE, THE WORLD REGARDS ORSON'S FRANTIC WARNINGS AS THE BEST JOKE OF THE YEAR!!

THEY'RE CLOSING IN ON ME!... I CAN'T HOLD THEM OFF ANY LONGER... THEY'RE GOING TO BLAST ME WITH THEIR RAY GUNS... PREPARE FOR THE MARTIAN ROCKET SHIPS!!

THIS IS THE FUNNIEST THING I'VE HEARD IN AGES!

BETTER THAN BOB HOPE!

IN THE MARTIAN RADIO STUDIO, WELLES FIGHTS DESPERATELY WITH AN ANCIENT SWORD AGAINST THE RAY GUNS OF THE SOLAZIS!

... THIS IS THE END! BEWARE, EARTH... PREPARE! THE MARTIANS ARE COMING!

AS THE RAY GUN TRIGGER TIGHTENS, AND THE DEADLY BEAM STABS OUT... ENTER SUPERMAN!

THE **MAN OF STEEL** TAKES ON HIS OWN INDESTRUCTIBLE CHEST THE MAN-DESTROYING BEAM WHICH WOULD HAVE SHRIVELED ORSON WELLES TO ASHES!

IT TICKLES!

THEN, ON THE INTER-COMMUNICATION TELEVISION SCREEN APPEARS THE IMAGE OF THE MARTIAN DICTATOR...

STOP THIS NONSENSE, ALL OF YOU! I WISH TO SEE SUPERMAN AND TALK WITH HIM!

215

217

THE FIRST PART OF THE **SUPERMAN**-ORSON WELLES PLAN WORKS AS THE MOON REACHES THE ROCKET SHIP FLEET AND PULLS THE SPACE SHIPS WITHIN ITS ORBIT. THE ROCKET SHIPS ARE POWERLESS TO CONTINUE AND ARE NOW MERE SATELLITES OF THE MOON.!

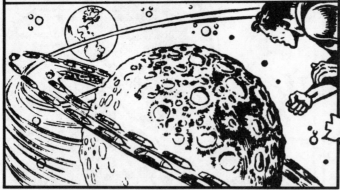

IT WORKED—AND JUST IN TIME! ANOTHER FEW MINUTES AND THE MARTIAN ROCKET SHIPS WOULD HAVE REACHED EARTH! NOW TO WORK OUT A PLAN WITH ORSON TO MAKE SURE THAT MARS NEVER AGAIN TRIES TO INVADE THE EARTH.!

SWIFTLY, ORSON WELLES AND **SUPERMAN** PUT THEIR SECOND PLAN INTO OPERATION...

I'VE LEARNED ENOUGH OF THE MARTIAN LANGUAGE TO MAKE MR. MARTLER SAY A FEW WORDS TO HIS MARTIAN SUBJECTS.!

AND WITH MY X-RAY VISION, I'VE LEARNED ENOUGH ABOUT THIS MACHINERY TO MAKE THE TELECAST! LET'S GO.!

SCAN MARS

FELLOW MARTIANS, THERE MUST BE NO MORE WAR. WE WILL STAY ON OUR OWN PLANET.!

SCAN MARS

YOU WILL RULE YOURSELVES— AND I SHALL RETIRE—

GREAT NEWS! NOW WE CAN GO HOME TO OUR FAMILIES! I NEVER DID WANT TO FIGHT ANYWAY.!

221

SUPERMAN

REG. U. S. PAT. OFF.

Superman, mighty man of steel whose super-powers have conquered catastrophes and wrecked wrong-doers! Batman, hooded foe of crime whose flashing feats have crushed crooks for years! Are any two names in the world more famous than these? Yet these two mighty champions of the right have never met -- *UNTIL NOW!* Yes, at long last Superman and Batman meet face to face on a voyage of peril -- and strange and startling is the outcome when two legendary figures form . .

"The MIGHTIEST TEAM in the WORLD!"

SUPER COMET

53412

A GREAT ADVENTURE CAN HAVE MANY BEGINNINGS--AND THIS ONE BEGINS IN GOTHAM CITY, WHEN THE FAMED *BATMAN* AND *ROBIN* CORNER A WANTED BANDIT-KILLER...

I'LL STOP YOU, *BATMAN*, NO MATTER WHAT HAPPENS TO ME!

NO YOU WON'T, GELL!

NICE GOING, *ROBIN*-- I CAN HANDLE HIM FROM HERE!

AND THE HAMMERING FISTS OF *BATMAN* SOON END ANOTHER CRIMINAL'S CAREER!

GELL WAS THE LAST CRIMINAL ON OUR "WANTED" LIST, *BATMAN*! NOW YOU AND *ROBIN* CAN TAKE A MUCH-DESERVED REST!

THANKS, COMMISSIONER! COME ON, *ROBIN*-- WE'LL TAKE THIS HOODLUM IN AND THEN GO HOME!

"HOME" IS THE MANSION OF WEALTHY PLAYBOY BRUCE WAYNE --FOR BRUCE AND HIS WARD, DICK GRAYSON, ARE SECRETLY *BATMAN* AND *ROBIN*!

NOW'S MY CHANCE TO VISIT MY RELATIVES UPSTATE--BUT I HATE TO LEAVE YOU ALONE, BRUCE!

THAT'S ALL RIGHT, DICK... I'M GOING TO GET A REAL VACATION, ON A COASTAL CRUISE! I'LL JUST RELAX AND FORGET CRIME, FOR A CHANGE!

BUT ANOTHER BEGINNING OF THIS STRANGE ADVENTURE TAKES PLACE IN METROPOLIS, WHERE THAT CITY'S MOST FAMOUS CITIZEN COMPLETES A TASK...

THIS FOSSIL I DUG OUT OF THE GOBI DESERT FINALLY COMPLETES THE NEW *HALL OF LEARNING*! NOW TO PUT THE ROOF BACK ON, AND I'M THROUGH!

LOOK--IT'S *SUPERMAN*!

YES, IT IS THE *MAN OF STEEL*, WHOSE AWESOME SUPER-POWERS HAVE RUNG AROUND THE WORLD! BUT HE IS ALSO SOMEONE ELSE...

I'D BETTER HURRY INTO MY STREET CLOTHES IF I'M TO KEEP MY DATE WITH LOIS!

FOR JUST AS PLAYBOY BRUCE WAYNE IS SECRETLY *BATMAN*, SO MIGHTY *SUPERMAN* HIDES HIS IDENTITY BENEATH THE GUISE OF MILD-MANNERED REPORTER CLARK KENT!

SO YOU START YOUR VACATION CRUISE ON THE *VARANIA* TOMORROW EVENING? I'LL COME DOWN AND SEE YOU OFF, CLARK!

THAT'LL BE SWELL, LOIS! I'M HOPING FOR A REAL REST ON THIS CRUISE!

THUS, FATE WEAVES A STRANGE PATTERN TO DRAW THE TWO MOST FAMOUS CHAMPIONS IN THE WORLD INTO AN UNPRECEDENTED ADVENTURE! FOR NEXT EVENING...

2

...AS PASSENGERS BOARD THE CRUISE-SHIP *VARANIA*...

ISN'T IT DIVINE? I'LL WAIT ON DECK WHILE YOU SEE THE PURSER, CLARK!

ALL RIGHT, LOIS!

LOOKS LIKE A FULL PASSENGER LIST! THANK GOODNESS I HAVE A CABIN TO MYSELF!

BUT SECONDS LATER, A DISMAYING SURPRISE...

I'M SORRY, MR. KENT, BUT THE SHIP'S SO CROWDED, I'VE PUT YOU IN WITH ANOTHER PASSENGER-- A MR. BRUCE WAYNE!

BUT-- BUT--

GOSH, I CAN'T MAKE TOO BIG A FUSS... LOIS WOULD SURELY GET SUSPICIOUS!

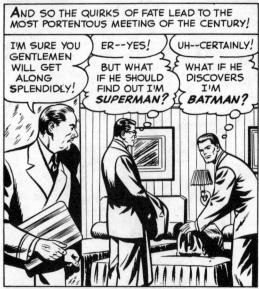

AND SO THE QUIRKS OF FATE LEAD TO THE MOST PORTENTOUS MEETING OF THE CENTURY!

I'M SURE YOU GENTLEMEN WILL GET ALONG SPLENDIDLY!

ER--YES! BUT WHAT IF HE SHOULD FIND OUT I'M *SUPERMAN*?

UH--CERTAINLY! WHAT IF HE DISCOVERS I'M *BATMAN*?

AT THAT MOMENT, OUT ON THE DOCK...

LOOK--THAT MAN! HE'S FIRED *INCENDIARY BULLETS* AT THAT TANK TRUCK!

IT'S CATCHING FIRE!

CUSTOMS OFFICE

JUST AS I PLANNED! THIS ASBESTOS SUIT PROTECTS ME FROM THE FLAMES WHILE I SNATCH THAT DIAMOND SHIPMENT!

CUSTOMS OFFICE

WHAT A SCOOP! IF I CAN ONLY GET A CLOSER LOOK!

AND ONCE AGAIN, LOIS LANE'S DARING LEADS HER INTO DANGER...

STOP HIM! HE'S GOT THE FABIAN DIAMONDS!

NO ONE CAN COME AFTER ME THROUGH THE FLAMES!

HELP! THE FIRE HAS CIRCLED AROUND--I'M TRAPPED!

3

Panel 1: BUT BEFORE CONTINUING THE PURSUIT, A VITAL MATTER MUST BE SETTLED...

SUPERMAN, YOU CAN DEPEND ON ME TO KEEP SECRET YOUR IDENTITY AS CLARK KENT! AND ONLY YOU AND MY PAL ROBIN KNOW THAT I'M BRUCE WAYNE!

I'LL KEEP YOUR SECRET, TOO, BATMAN! BUT WHAT'LL WE DO ABOUT THAT BANDIT?

Panel 2: EVEN IF HE'S ON THAT SHIP, IF WE SUDDENLY APPEAR AS BATMAN AND SUPERMAN WHILE AT SEA, OUR IDENTITIES MAY BE SUSPECTED!

THEN WE MUST SAIL ON THE VARANIA AS BATMAN AND SUPERMAN -- AS WELL AS IN OUR EVERY-DAY IDENTITIES!

Panel 3: THUS, AN AMAZED CAPTAIN FINDS THAT HE IS TO HAVE TWO WORLD-FAMOUS PASSENGERS!

YOU SEE, WE BELIEVE THIS CROOK IS A PASSENGER WHO BOARDED SHIP IN THE UPROAR, AND WE'RE GOING ALONG TO CATCH HIM!

WHY--WHY, I'M HONORED, GENTLEMEN! I'LL GIVE YOU TWO MY OWN CABIN... I CAN SHARE THE MATE'S!

Panel 4: BUT AWHILE LATER, AS THE VARANIA FORGES OUT TO SEA, SUPERMAN GETS AN UNEXPECTED SURPRISE...

LOIS! WHAT ARE YOU DOING ON BOARD?

I'M GOING ALONG! I PHONED THE CHIEF FOR PERMISSION TO TAKE MY VACATION NOW, AND HAD A SUITCASE RUSHED DOWN! NO ONE ELSE IS GOING TO GET THIS STORY!

Panel 5: BUT IT'S IMPOSSIBLE-- THERE'S NO CABIN-SPACE!

A WOMEN WHO WAS UPSET BY THE FIRE CANCELLED HERS, SO I WAS GIVEN HER CABIN! AND BY THE WAY, SUPERMAN, YOUR FRIEND CLARK KENT IS ABOARD... I'LL TELL HIM YOU'RE HERE!

Panel 6: AN EMERGENCY THAT BOTH CRIME-FIGHTERS HAVE OFTEN FACED CALLS FOR QUICK ACTION...

WE'VE GOT TO REACH OUR CABIN AND SWITCH TO CLARK AND BRUCE BEFORE LOIS GETS THERE! GOSH-- WHY DID SHE HAVE TO COME ALONG?

WHY NOT? SHE SEEMS LIKE A CHARMING GIRL!

6

SHE IS-- BUT IF YOU ONLY KNEW THE TROUBLE THAT GIRL HAS CAUSED ME, *BATMAN*...

OH, OH... HERE SHE COMES NOW! QUICK-- GET INTO YOUR BUNK!

AND WHEN LOIS ENTERS...

HE SEEMS PRETTY SEASICK, MISS LANE! I'LL HAVE TO STAY HERE AND TAKE CARE OF HIM!

CLARK KENT, YOU *WOULD* BE SEASICK! WELL, I DON'T CARE-- NOT WITH *SUPERMAN* AND *BATMAN* ABOARD!

WHEW! THAT'LL EXPLAIN WHY BRUCE AND CLARK DON'T APPEAR DURING THE VOYAGE!

BUT LOIS WILL BE TAGGING EVERYWHERE AFTER *BATMAN* AND *SUPERMAN!* HOW CAN WE ROOT OUT THE CRIMINAL ON BOARD WITH HER GETTING IN OUR HAIR?

LATER, ON DECK...

SAY-- I JUST THOUGHT OF A WAY TO KEEP LOIS OUT OF MY HAIR! IF YOU COULD PAY ATTENTION TO HER-- MAKE HER THINK YOU'RE FALLING FOR HER-- AND I PRETEND TO BE JEALOUS, SHE'D BE TOO OCCUPIED FOR AMATEUR DETECTIVE WORK!

WELL-- IF YOU SAY SO... ALL RIGHT!

SO THAT'S HIS SCHEME! WELL, I'LL JUST TEACH *SUPERMAN* A LESSON!

OH, *BATMAN*, I *SO* WANT TO TALK TO YOU! ER... *SUPERMAN*, WHY DON'T YOU GO SMOOTH OUT THESE ROUGH WAVES, SO THE SHIP WILL STOP PITCHING?

HMPH! SINCE YOU SEEM TO PREFER *BATMAN'S* COMPANY, I WILL!

AND THE *MAN OF STEEL* TAKES A QUICK METHOD TO STOP THE SHIP FROM PITCHING...

LOIS DOES SEEM RATHER TAKEN BY *BATMAN!* OH, WELL... IT'LL HELP OUR GAG! AND WHILE I'M DOING THIS, I'LL LOOK THROUGH THE SHIP FOR THE STOLEN DIAMONDS!

7

SO THAT NIGHT, BEFORE AWED SPECTATORS, A DAZZLING DISPLAY OF *BATMAN'S* LEGENDARY ACROBATIC SKILL!

HE'S REALLY TERRIFIC!

OH, ISN'T HE? AND SO GLAMOROUS, TOO!

GUESS *I'LL* DO A FEW STUNTS FOR THE AUDIENCE TOO, LOIS! BE BACK IN JUST A MOMENT!

HO, HUM-- YOU CAN IF YOU LIKE!

A TRIP TO NORTHERN WATERS AND BACK AGAIN TAKES ONLY A MOMENT AT THE *MAN OF STEEL'S* SUPER-SPEED! THEN, SOME *SUPER-JUGGLING*...

WOW! LOOK AT HIM JUGGLE THOSE ICEBERGS! WHAT A GUY!

OH, YES-- (YAWN)--BUT HE'S SO CORNY! I GUESS (YAWN) I'LL POLISH MY NAILS!

AND WHEN THE PERFORMANCE IS OVER...

MY *SUPER-HEARING* CAUGHT WHAT LOIS SAID, *BATMAN,* AND...WELL-- I GUESS THE BETTER MAN WON!

BUT I ONLY PAID ATTENTION TO KEEP HER FROM MESSING UP OUR SEARCH--AS YOU SUGGESTED,

I'M SURE SMILTER IS OUR MAN...YET, IF YOU COULDN'T SEE THE DIAMONDS ON BOARD, WHAT DID HE DO WITH THEM?

I CAN'T IMAGINE-- BUT ANYWAY, HE CAN'T LEAVE THE SHIP UNTIL WE REACH PORT!

BUT *SUPERMAN* IS WRONG! FOR AT THAT VERY MOMENT...

THE HELICOPTER WILL BE HERE SOON, TO PICK ME UP... AND A LITTLE SABOTAGE WILL KEEP *SUPERMAN* TOO BUSY TO FOLLOW! BUT JUST TO MAKE SURE, I'LL TAKE ALONG A HOSTAGE!

9

Panel 1: SHOOT HIM!

NO--I *CAN'T* *SHOOT!* MUST TRY TO THROW HIM OFF!

Panel 2: BUT *BATMAN* HANGS ON, AND LUNGES INTO THE COCKPIT...

OH, *BATMAN*-- I KNEW YOU'D COME TO SAVE ME!

Panel 3: LATER, WHEN *SUPERMAN* HAS TOWED THE DISABLED LINER TO PORT...

YOU GOT HIM AND SAVED LOIS, BUT WE STILL DON'T HAVE THE DIAMONDS!

YES WE DO! HE HID THE GEMS INSIDE THE *LEAD BULLETS* OF THIS GUN, WHERE YOUR *X-RAY VISION* COULDN'T SEE THEM! I GUESSED IT WHEN HE REFUSED TO FIRE AT ME!

Panel 4: AND AFTER THE CRIMINALS HAVE BEEN TURNED OVER TO THE POLICE...

YOU'RE BOTH LEAVING THE CRUISE HERE?

YES-- OUR JOB IS DONE!

AND WE HAVE TO SLIP BACK INTO THE SHIP AND BECOME CLARK KENT AND BRUCE WAYNE AGAIN!

Panel 5: BUT LATER, AS THE *VARANIA* STARTS HOMEWARD...

YOU GOT OVER YOUR "SEA-SICKNESS" MIGHTY QUICK, CLARK KENT! AS SOON AS *SUPERMAN* AND *BATMAN* LEFT, YOU AND BRUCE APPEAR AGAIN!

ER--YES, THE STOP AT THAT PORT--ER-- REVIVED ME!

Panel 6: THAT DID IT! NOW SHE'S SURE WE'RE *SUPERMAN* AND *BATMAN*!

I CAN COVER YOUR SECRET IDENTITY, BRUCE-- BUT I'M AFRAID NOTHING WILL COVER MINE NOW! WAIT UNTIL TONIGHT!

11

THAT NIGHT, AS DARKNESS SHROUDS THE HOMEWARD-BOUND *VARANIA*...

YOU CAN MAKE A BRIEF APPEARANCE IN GOTHAM CITY, AND I CAN BRING YOU BACK TO THE SHIP AT *SUPER-SPEED!*

SO MINUTES LATER, IN GOTHAM CITY...

LOOK--BATMAN! HE'S WATCHING OUT FOR CRIME, AS USUAL!

NEXT MORNING...

WHY, THE SHIP'S RADIO NEWS-SHEET SPEAKS OF *BATMAN* APPEARING IN GOTHAM CITY LAST NIGHT! THEN HE COULDN'T POSSIBLY BE BRUCE WAYNE!

THAT CONVINCED HER--BUT I'M AFRAID THERE'S NO HELP FOR ME!

YES THERE IS! WHEN WE NEAR PORT CITY, YOU ZIP AHEAD AS *SUPERMAN*, AND GREET THE SHIP! I'LL FIX THINGS FOR YOU!

AND WHEN THE *VARANIA* DOCKS, LOIS AND CLARK KENT DISEMBARK TO BE GREETED BY...

SUPERMAN!

WELCOME HOME, LOIS! OH, HELLO, CLARK--SORRY YOU WERE SO SEASICK!

LATER, IN A SECLUDED CORNER...

YOUR WONDERFUL SKILL IN DISGUISING AS CLARK KENT SAVED MY SECRET, *BATMAN!* BUT WE STILL DON'T KNOW WHICH OF US LOIS REALLY PREFERS!

LET'S SEE WHICH OF US SHE'LL GO OUT TO DINNER WITH...THAT'LL PROVE HER PREFERENCE!

12

BUT WHEN THEY RETURN TO THE CROWD...

HI, *BATMAN!* WHAT DO YOU THINK?...I'M TAKING MISS LANE OUT TO DINNER!

OH, NO!

ISN'T HE THE CUTEST LITTLE CHAP?

The End

234

235

237

"... I REMEMBER HOW *SUPERBOY* ONCE ENCOUNTERED AN ESCAPING BANDIT GANG IN SMALLVILLE ..."

"HE STOPPED THEM BY SWIFTLY SHAPING A ROCK INTO A GREAT PRISM THAT DAZZLED THEM WITH MAN-MADE RAINBOWS!"

"I ALSO REMEMBER THE TIME AN AVALANCHE BROUGHT A GREAT ROCK-FALL TO THREATEN SMALLVILLE ..."

THESE HOME-RUNS WILL *SAVE* HOMES! AND THEY'LL FALL IN THAT UNINHABITED SWAMP!

"I ALSO REMEMBER HOW, WHEN CRIMINALS USING STOLEN ARMY TANKS THREATENED SMALLVILLE, *SUPERBOY* CONVERTED A LOCOMOTIVE INTO A HUGE MAGNET TO SAVE THE DAY!"

LOOK, *SUPERBOY* HAS GRABBED UP THOSE TANK-MOBSTERS!

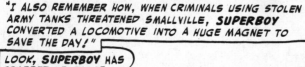

5

"AND THE TIME WHEN *SUPERBOY* AVERTED THE CLEVER 'MOVIE' HOLD-UP OF SMALLVILLE'S BANK! I SAW IT FROM THE START..."

LOOK, THEY'RE MAKING A CRIME MOVIE!

A MOVIE... I WANT TO SEE THAT!

"NOBODY REALIZED THE MOVIE WAS A FAKE TO COVER A *REAL* HOLD-UP, UNTIL *SUPERBOY* POPPED OUT OF THAT BLIND ALLEY BESIDE THE BANK! "

SILENT MOVIES WENT OUT A FEW YEARS AGO... AND HAVING NO SOUND-EQUIPMENT PROVES YOU'RE FAKING FOR A REAL HOLD-UP!

HE'S CAUGHT ONTO THE GAG... I'M GETTING OUT OF HERE!

"BUT THE CAMERAMAN-ACCOMPLICE GOT ONLY A FEW MILES AWAY BEFORE *SUPERBOY* CAUGHT UP TO HIM!"

I BROUGHT BACK THE OTHER CROOK, TOO!

THANKS, *SUPERBOY*... IF YOU HADN'T SPOTTED THEM, THEIR GAG WOULD HAVE WORKED!

BUT AS LANA LANG IS ABOUT TO TURN IN *THAT SUPERBOY* STORY, A RED-HOT IDEA COMES TO HER!

WHY, I NEVER THOUGHT TILL NOW... THE *CAMERA* THAT CROOK USED WAS GONE WHEN *SUPERBOY* CAUGHT UP TO HIM! HE MUST HAVE HIDDEN IT SOME-WHERE BEFORE HE WAS CAUGHT!

ONLY ONE REASON WOULD MAKE HIM HIDE IT... THERE WAS REAL FILM IN IT, A REAL PICTURE! AND THAT PICTURE WOULD SHOW WHO DUCKED *INTO* THAT BLIND ALLEY BEFORE *SUPERBOY* POPPED OUT OF IT! IT WOULD SHOW WHO *SUPERBOY* REALLY WAS!

WHERE AM I GOING, LOIS? FOR THE BIGGEST STORY IN HISTORY... AND IT'LL INTEREST CLARK KENT MORE THAN ANYONE!

THAT CAN ONLY MEAN THAT LANA'S TRYING TO PROVE CLARK IS REALLY *SUPERMAN!* I'D BETTER FOLLOW HER!

MEANWHILE, AS FATE WOULD HAVE IT, "LENS" LEWIS, THE CAMERAMAN CROOK, IS ABOUT TO BE RELEASED FROM THE METROPOLIS PRISON, WHERE HE HAS JUST FINISHED SERVING THE SENTENCE FOR HIS CRIME...

WHY, LANA'S TALKING TO THAT CRIMINAL WHO WAS JUST RELEASED! NOW WHAT ON EARTH...

SURE, THERE WAS FILM IN THAT CAMERA! I FIGURED I COULD USE A FILM OF THE ROBBERY TO FORCE THE BOYS INTO GIVING ME A BIGGER CUT!

IF IT'S STILL WHERE YOU HID IT, WILL YOU SELL IT TO ME? I WANT A SOUVENIR OF THAT CASE!

SURE, WHY NOT? I HID IT SO IT COULDN'T BE USED AS EVIDENCE AGAINST ME, TOO... BUT I'VE SERVED MY TIME AND THE FILM CAN'T HURT ME NOW!

I THINK I CAN GUESS WHAT'S ON THAT FILM...AND I'VE GOT TO MAKE SURE LANA DOESN'T USE IT!

SOON, IN A SECLUDED SPOT OUTSIDE SMALLVILLE...

I DUCKED IT HERE WHEN I WAS TRYING TO GET AWAY FROM SUPERBOY... AND IT'S STILL SAFE!

WONDERFUL! I HAVE YOUR MONEY, MR. LEWIS!

BUT AS "LENS" LEWIS WALKS AWAY...

BY WRAPPING THIS LEAD FOIL I BROUGHT ALONG AROUND THE FILM, IT WILL PREVENT SUPERMAN FROM FOGGING IT WITH X-RAY VISION AND... WHY, LOIS! YOU FOLLOWED ME

LANA, IF THAT FILM CONTAINS THE SECRET OF SUPERBOY'S IDENTITY, YOU MUSTN'T USE IT! IT WOULD WRECK SUPERMAN'S CAREER!

OF COURSE, IF SUPERMAN WERE MY BOY FRIEND, I MIGHT FEEL ABOUT IT AS YOU DO!

ALL RIGHT...SIGH!...I'LL GIVE HIM UP TO YOU IF YOU'LL DESTROY THAT FILM!

OH, NO, YOU DON'T! I CAN USE THE FILM NOW...TO LEARN SUPERMAN'S IDENTITY! DON'T TRY ANYTHING...THIS GUN I HID WITH THE CAMERA STILL WORKS!

240

7

SOON, HEADING BACK TOWARD METROPOLIS IN LANA'S CAR...

THE SECRET OF *SUPERMAN'S* IDENTITY! WHY, I CAN MAKE A FORTUNE SHOWING THIS, AND CHARGING EVERY CROOK IN METROPOLIS A GRAND TO SEE IT!

I HOPE YOU'RE SATISFIED WITH WHAT YOU'VE DONE, LANA!

MEANWHILE, BACK AT THE *PLANET* OFFICE, PERRY WHITE HAS A PROBLEM...

LANA LANG WENT OFF TO TALK TO SOME CROOK GETTING OUT OF PRISON, AND HASN'T COME BACK! HER "I REMEMBER SUPERBOY!" ARTICLE FOR TODAY ISN'T FINISHED!

WHY DON'T YOU GET LOIS TO DO IT?

SHE'S DISAPPEARED, TOO! *YOU'LL* HAVE TO FINISH THE ARTICLE, CLARK!

WELL...ER...ALL RIGHT, BUT MY TYPEWRITER'S NOT WORKING WELL! I'LL HAVE TO USE THE ONE IN THE NIGHT EDITOR'S OFFICE!

IN THE PRIVACY OF THE SMALL OFFICE, CLARK KENT BECOMES *SUPERMAN* FOR AN URGENT REASON!

THAT UNFINISHED ARTICLE OF LANA TELLS ME WHAT SCHEME SHE HAD IN MIND... AND IT MIGHT WORK! I CAN GUESS WHERE SHE AND THAT CROOK WOULD GO, AND I'D BETTER GET THERE FAST!

BUT, ZIPPING AT SUPER-SPEED OVER THE COUNTRY-SIDE TOWARD SMALLVILLE...

IT WAS NEAR HERE I CAUGHT LENS AFTER THE HOLD-UP, SO HE MUST HAVE HIDDEN HIS CAMERA SOMEWHERE NEAR... OH, OH! THAT CAR...MY TELESCOPIC VISION TELLS ME THAT LANA AND LOIS ARE *BOTH* IN IT, AND IN TROUBLE!

SO THERE *WAS* FILM IN THAT CAMERA... I DIDN'T DREAM THERE COULD BE, SINCE IT WAS A FAKE "MOVIE"! NOW I'VE GOT TO GET HOLD OF IT SOMEWAY, BUT I CAN'T ENDANGER THE GIRLS!

241

UNWILLING TO RISK HARM TO LANA OR LOIS, THE MAN OF STEEL FOLLOWS UNSEEN TO THE OUT-SKIRTS OF METROPOLIS!

I REMEMBER LEWIS HAD A HOUSE AND PHOTOGRAPHIC STUDIO... AND THAT WOULD BE IT! BUT WHAT'S HIS PLAN? IF I CAN EAVESDROP WITH SUPER-HEARING!...

I'LL DEVELOP THIS FILM QUICK AND THEN I'M GIVING A MOVIE... AT A THOUSAND DOLLARS A SEAT!

OH, WHAT A TERRIBLE MISTAKE I MADE!

I CAN'T JUST GRAB LOIS AND LANA...THEY MIGHT GET SHOT! AND IF I JUST GRAB THE FILM, THE GIRLS WOULD STILL BE SURE THAT CLARK KENT WAS SUPERBOY... ER, I MEAN, IS SUPERMAN... ER, ANYWAY, I HAVE AN IDEA!

SOON, IN A DESERTED TRACT OF LAND SOME DISTANCE FROM METROPOLIS, AN ASTOUNDING ACTIVITY BEGINS!

THAT PATCH OF FOREST HAD TO BE CLEARED ANYWAY FOR A NEW ROAD... AND THIS TIMBER AND THE STONE I QUARRIED WILL PROVIDE ALL THE MATERIALS I NEED!

FASTER THAN AN ARMY OF CONSTRUCTION MEN COULD WORK, THE MAN OF STEEL STARTS HIS TASK...AND ON THE PLAIN THERE RISES A STREET OF GIANT SIZE!

THANKS TO MY PHOTOGRAPHIC MEMORY, EVERY DETAIL WILL BE PERFECT... AND IN EXACT SCALE!

SMALLVILLE BANK

BANK

9

THESE ADULT-SIZED TEEN-AGED CLOTHES AND THE OVERSIZED SCHOOL BOOKS OUGHT TO DO THE TRICK! THEN TO SET UP THAT AUTOMATIC MOVIE CAMERA I BORROWED...

NOW FOR SOME ACTING! BUT THIS MAKES ME FEEL STRANGE... AS THOUGH I REALLY WAS A BOY AGAIN, WALKING HOME FROM SCHOOL!

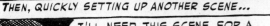

THEN, QUICKLY SETTING UP ANOTHER SCENE...

I'LL NEED THIS SCENE FOR A CONVINCING DOUBLE-EXPOSURE... AND THOSE OVERSIZED MECHANICAL DUMMIES I MADE WILL DO VERY WELL FOR BANDITS!

AGAIN DONNING THE **SUPERMAN** COSTUME, THE MAN OF STEEL APPEARS AS THE **BOY** OF STEEL AGAINST THE BACKGROUND OF GIANT BUILDINGS!

WHEN I COMBINE THIS PICTURE WITH THE ONE I JUST TOOK, IT SHOULD CONVINCE EVEN LANA THAT SHE'S WRONG!

MOMENTS LATER AFTER DISMANTLING HIS GIANT SET...

NOW TO RETURN THIS CAMERA AND DO SOME SUPER-FAST DEVELOPING ON THIS FILM!

MEANWHILE, THE JUBILANT "LENS" LEWIS GETS ON WITH HIS PLAN TO MAKE A FORTUNE...

YEAH, I'M RUNNING THE FILM TONIGHT... AND IT'LL COST A THOUSAND CASH DOLLARS TO SEE IT!

A THOUSAND BUCKS IS CHEAP TO SEE THAT FILM, IF IT REALLY GIVES AWAY **SUPERMAN'S** IDENTITY!

10 243

ONE DAY, AT AN AMUSEMENT PARK IN THE OUTSKIRTS OF METROPOLIS, WE SEE AN OLD AND FAMIL... WELL, NOT *QUITE* SO FAMILIAR A FIGURE...

HA,-HA,-HA! THIS CRAZY MIRROR MAKES ME LOOK ALL OUT OF SHAPE!

YES, IT IS *SUPERMAN'S* OLD ENEMY--THE PRANKSTER.

AND ELSEWHERE IN THE SAME AMUSEMENT PARK...

THIS GIANT DUCK IS LIKE ONE OF MY TOYS--THAT I USED IN CRIME! SIGHH! THOSE WERE THE GOOD OLD DAYS, BEFORE *SUPERMAN* DROVE ME OUT OF BUSINESS!

YOU GUESSED IT, DEAR READER, THIS PLUMP FELLOW IS NONE OTHER THAN THE TOYMAN!

BY A STRANGE COINCIDENCE, A THIRD WELL-KNOWN GENIUS IS ALSO PRESENT...

BAH! IF I WANTED TO DEVOTE MY GENIUS TO SUCH INVENTIONS, WHAT A SENSATION I COULD CREATE!

THIS THIRD CHARACTER IS LUTHOR, RENEGADE MASTER-MIND OF SCIENCE AND ARCH-FOE OF *THE MAN OF STEEL!*

SHORTLY AFTERWARDS, A WHIM OF FATE BRINGS THE 3 MASTERS OF MENACE TOGETHER IN A SURPRISING FASHION!

WHY DON'T YOU WATCH WHERE-- SAY, YOU'RE THE TOYMAN!

AND YOU'RE THE PRANKSTER!

LOOK OUT!

LUTHOR!

OUCH! WHY BLESS ME, THAT'S WHO HE IS.

MOMENTS AFTER THEIR EXPLOSIVE MEETING...

THIS CHANCE MEETING MAY BE THE LUCKIEST THING THAT EVER HAPPENED! WHAT HAVE YOU FELLOWS BEEN DOING LATELY?

IT'S *SUPERMAN,* YOU KNOW. HE'S ALWAYS INTER-FERING!

NOT MUCH!

247

WHY DON'T THE THREE OF US COMBINE OUR TALENTS AND FIGHT **SUPERMAN?** HE'S HAD TROUBLE ENOUGH BEATING ANY ONE OF US! HOW COULD HE DEFEAT ALL THREE?

SOUNDS LIKE A GREAT IDEA, LUTHOR!

LATER.. WE'VE AGREED TO BECOME PARTNERS! NOW WE'LL DRAW LOTS TO DECIDE WHICH ONE OF US PLANS THE FIRST CRIME!

I WIN! I DREW THE SLIP WITH THE X MARKED ON IT!

I'VE GOT JUST THE PRANK FIGURED OUT FOR THIS JOB, TOO. I ALWAYS WANTED TO TRY IT BUT I DIDN'T HAVE THE NERVE! THIS OUGHT TO BE FUN!

AND THE NEXT DAY, AS A CROWD GATHERS TO VIEW A DAZZLING JEWELRY STORE EXHIBIT...

GOLLY! LOOK AT THAT MODEL OF METROPOLIS BRIDGE--ALL MADE OF PRECIOUS STONES! IT'S WORTH A FORTUNE!

HMM! WHAT'S THIS?

DON'T TRY TO PICK IT UP, MISTER! SEE THAT STRING ATTACHED? THE KIDS WILL YANK IT OUT OF SIGHT BEFORE YOU TOUCH IT!

SAY, YOU'RE RIGHT! THAT'S AN OLD CHILDREN'S PRANK!

THE KIDS IN THIS NEIGHBORHOOD ARE FULL OF MISCHIEF! SEE WHAT'S HAPPENING TO THAT GENTLEMAN!

GREAT SCOTT! IT'S **LUTHOR,** THE CRIMINAL SCIENTIST!

HEY!

3

SUDDENLY, FROM THE STRANGE HAT ON THE PAVEMENT, THERE POURS CHOKING CLOUDS OF SUFFOCATING GAS!

GAS? I--I CAN'T BREATHE!

BUT EVEN AS THE FUMES FELL THE OTHERS, REPORTER CLARK KENT CHANGES COSTUMES TO BECOME SUPERMAN!

THE GAS IS HARMLESS--SO I CAN CONCENTRATE ON CATCHING LUTHOR! QUEER--THIS DOESN'T SEEM TO BE THE SORT OF CRIME LUTHOR WOULD HAVE PLANNED!

BUT I GUESS EVEN AN OLD DOG CAN LEARN NEW TRICKS!

SUPERMAN!

AS SUPERMAN'S STEELY FINGERS CLOSE ON HIS QUARRY, THE PRANKSTER PULLS THE REST OF HIS PLAN INTO ACTION!

I KNEW NOBODY WOULD TOUCH THIS WALLET-- THINKING IT TO BE A CHILDISH PRANK! HA-HA! ACTUALLY, THAT STRING IS ATTACHED TO A DETONATOR THAT SETS OFF DYNAMITE PLANTED BY THAT BUILDING WALL!

BOOM!

SO THAT'S IT! DURING THE CONFUSION, YOUR HENCHMEN ARE BLASTING THEIR WAY INTO THE JEWELRY BUILDING! WELL, I'LL JUST PUT YOU HERE FOR SAFEKEEPING!

AND THEN I'LL TAKE CARE OF... GOOD GLORY! THE PRANKSTER AND THE TOYMAN!

ULP!

4 249

PUFFS OF SUPER-BREATH WRENCH THE JEWELED BRIDGE MODEL FROM THE PRANKSTER'S GRASP AND SEND HIM HURTLING BACK...

UGHHH! QUICK, TOYMAN! *DO* SOMETHING!

I ALWAYS HAVE SPECIAL TOYS PREPARED FOR EMERGENCIES!

AND THERE'S NO DENYING *THIS* IS AN EMERGENCY!

WHA-? TINY, FLYING PUPPETS OF ME!

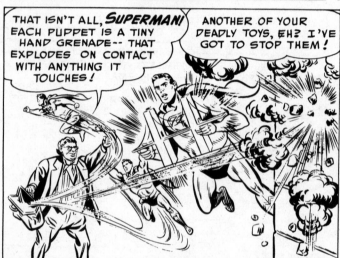

THAT ISN'T ALL, *SUPERMAN!* EACH PUPPET IS A TINY HAND GRENADE-- THAT EXPLODES ON CONTACT WITH ANYTHING IT TOUCHES!

ANOTHER OF YOUR DEADLY TOYS, EH? I'VE GOT TO STOP THEM!

CAN'T RISK THE EXPLOSION DESTROYING THIS MODEL BRIDGE! SO I'LL SET OFF THE GRENADES-- WITH MY TEETH!

AT DAZZLING SPEED, *SUPERMAN* INTERCEPTS THE EXPLOSIVE PUPPETS BEFORE THEY TOUCH ANYTHING! ALL EXCEPT ONE...

I CAN'T EXPLODE THAT GRENADE -- WITHOUT DANGER OF FLYING PARTICLES HURTING THAT WOMAN! ONLY ONE THING TO DO!

OPENING HIS MOUTH WIDE, THE *MAN OF STEEL* SWALLOWS THE DEADLY GRENADE!

HMM! THIS FLAVOR IS DELICIOUS!

BUT WHILE *SUPERMAN* IS VERY BUSY, THE THREE OUT-LAWS MAKE GOOD THEIR ESCAPE IN ONE OF LUTHOR'S INVENTIONS.

FORTUNATELY, I HAD MY JET-MOBILE READY! WE'LL BE MILES AWAY BEFORE *SUPERMAN* STARTS TO LOOK FOR US!

DON'T FORGET! IT WAS MY TOYS THAT KEPT *SUPERMAN* BUSY AND GAVE US THE CHANCE TO ESCAPE!

WE CARRIED OUT *OUR* PART OF THE JOB PERFECTLY, TOYMAN! IT WAS THE PRANKSTER'S FAULT THAT WE FAILED!

THE NEXT JOB IS MINE, THOUGH! AND I'VE ALREADY FIGURED OUT WHAT IT WILL BE! THERE WILL BE NO MISTAKES *THIS* TIME!

SEVERAL DAYS LATER, IN THE DAILY PLANET OFFICE WHERE REPORTERS CLARK KENT AND LOIS LANE ARE EMPLOYED...

I GUESS LUTHOR, THE PRANKSTER AND THIS TOYMAN HAVE GIVEN UP TRYING TO DEFEAT *SUPERMAN* AFTER THEIR FIRST ATTEMPT FAILED!

MORE LIKELY, THEY'RE WAITING FOR THE RIGHT OPPORTUNITY TO STRIKE AGAIN!

HMM! AND THIS FRONT PAGE STORY COULD BE IT!

LATER, WHEN CLARK KENT IS ALONE...

THAT STORY MENTIONED THE "JACK IN THE BOX" CONTEST! IT TOLD ABOUT A CONTEST IN WHICH $1,000,000 IN PRIZE MONEY IS TO BE GIVEN AWAY TO SOME LUCKY WINNER!

THAT'S JUST THE SET-UP THAT WOULD INTEREST THE TOYMAN! EVEN THE NAME OF THE CONTEST IS THAT OF A *TOY!*

AT THIS MOMENT, OUTSIDE THE BUILDING WHERE THE CONTEST IS BEING HELD...

CAREFUL WITH THOSE CRATES! THEY'RE MARKED "HANDLE WITH CARE"!

THEY SURE ARE HEAVY! I WONDER WHAT'S IN 'EM--AND WHY WE GOT ORDERS TO LEAVE THEM RIGHT HERE ON THE SIDEWALK?

JACK IN THE BOX CONTEST HEADQUARTERS

THIS SIDE UP
HANDLE WITH CARE

THIS SIDE UP
HANDLE WITH CARE

AS YOU'VE GUESSED, READER, THESE ARE NO ORDINARY CRATES! IN FACT, THEY CONCEAL...

6

WHOOOOSH

JACK IN THE BOX

THIS END UP

HANDLE WITH CARE

MOMENTS AFTERWARD...

NOT BAD, TOYMAN, USING REAL JACK-IN-THE-BOXES TO GET-- THIS JACK IN THE BOX!

HA-HA! AND FOR A FINAL TOUCH, I'LL OPEN THE SAFE WITH MY TOY CAN-OPENER! IT'S REALLY A MINIATURE ACETYLENE TORCH!

BUT SUDDENLY... SUPERMAN AGAIN!

OH, NO! NOBODY'S LUCK CAN BE THIS BAD!

SAFE LOCK

SWIFTLY, THE TERRIBLE TRIO TAKES TO FLIGHT...

TO THE ROOF! IT'S OUR ONLY CHANCE!

OUT OF MY WAY!

THE SAFE-- IT'S FALLING! THE TOYMAN'S TINY TORCH CUT THROUGH THE FLOOR SUPPORT!

THAT HEAVY SAFE WILL PLUNGE THROUGH TO THE LOWER FLOORS OF THE BUILDING! IT'S BOUND TO HURT SOMEBODY!

SORRY TO BOTHER YOU, MISS!

EEEK! YOU SAVED MY LIFE, SUPERMAN!

7

I CAN KNOCK LUTHOR'S LAND MINES OUT OF THE SKY BEFORE HE HAS A CHANCE TO DROP THEM! HMM! THAT ONE WILL CHANGE THE MOON'S GEOGRAPHY A LITTLE!

BUT AS *SUPERMAN* LANDS ON ANOTHER OF THE GIANT ENGINES OF DESTRUCTION...

SOMETHING'S AFFECTING... ME! I FEEL... WEAK! I--I HAVEN'T STRENGTH ENOUGH TO... DESTROY IT!

AND AT LUTHOR'S HEADQUARTERS...

HA-HA! THE SYNTHETIC KRYPTONITE I COVERED *THAT* MINE WITH IS TAKING EFFECT! IT'S THE ONLY SUBSTANCE THAT CAN AFFECT *SUPERMAN*! HE'S COMPLETELY AT MY MERCY!

GOSH!

NOW I'LL THROW THE DEGRAVITATIONAL SWITCH-- AND SEND THE LAND MINE AND *SUPERMAN*-- HURTLING INTO SPACE!

IT--IT'S HARD TO BELIEVE!

SIGHH! I GUESS LUTHOR IS A GENIUS AFTER ALL!

RELEASED OF GRAVITATIONAL PULL, THE MASSIVE METAL DISC--WITH *SUPERMAN* A HELPLESS PRISONER UPON IT-- WHIRLS OUT INTO SPACE!

I'VE GOT TO DO SOMETHING! OR I'LL KEEP TRAVELLING INTO SPACE FOREVER!

THAT TRIGGER WIRE CONTROLS THE EXPLOSIVE MECHANISM! PERHAPS I CAN SET IT OFF BY FUSING THE TRIGGER CONNECTION WITH HEAT FROM MY X-RAY VISION!

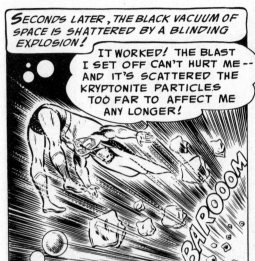

SECONDS LATER, THE BLACK VACUUM OF SPACE IS SHATTERED BY A BLINDING EXPLOSION!

IT WORKED! THE BLAST I SET OFF CAN'T HURT ME-- AND IT'S SCATTERED THE KRYPTONITE PARTICLES TOO FAR TO AFFECT ME ANY LONGER!

BAROOOM

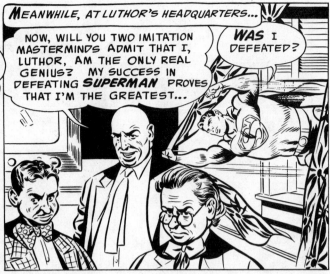

MEANWHILE, AT LUTHOR'S HEADQUARTERS...

NOW, WILL YOU TWO IMITATION MASTERMINDS ADMIT THAT I, LUTHOR, AM THE ONLY REAL GENIUS? MY SUCCESS IN DEFEATING *SUPERMAN* PROVES THAT I'M THE GREATEST...

WAS I DEFEATED?

TELL ME MORE, LUTHOR--BUT WHILE I LISTEN, I'LL JUST TIE YOU UP WITH THIS ROPE I'M MAKING OUT OF THE DRAPERIES!

I--I DON'T UNDERSTAND! MY PLAN WAS FOOLPROOF! W-WHAT *COULD* HAVE GONE WRONG?

10

SECONDS LATER, ON THE WAY TO PRISON...

HA, HA, HA! *YOU* THOUGHT YOU WERE A GENIUS!

LUTHOR GOT US ALL CAPTURED BY *SUPERMAN!* HA, HA, HA!

THE PRANKSTER AND THE TOYMAN ARE SO HAPPY LUTHOR CAN'T GLOAT OVER THEM--THAT THEY DON'T EVEN MIND GOING TO PRISON! WHAT A PRIZE PACKAGE OF CONCEITED HAMS THESE THREE ARE!

THE END

"SUDDENLY, A BOILER EXPLODED AND THE FLOATING AQUARIUM NEARLY SPLIT IN TWO..."

EEEE! HELP!

A JOB FOR SUPERMAN COMING UP!

BOOM!

"EVERYONE JUMPED INTO THE WATER AND SWAM TO SHORE A FEW YARDS AWAY--SO I WAS UNOBSERVED AS I DIVED TO AN UNDERWATER CAVERN..."

I'M GLAD I MADE A HABIT OF CARRYING MY SUPER-COSTUME IN MY SCHOOL BRIEFCASE!

"THEN I BECAME AN UNDERWATER "COWBOY", HERDING TOGETHER ALL THE FISH THAT HAD ESCAPED FROM THE AQUARIUM..."

GIT ALONG, LITTLE DOGIE!

NOW I'LL WEAVE THESE LONG STRANDS OF SEA WEED INTO A NET "CAGE" ABOUT THE SPECIMENS UNTIL THE AQUARIUM IS REPAIRED AND READY TO STOCK THEM AGAIN!

"SUDDENLY, I SAW A FAMILIAR STUDENT--A STUDENT NOW IN TERRIBLE DANGER!"

LORI--IN THE GRIP OF A GIANT OCTOPUS!

"EVEN AS I SHOT FORWARD, I WAS AMAZED TO SEE THAT LORI WAS NOT FRIGHTENED, BUT CALMLY REGARDING THE CREATURE..."

HER LIPS ARE MOVING! IF I DIDN'T KNOW BETTER, I'D ALMOST BELIEVE SHE WAS TALKING TO THE OCTOPUS!

"SUDDENLY, TO MY ASTONISHMENT, THE OCTOPUS SLID HIS TENTACLES FROM HER AND PLACIDLY SWAM AWAY!"

GREAT SCOTT! IT'S LEFT HER UNHARMED!

YOU'RE LUCKY YOU WEREN'T HURT! I'M STILL WONDERING WHY THE OCTOPUS LEFT YOU SO SUDDENLY!

WELL, *SUPERMAN...* HE PROBABLY SAW YOU STREAKING NEAR AND WAS FRIGHTENED AWAY!

"AS DAYS SPED BY, I BECAME INTRIGUED WITH THIS MYSTERIOUS GIRL AND DATED HER STEADILY, MEETING HER AT THE SCHOOL SODA SHOP..."

CLARK, BEING WITH YOU HAS BEEN WONDERFUL, BUT IT'S GETTING LATE! I MUST BE HOME BY EIGHT O'CLOCK!

WHY DOES SHE ALWAYS HAVE TO BE HOME EVERY NIGHT BY EIGHT, I WONDER?

" I THOUGHT OF LORI CONSTANTLY NOW -- IN OUR ASTRONOMY CLASS, I DAY-DREAMED OF IMPRESSING HER BY ACTUALLY FLYING HER TO THE PLANETS IN MY *SUPERMAN* IDENTITY..."

"IN OUR ART CLASS, I DAY-DREAMED OF SCULPING MT. EVEREST IN HER IMAGE TO PROVE MY LOVE FOR HER..."

4

" IN OUR MUSIC CLASS, I DAY-DREAMED OF FLYING A GREAT ORCHESTRA AROUND THE WORLD, SO ALL WOULD HEAR A LOVE SONG I'D WRITE FOR HER..."

LORI, LORI IS

MY LOVE

"THEN, ONE MORNING..."

CLARK, I'M AFRAID OUR DATE LATER WILL BE OUR LAST ONE! I MUST RETURN TO MY PARENTS TONIGHT!

LORI--YOU'RE GOING AWAY? OH, NO...

"I KNEW THEN THAT I COULD NOT STAND THE THOUGHT OF NEVER SEEING LORI AGAIN..."

I LOVE HER! SHE'S THE KIND OF GIRL I'VE ALWAYS DREAMED OF MARRYING-- A GIRL OF RARE BEAUTY AND COURAGE! I'M GOING TO ASK HER TO BE MY WIFE!

BUT MY CRIME-FIGHTING CAREER AS SUPERMAN WOULD ENDANGER MY FUTURE WIFE! IF CRIMINALS EVER LEARNED MY CLARK KENT IDENTITY, THEY COULD SEIZE MY WIFE AS A HOSTAGE TO FORCE ME TO STOP FIGHTING THEM!

"THEN I KNEW WHAT I HAD TO DO..."

THERE'S ONLY ONE WAY I CAN MARRY LORI AND BE SURE SHE'LL NEVER BE ENDANGERED! I MUST TELL HER MY SECRET IDENTITY--THEN GIVE UP MY SUPERMAN CAREER AND REMAIN ONLY IN MY CLARK KENT IDENTITY!

"BUT THAT NIGHT, AS PART OF MY FRATERNITY INITIATION, I WAS RESTRICTED TO MY QUARTERS WITH OTHER STUDENTS..."

I CAN'T SNEAK OUT WHILE THE OTHER STUDENTS ARE IN THIS DORMITORY-- BUT SOMEHOW I MUST GET OUT TO MEET LORI! HMM... THE FIREPLACE!

I'LL JUST SUCK IN AIR FROM THE FIREPLACE AND CREATE A DOWNDRAFT IN THE CHIMNEY FLUE SO THAT THE FIRE WILL START SMOKING!

COUGH! COUGH!

SOMETHING'S GONE WRONG WITH THE CHIMNEY FLUE!

COUGH! WE'LL HAVE TO GET OUT TILL THE SMOKE CLEARS!

NOW I'LL BE ABLE TO SLIP AWAY UNNOTICED!

"LATER, I MET LORI, TOOK HER TO A ROMANTIC SPOT--AND PROPOSED!"

LORI-- I LOVE YOU; WILL YOU MARRY ME? BEFORE YOU GIVE ME YOUR ANSWER, I MUST TELL YOU THE TRUTH ABOUT MYSELF...

YOU DON'T HAVE TO TELL ME, CLARK--I'VE KNOWN FROM THE VERY BEGINNING THAT *YOU ARE SUPERMAN!*

Y-YOU KNEW? BUT HOW...?

THAT'S NOT IMPORTANT! WHAT IS IMPORTANT IS THAT ALTHOUGH I LOVE YOU, I CAN NEVER MARRY YOU!

BUT--IF IT'S BECAUSE OF YOUR LEGS, THAT DOESN'T MATTER TO ME! AFTER ALL, I'M *SUPERMAN!* I'LL SEARCH THE UNIVERSE FOR A CURE THAT CAN MAKE YOU WALK AGAIN!

PLEASE, DON'T QUESTION ME ANYMORE! NOW I REALLY HAVE TO GO! I MUST BE HOME BY EIGHT!

WHY CAN'T SHE MARRY ME? AND WHY DOES SHE ALWAYS HAVE TO LEAVE ME AT EIGHT? DOES SHE GO TO MEET ANOTHER MAN?

"I'M AFRAID I LET MY JEALOUSY GET THE BETTER OF ME--AND LATER USED MY X-RAY VISION TO LOOK INTO HER TRAILER HOUSE OFF THE CAMPUS..."

LORI REPORTING! I LEAVE FOR HOME TONIGHT! MY MISSION IN AMERICA IS COMPLETE!

THIS IS WHY SHE RETURNS AT EIGHT-- TO MAKE SECRET RADIO REPORTS! HER "MISSION", SHE SAID! IS IT POSSIBLE LORI IS A FOREIGN AGENT--A SPY?

I LOVE LORI--BUT I LOVE MY COUNTRY, TOO! IF SHE IS AN ENEMY, SHE MAY BE AFTER SECRET DATA ON THE SECRET SCIENTIFIC RESEARCH BEING DONE AT THIS COLLEGE! I MUST SEARCH HER ROOM FOR EVIDENCE WHEN SHE GOES OUT TO DINNER!

"LATER WHEN I SEARCHED HER ROOM, I FOUND NO SECRET DOCUMENTS--BUT I DID COME ACROSS SOME PUZZLING THINGS..." A LARGE TANK FILLED WITH SALT WATER? WHY WOULD SHE NEED THAT? AND WHY IS THERE **NO BED** IN HER ROOM? SURELY SHE CAN'T SLEEP ON THE FLOOR!

"SUDDENLY, LIKE A LIGHTNING FLASH, THE TRUTH ABOUT LORI'S MYSTERIOUS ACTIONS DAWNED ON ME!" OF COURSE, IT'S FANTASTIC--BUT IT'S THE ONLY POSSIBLE EXPLANATION!

"LATER, I CONFRONTED LORI, BUT BEFORE I COULD SAY A WORD SHE LOOKED AT ME WITH THOSE EYES THAT SEEMED TO LOOK RIGHT INTO MY MIND..." SO YOU'VE GUESSED THE TRUTH ABOUT ME, HAVEN'T YOU, **SUPERMAN**? YES--BUT HOW...?

"BEFORE SHE COULD ANSWER, WE HEARD A THUNDEROUS ROAR, WHICH MY TELESCOPIC VISION REVEALED TO BE CAUSED BY A SUDDEN DISASTER!" SUPERMAN, WHAT IS IT? ROOAA-RR THE STATE DAM HAS BURST! THERE ARE HOMES IN THE VALLEY! I'VE GOT TO STOP THE FLOOD AS SWIFTLY AS POSSIBLE!

WAIT, **SUPERMAN!** I CAN BE OF USE! I WANT TO DO WHAT I CAN TO REPAY THE PEOPLE HERE WHO HAVE BEEN SO KIND TO ME! I UNDERSTAND! ALL RIGHT, LORI!

"I SUPPOSE IT WOULD HAVE SEEMED CRAZY TO ANYONE ELSE! AFTER ALL, WHAT COULD A PARALYZED GIRL DO TO HELP **ME** ON A MISSION REQUIRING SUPER-POWERS!"

⑦

"BUT I KNEW THE TRUTH ABOUT LORI--AND WHEN WE REACHED THE FLOOD SCENE, SHE SUDDENLY THREW OFF HER BLANKET--AND *DOVE INTO THE WATERS!*"

JUST AS I SUSPECTED-- AMAZING AS IT MAY SEEM -- LORI IS A **MERMAID** !

"THEN, THIS **MERMAID** AND I WORKED AS A RESCUE TEAM--I PLUCKED TRAPPED PEOPLE FROM THE WATERS!"

"WHILE LORI TOWED THEM ON A RAFT TOWARDS HIGHER GROUND!"

"WORKING AS PERFECT PARTNERS, LORI AND I CONSTRUCTED A DAM OF SANDBAGS TO STOP THE RAGING WATERS!"

"AND FINALLY SHE HELPED ME LASH A LINE OF HOUSES TOGETHER THAT I TOWED LIKE A FLOTILLA TO DRY LAND!"

NOW THAT THE RESCUE WORK IS FINISHED, I CAN REPAIR THE DAM AND RESTORE THINGS TO NORMAL HERE !

8

268

4400 FATHOMS DOWN, BY SHEER BAD LUCK, IT *STRIKES* THE BATHYSCAPH!

SOS! METEOR SMASHED OUR FUEL PIPES! CANNOT START ENGINE AND RISE! WE'RE *MAROONED* DOWN HERE! SOS! SOS!...

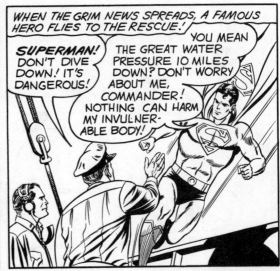

WHEN THE GRIM NEWS SPREADS, A FAMOUS HERO FLIES TO THE RESCUE!

SUPERMAN! DON'T DIVE DOWN! IT'S DANGEROUS!

YOU MEAN THE GREAT WATER PRESSURE 10 MILES DOWN? DON'T WORRY ABOUT ME, COMMANDER! NOTHING CAN HARM MY INVULNERABLE BODY!

YES, BUT I RECOGNIZED THAT GLOWING METEOR AS *RED KRYPTONITE!* IT'S MORE DANGEROUS TO YOU THAN GREEN *KRYPTONITE!*

GREAT SCOTT! IN THAT CASE, I'LL SEND AN X-RAY BEAM TO MY *FORTRESS OF SOLITUDE* HIDDEN IN THE ARCTIC, AND...

...ACTIVATE ONE OF MY *SUPERMAN* ROBOTS! I'LL SUMMON HIM HERE AT SUPER-SPEED TO PINCH-HIT FOR ME!

SHORTLY...

THE WATER-PRESSURE 10 MILES DOWN IS 20,000 POUNDS PER SQUARE INCH! THE BATHYSCAPH HAS STEEL WALLS A FOOT THICK TO WITHSTAND IT!

B-BUT MY ROBOT'S OUTER STEEL IS ONLY ONE INCH THICK! WILL HE SURVIVE?

AS *SUPERMAN* WATCHES DEEP BELOW WITH HIS SUPER-EYES...

THE RED *KRYPTONITE* RAYS DID NOT AFFECT MY ROBOT... BUT THE GREAT PRESSURE CRUSHED HIM LIKE AN EGG-SHELL! THAT MEANS I...I'LL HAVE TO GO DOWN *MYSELF!*

B-BUT YOU'RE TOO IMPORTANT TO THE WORLD TO RISK YOUR LIFE DOWN THERE! WHY NOT CALL IN *KRYPTO*, YOUR *SUPERDOG*, FROM SPACE?

NO! I...I'D BE A COWARD TO SEND MY FAITHFUL DOG TO HIS DOOM!

AND *SUPERMAN*, IN HIS PRIVATE THOUGHTS, REJECTS ANOTHER SUBSTITUTE!

NOR CAN *SUPERGIRL*, WHOSE EXISTENCE IS UNKNOWN ON EARTH, TAKE MY PLACE! *RED KRYPTONITE* IS AS DANGEROUS TO HER AS TO ME!

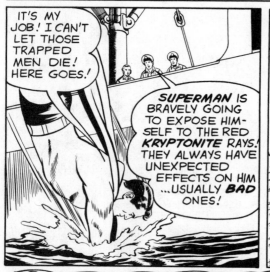

IT'S MY JOB! I CAN'T LET THOSE TRAPPED MEN DIE! HERE GOES!

SUPERMAN IS BRAVELY GOING TO EXPOSE HIM-SELF TO THE RED *KRYPTONITE* RAYS! THEY ALWAYS HAVE UNEXPECTED EFFECTS ON HIM ...USUALLY *BAD* ONES!

AS THE *MAN OF STEEL* DIVES, HIS SUPER-SWIFT THOUGHTS REVIEW THE ORIGIN OF THIS STRANGE DEADLY MINERAL...

WHEN A 'RADIOACTIVE CHAIN REACTION EXPLODED MY NATIVE PLANET *KRYPTON*, LONG AGO, CHUNKS OF *GREEN KRYPTONITE* WERE FORMED! THEY SCATTERED THROUGHOUT SPACE AS METEORS!

"THEIR PECULIAR RADIOACTIVE RAYS CAN BRING *KRYPTONITE-FEVER* AND DEATH TO ANY PERSON FROM *KRYPTON*...BUT ARE *HARMLESS* TO EARTH PEOPLE!"

I DON'T FEEL A THING, *SUPERMAN*! I'LL TAKE AWAY THIS GREEN *KRYPTONITE* METEOR THAT FELL NEAR YOU!

¿GASP!¿... I... I FEEL... TERRIBLE PAIN... OHHHHH!

"BUT ONE FLOCK OF THE ORIGINAL GREEN *KRYPTONITE* METEORS WENT THROUGH A STRANGE COSMIC CLOUD AND TURNED TO *RED KRYPTONITE*...EACH OF THESE RED METEORS ALWAYS CAUSED AN UNEXPECTED EFFECT ON ME!"

3

271

MORE SUPER-SWIFT MEMORIES UNREEL AS **SUPERMAN** CONTINUES HIS 10-MILE DIVE TO THE SEABOTTOM...

THEN, ONE TIME, WHILE I WAS JUDGING THE BEST MINERAL COLLECTION AT **METROPOLIS HIGH**, A YOUTH HELD UP A SMALL ROCK HE HAD FOUND, NOT REALIZING IT WAS **RED KRYPTONITE**!

TH- THE RAYS HIT ME! BUT...UH... **NOTHING** HAPPENED TO ME! I FEEL NO PAIN....I'M COMPLETELY NORMAL!

"SO IT SEEMED, AS I LATER REPAIRED A CRACKED PLATE-GLASS WINDOW FOR A SHOPKEEPER..."

THE HEAT OF MY X-RAY VISION WILL MELT THE GLASS AND I'LL SMOOTH OUT THE CRACK! I GUESS THE **RED KRYPTONITE** DIDN'T AFFECT MY SUPER-POWERS IN ANY WAY!

"BUT THEN I FOUND OUT THE REACTION WAS ONLY **DELAYED!**"

GREAT FIREBALLS! I...I CAN'T **TURN OFF** MY X-RAY VISION! NO MATTER WHICH WAY I TURN, I'M CAUSING DAMAGE! I CAN'T CONTROL MY X-RAY VISION!

"EVEN THOUGH I MADE SPECTACLES WITH **LEADEN** LENSES THAT CAN STOP X-RAYS, I WAS IN TROUBLE ALL DAY!"

TURN, **SUPERMAN!** YOU'RE HEADING STRAIGHT INTO A SKYSCRAPER!

GOOD HEAVENS! I NEARLY RAN INTO SOMETHING! I'LL BE "BLIND" UNTIL THE EFFECTS OF THE **RED KRYPTONITE** WEAR OFF!

AS **SUPERMAN** CONTINUES HIS GREAT DIVE, HE RECALLS ANOTHER FEARFUL ENCOUNTER WITH **RED KRYPTONITE**...

ONE OF MY WORST EXPERIENCES WITH **RED KRYPTONITE** WAS WHEN A DOSE OF ITS RAYS LATER GAVE ME **HALLUCINATIONS!**

I'LL PATROL FOR SHIPS IN TROUBLE...**GREAT SCOTT!** H-HOW CAN THAT ICEBERG BE... BE **ON FIRE?**

WELL, I'LL BLOW OUT THE FLAMES WITH MY SUPER-BREATH... **WHAT?** IT...IT DIDN'T WORK! WHAT KIND OF A...A FIRE IS **THAT?**

STOP, **SUPERMAN**... STOP!

BUT LATER, IN HIS FORTRESS OF SOLITUDE...

AH, I HAVE IT! I'LL SUMMON BOTH SUPERGIRL AND KRYPTO HERE! THIS ELECTRONIC WHISTLE'S "SILENT SOUND" WILL REACH KRYPTO IN SPACE! I'LL ALSO USE A WHISTLING CODE THAT SUPERGIRL WILL UNDERSTAND!

WHEEE-WHEEET-WHEE-WHEE-WHEEET-WHEEE

S-U-P-E-R-G-I-R-L, C-O-M-E T-O F-O-R-T-R-E-S-S... U-R-G-E-N-T!

WHEN SUPERMAN'S FAITHFUL PET SUPER-DOG AND HIS SUPER-COUSIN ARRIVE...

YIPE, YIPE?

DON'T WORRY, KRYPTO, ...IT'S STILL ME, YOUR MASTER!

GOODNESS! ARE YOU SURE YOU'RE SUPERMAN? YOU LOOK LIKE THE SUPER-WILD MAN FROM BORNEO!

AFTER SUPERMAN TELLS HIS STORY...

FORTUNATELY, THERE'S ONE WAY OF DESTROYING MY EXTRA HAIR AND LONG NAILS! BOTH OF YOU FOCUS YOUR X-RAY VISION ON MY BEARD AT FULL POWER!

BUT WHAT GOOD IS THAT, SUPERMAN? YOU SAID YOUR OWN X-RAY VISION FAILED BEFORE!

YES, BUT YOUR COMBINED X-RAY VISION IS DOUBLE THE POWER OF MINE! SEE? IT'S DISINTEGRATING MY BEARD!

WE'LL GIVE YOU A SHAVE, HAIRCUT AND MANICURE!

LATER...

THAT'S THAT! THANKS, SUPERGIRL AND KRYPTO! NOW I CAN RETURN TO METROPOLIS... AND SHOW UP AT THE DAILY PLANET AS CLARK KENT!

FINALLY, AT THE OFFICE...

MY QUICK RETURN LULLED LOIS LANE'S SUSPICIONS! HMM... I WONDER WHAT UNPREDICTABLE EFFECT RED KRYPTONITE WILL HAVE ON ME NEXT TIME!

9

THE END.

FAR OFF IN SPACE SPINS THE STRANGEST PLANET IN EXISTENCE... A *SQUARE* WORLD!

THE CAPITAL OF THIS INCREDIBLE WORLD IS A CITY OF CROOKED STRUCTURES, SEEMINGLY DESIGNED BY A MAD ARCHITECT!

HOURS ARE NUMBERED THE WRONG WAY ON ITS CRAZY CLOCKS, AND FLAGS ARE UPSIDE-DOWN WITH THE STARS AND STRIPES WRONGLY COLORED!

ON THIS MIXED-UP WORLD, *COAL* IS USED FOR MONEY... AND WORDS ARE ALL MISSPELLED!

QUEEREST OF ALL, THE PEOPLE ARE ALL IMPERFECT DOUBLES OF *SUPERMAN* AND *LOIS LANE*, LIVING IN A WORLD WHERE EVERYTHING IS THE *OPPOSITE* OF THINGS ON EARTH!

HELLO, BIZARRO!

HELLO, BIZARRO!

HI, BIZARRO-LOIS!

HI, BIZARRO-LOIS!

US GO SEE WESTERN MOVIE WHERE *BADMEN* WIN!

YOU...THE *BIZARRO* STREET CLEANER! BE SURE TO *SPREAD* DIRT ALL OVER! STREETS LOOK TOO CLEAN!

ARRIVING ON A FARAWAY WORLD, *BIZARRO'S* IMPERFECT REPLICA OF *SUPERMAN'S* SUPER-KEEN MIND HAD A MOMENTARY FLASH OF INSPIRATION, AND...

ME MADE *IMITATOR MACHINE* TO FORM MANY *MORE BIZARRO-LOISES!* ME WILL USE RAY ON MYSELF TO MAKE MORE MEN *BIZARROS,* TOO! THEN OUR BIZARRO PEOPLE WILL BUILD CITY!

FINALLY, THE ORIGINAL *BIZARRO* AND *BIZARRO-LOIS* APPOINTED THEMSELVES THE RULERS, AND MADE THEIR HATRED OF EARTH A LAW! LISTEN TO *BIZARRO CODE!* "US DO *OPPOSITE* OF ALL EARTHLY THINGS! US *HATE* BEAUTY! US *LOVE* UGLINESS! IS BIG *CRIME* TO MAKE ANYTHING *PERFECT* ON *BIZARRO WORLD!*"

A STRANGE STORY INDEED! BUT NOW, ON THIS TWISTED WORLD, *BIZARRO* NUMBER ONE IS ANNOYED ONE DAY, AS...

BAH! *BIZARRO* SERVANT... *BIZARRO* GARDENER... *BIZARRO* MAILMAN... *BIZARRO* PALACE GUARD... EVERYWHERE ME LOOK, ME SEE *MYSELF!* ME GETTING TIRED OF IT!

POSSESSING DIM DUPLICATED MEMORIES OF ALL THAT *SUPERMAN* KNOWS, THE *BIZARRO* LEADER HAS AN IDEA...

AH! *SUPERMAN* HAS *FORTRESS OF SOLITUDE* ON EARTH! ME GO BUILD PRIVATE PLACE LIKE THAT, TOO!

LATER, ALWAYS DOING THINGS THE *OPPOSITE*...

SUPERMAN'S FORTRESS IS IN *COLD ARCTIC*... SO ME MAKE MINE IN *HOT DESERT!*

WHEN IT IS DONE, THE DIM-WITTED BUILDER HAS MADE A TYPICAL *BIZARRO BLUNDER*...

ME... ER... FORGOT DOOR! WELL, ME JUST BUST HOLE IN WALL! THAT MAKES IT IMPERFECT, TOO! THEN ME MAKE EXHIBITS LIKE *SUPERMAN* HAS... ONLY *DIFFERENT!*

FOURTRISS UV BIZARRO

4

LATER, AFTER *BIZARRO* GATHERS "TROPHIES" FROM AREAS OF HIS WORLD...

HAH! *SUPERMAN* HAS *VALUABLE* THINGS! BUT ME PROUD OF MY COLLECTION OF *WORTHLESS JUNK!*

BIZARRO ALSO BRINGS ANOTHER SPECIAL MACHINE HE PREVIOUSLY INVENTED, AND MAKES STATUES FOR AN EXHIBIT...

ONCE, *SUPERMAN* VISITED *BIZARRO WORLD* AND BROKE OUR CODE! US PUT *KRYPTONITE* HANDCUFFS ON HIM, THEN EXECUTIONER WAS READY TO USE *BIZARRO RAY* TO TURN *SUPERMAN* INTO *BIZARRO* FORM!

BUT *SUPERMAN* WAS PARDONED AT LAST MOMENT AND SENT HOME TO EARTH! WELL, ME HAD NICE VACATION ALONE HERE AT FORTRESS! NOW ME GO HOME TO MY WIFE, *BIZARRO-LOIS!*

RETURNING, *BIZARRO* MEETS A THRILLING SURPRISE!

LOIS! YOU HAD *BABY* WHILE ME WAS GONE! OH, ME HAPPY FATHER NOW!

Y-YOU NOT BE SO...UH... HAPPY WHEN YOU SEE BABY'S FACE, *BIZARRO!* OUR CHILD IS A...A *FREAK!*

YOU RIGHT, *LOIS!* OH, H-HOW *AWFUL!* IT...IT LOOKS LIKE *HUMAN* BABY OF EARTH!

Y-YES, IS *UGLY!* IS A *DISGRACE* TO NAME OF *BIZARRO!*

WHILE YOU OUT BEFORE, ME FOUND BABY CRYING! HIS SUPER-GRIP HAD WRECKED ALL *ORDINARY* TOYS! SO ME MADE HIM DOLLY OUT OF SOLID *IRON!*

NOW YOU TELL ME!

TIME PASSES AND ONE DAY, AS BABY *BIZARRO* PLAYS IN THE YARD AND SEES HIS FATHER LEAVING...

ME WANNA GO WITH DADDY!

STOP, BABY!...OH! TOO LATE! HIM DISCOVERED HIM COULD *FLY* LIKE HIS FATHER! AND ME CAN'T CHASE HIM!

CLUMSY ON HIS FIRST FLIGHT, THE CHILD STRIKES TREES DOWN, AND...

OOPS! ME JUMPED BACK IN TIME! BUT DADDY *BIZARRO* NOW OUT OF SIGHT! MAYBE BABY COME BACK!

INSTEAD, AFTER GAINING MORE SKILL IN FLYING, CURIOSITY SENDS THE BABY ON...

WHY MOMMY AND DADDY NEVER TOOK ME TO VISIT *OTHER* PEOPLE? ME GO SAY HELLO TO LADY IN THIS HOUSE!

INSIDE, WHERE ANOTHER *BIZARRO-LOIS* HOUSEWIFE IS SWEEPING...

ME HELP HER! ME USE MY SUPER-BREATH AND BLOW OUT DUST! THEN MAYBE SHE BE MY FRIEND AND GIVE ME CANDY!

BUT INSTEAD...

IT'S THAT *PERFECT* BABY WHO LOOKS LIKE EARTH BABIES! GET OUT! NOBODY WANT *UGLY BRAT* LIKE YOU AROUND!

SH-SHE CHASING ME OUT! WHY SHE *HATE* ME? WELL, ME MAKE FRIENDS WITH OTHER PEOPLE!

7   283

BUT BABY **BIZARRO** MEETS THE SAME RECEPTION EVERYWHERE!

HUMAN MONSTER! HOW DARE YOU BOTHER DECENT PEOPLE? GO HOME AND STAY THERE!

WH- WHY THEY ALL CHASE ME AWAY? WHAT'S WRONG WITH ME?... SOB!...ME ASK MOMMY AND DADDY!

AT HOME THE **BIZARRO** PARENTS TRY TO HIDE THE TRUTH...

ER...NEVER MIND WHAT PEOPLE SAY ABOUT YOU, BABY **BIZARRO!** ME GLAD YOU CAME HOME! ME CUDDLE YOU!

NO! ME WANT TO SEE WHY THEY CALL ME "UGLY"! ME LOOK IN MIRROR!

WHEW! ME SMASHED MIRROR JUST IN TIME! ME WILL FORBID MIRRORS IN HOUSE AFTER THIS! BABY MUST NEVER SEE HIS H-HORRIBLE FACE! HIM WILL PLAY NOW AND FORGET WHAT PEOPLE SAID!

BUT SOON, AFTER A RAIN...

MOMMY! DADDY! WHY ME LOOK SO DIFFERENT FROM YOU?

IT DID NO GOOD TO KEEP MIRRORS AWAY! BABY **BIZARRO** SAW HIS REFLECTION IN **RAIN PUDDLE!**

PATHETICALLY, SOBS WRACK THE CHILD AT THE BEWILDERING REVELATION!

WAHAHHH! ME NOT LOOK LIKE YOU OR OTHER PEOPLE!

BUT WE STILL LOVE YOU, BABY **BIZARRO!** YOU BE OURS! EVEN IF YOU ARE A ... A **FREAK!**

MEANWHILE, AN ANGRY MOB APPROACHES!

EXISTENCE OF BABY **BIZARRO** IS AGAINST CODE! HIM GUILTY OF **CRIME** OF BEING **PERFECT!** HIM MUST BE **WIPED OUT!**

BUT CHILD IS INVULNERABLE! YOU CAN'T DESTROY HIM!

BUT HOURS LATER, *BIZARRO* RETURNS WITH HEART-BREAKING NEWS.!

ME SEARCHED A MILLION MILES B-BUT BABY *BIZARRO* LOST FOREVER!

OH, US NEVER SEE OUR SON AGAIN... SOB!: MAYBE POOR CHILD WILL LAND ON LONELY WORLD WHERE NO PEOPLE LIVE!

BUT UNKNOWN TO THE *BIZARRO* PARENTS, THE STEEL SHELL WAS A *SPACE ROCKET* THAT IS NOW ORBITING BACK TO *EARTH* UNDER AUTOMATIC CONTROLS.!

ATTENTION! SPACE PROBE RETURNING! WILL FALL IN AREA Z-13! RUSH THERE TO RESCUE SPACE PHOTO-GRAPHS FROM WRECKAGE!

STRANGELY, IT IS ALMOST LIKE WHEN THE *KRYPTON* ROCKET OF *JOR-EL* LANDED HIS INFANT SON ON EARTH, WHO BECAME *SUPER-BABY* AND GREW UP INTO *SUPERBOY* AND *SUPERMAN!*

ZZZZZ

CRASH!

UNHARMED BY THE CRASH, AND NOT EVEN WAKENING, THE SON OF *BIZARRO* SLEEPS ON, HIDDEN FROM THE SCIENTIFIC CREW THAT ARRIVES SOON...

WE'LL HAUL THE WRECKAGE TO OUR LAB, THEN EXAMINE THE FILM! GOOD THING NO PILOT WAS IN THIS SPACE PROBE! *NOBODY* COULD HAVE COME OUT OF THIS WRECK *ALIVE!*

ZZZZ-ZZ

LATER, JUST LIKE AFTER *SUPERBABY* CRASHED ON EARTH, THE *BIZARRO* BABY IS FOUND WHEN IT AWAKENS AND CRIES...

LOOK, DEAR... THAT BABY MUST HAVE BEEN ABANDONED HERE! WE'LL TAKE IT TO THE NEAREST ORPHANAGE, POOR THING!

WAH-H-HH!

BY A STRANGE TWIST OF FATE, THE ORPHANAGE CHOSEN IS...

MIDVALE ORPHANAGE

10

...MIDVALE ORPHANAGE, WHERE *SUPERGIRL* LIVES UNDER THE SECRET IDENTITY OF LINDA LEE! WHAT WILL HAPPEN AS THIS SUPER-BABY LIVES ON EARTH, WITH NO ONE AWARE IT CAME FROM THE *BIZARRO WORLD?* SEE THE NEXT THRILLING CHAPTER IN THIS ISSUE! **END - PART I.**

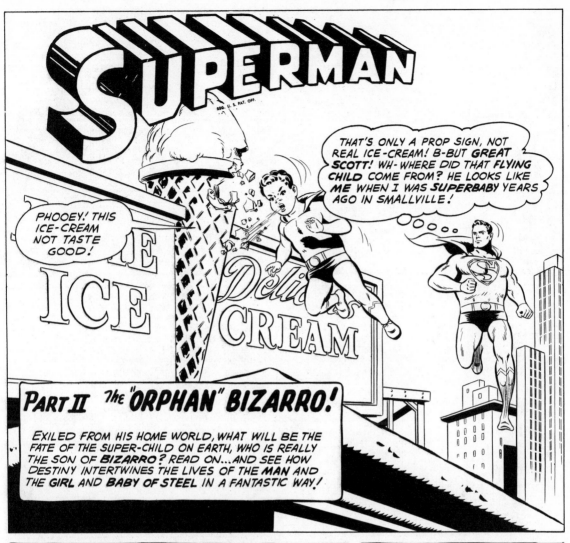

287

OH, THAT RATTLE MUST HAVE BEEN MADE OF A FLIMSY KIND OF PLASTIC!

I'LL PUT YOU DOWN, **BABY BUSTER!**

ME PLAY WITH SHINY BALL!

AGAIN, AS THE CHILD USES HIS SUPER-ABILITIES...

WHEEE! ME PLAY BOUNCE!

WH-WHAT? HE MADE THE BALL BOUNCE BETWEEN THE FLOOR AND CEILING MANY TIMES AT SUPER-SPEED! C-CAN THAT CHILD HAVE...UH... **SUPER POWERS?**

MOMENTS LATER, ALL DOUBTS VANISH AS A STRAY BUTTERFLY FLITS IN AN OPEN WINDOW, AND...

ME CATCH PRETTY BUG!

NOW HE'S **FL-FLYING!** HE'S A...A **SUPER BABY!** B-BUT THEN HE CAN'T BE AN EARTH BABY! WHERE DID HE COME FROM? I'LL ASK HIM...

LINDA'S QUESTIONS BRING TEARFUL ANSWERS THAT EXPLAIN NOTHING!

ME COME FROM WORLD WHERE MY MOMMY AND DADDY LIVE...OH, ME MISS THEM!... ⸺SOB!⸺

MY QUESTIONS ONLY REMINDED THE POOR CHILD OF HIS LOVING PARENTS! OUT OF THE MANY MILLIONS OF PLANETS IN SPACE, **WHICH** WORLD IS HIS?

LINDA HAS NO CLUE FROM THE CHILD'S **HUMAN** APPEARANCE THAT HE IS REALLY FROM THE **WORLD OF BIZARROS!**

OH, OH! NOW BUSTER'S CHASING THE BUTTERFLY OUTSIDE! TO FLY AFTER HIM I'LL HAVE TO CHANGE TO MY SUPER-COSTUME!

BUT AS **SUPERGIRL**, SHE FACES A NEW PROBLEM!

OMIGOSH! THE ATHLETIC DIRECTOR AND THOSE BOYS WILL SEE ME! MY EXISTENCE ON EARTH MUST REMAIN A SECRET! HMM... I'LL USE SUPER-BREATH TO OBSCURE THEIR VISION UNTIL I FLASH PAST!

OOPS! A GUST OF WIND KICKED UP DUST!

2

THEN, AS THE CHASE LEADS OUT OF TOWN, **SUPERGIRL** ZOOMS FROM HIDING, AND...

WE'LL COME AT HIM FROM TWO SIDES, **SUPERMAN!**

THAT WAY WE'LL TRAP HIM BETWEEN US! BUT WHY ARE YOU HERE, **SUPERGIRL?**

AFTER CATCHING THE FLYING CHILD, **SUPERGIRL** TELLS HER STORY...

HMM...MAYBE THE BABY CAME FROM ANOTHER WORLD OF HEAVY GRAVITY, LIKE **KRYPTON!** THUS HE GAINED SUPER-POWERS ON EARTH, LIKE YOU AND I DID, **SUPERGIRL!**

BUT HIS HOME WORLD IS UNKNOWN, **SUPERMAN!** SHALL WE TURN HIM OVER TO THE AUTHORITIES AS A...A...ER... **"SECOND SUPERBABY?"**

NO, **SUPERGIRL!** JUST THINK! BEING A BOY, HE COULD GROW UP AND BE MY **SUCCESSOR** SOME DAY! HE MUST REMAIN IN THE ORPHANAGE UNDER HIS...UH...SECRET IDENTITY OF BABY BUSTER!

YOU MEAN I MUST KEEP HIS SUPER-POWERS **COVERED UP?** G-GOSH, WHAT A SUPER-JOB!

IT'LL ONLY BE FOR A SHORT TIME, **SUPERGIRL!** I'LL TRY TO THINK OF A PLAN TO SOLVE THE SITUATION!

MIDVAL
ORPHAN

SOON, IN THE NURSERY, AFTER **SUPERGIRL** CHANGES BACK TO LINDA LEE JUST BEFORE THE NURSE RETURNS...

I'VE GOT TO KEEP THIS **"SUPERBABY"** FROM REVEALING HE HAS SUPER-POWERS!

GOOD IDEA, LINDA! TAKE CHARGE OF HIM ALL DAY!

MAY I TAKE BABY BUSTER OUT TO THE PLAYGROUND? I WANT TO...ER...MAKE HIM FEEL AT HOME HIS FIRST DAY HERE!

THOUGH THE PLAYGROUND IS EMPTY, TROUBLE ARISES WHEN...

IS TOO EASY SLIDING DOWN! ME GO **UP** THIS SLIDE!

OMIGOSH! THAT CLEANING WOMAN WILL SEE FROM HER WINDOW HOW BABY BUSTER IS DEFYING GRAVITY, UNLESS...

4

...I USE THE HEAT OF MY X-RAY VISION AND CREATE A CLOUD OF *STEAM* FROM THAT DRINKING FOUNTAIN!

DEAR ME! A SUDDEN *FOG* ROLLED UP!

NEXT, AS THE *BABY OF STEEL* DOES ACROBATIC STUNTS...

ME SWING AROUND REAL FAST!

I'LL STOP HIM...HEAVENS! HIS FOOT CAUGHT MY FALSE WIG AND IS KICKING IT UP IN THAT TREE! THAT REVEALS MY BLONDE HAIR I HAVE AS *SUPER-GIRL!*

AS THE RECESS BELL RINGS AND OTHER YOUNGSTERS RUSH OUT TO PLAY...

I...I JUST HAVE A SECOND TO GIVE THE TREE A SUPER-SHAKE! AH, MY WIG IS DROPPING DOWN!

WHEW! I PUT MY WIG BACK ON JUST IN TIME! BABY BUSTER'S SUPER-TRICKS ARE NOT ONLY THREATENING TO REVEAL *HIS* EXISTENCE...BUT *MINE* AS *SUPERGIRL!*

THINGS TAKE AN EVEN WORSE TURN AS A COUPLE VISITS THE ORPHANAGE LATER, AND...

LOOK, HENRY! JUST THE KIND OF BABY BOY WE ALWAYS WANTED! WE'LL APPLY FOR ADOPTION RIGHT NOW!

GOODNESS! IF THEY TAKE THE BABY HOME, THEY'LL FIND OUT HE HAS SUPER-POWERS! IF *SUPERMAN* PLANNED ANYTHING, IT'S TOO LATE NOW!

LINDA GETS A REAL SHOCK, AS...

PSST! *SUPERGIRL!* READ THIS!

SHE'S SLIPPING ME A NOTE! AND SH-SHE KNOWS *WHO* I AM... ⸘GASP!⸘ H-HOW DID SHE FIND OUT MY BIG SECRET?

⑤

ALSO, *KRYPTO* HAS HIS ORDERS TO BE A SUPER-WATCHDOG AND KEEP BABY BUSTER FROM *LEAVING* THE FORTRESS!

KRYPTO IS HOLDING BACK THE CHILD SO HE CAN'T FOLLOW US! YOU'VE TAKEN CARE OF EVERY-THING, *SUPERMAN!*

ALONE IN THE FORTRESS, THE SUPER-TOT SOON TIRES OF PLAYING WITH *KRYPTO* AND SEEKS OTHER AMUSEMENT AMONG *SUPERMAN'S* EXHIBITS!

LOOK, *KRYPTO!* ME PLAY WITH BIG DOLLIES!

STAFF OF DAILY PLANET

WHEN *SUPERMAN* AND *SUPERGIRL* RETURN...

ME DRESSED UP DOLLIES DIFFERENT WAY!

I'LL...ER...SAY YOU DID, BABY BUSTER! THESE WAX DUMMIES OF CLARK KENT AND LOIS LANE ARE WEARING EACH OTHER'S CLOTHING!

AT NIGHT, WHEN *SUPERMAN* GOES ON HIS CRIME PATROL, LEAVING *SUPERGIRL* IN CHARGE...

I'LL BE YOUR...ER...*MOMMY! SUPERMAN* WILL BE YOUR *DADDY!* I BAKED YOU A GIANT CAKE IN THIS SUPER-KITCHEN, BABY BUSTER!

YUM!

TIME PASSES...AND MEANWHILE, FAR AWAY ON THE *BIZARRO WORLD, BIZARRO* IS IN HIS OWN FORTRESS...

ME NEED SOMETHING TO FILL EMPTY CORNER! AH, ME SEND MY SUPER-VISION ACROSS SPACE TO *SUPERMAN'S* FORTRESS ON EARTH! THEN ME MAKE *OPPOSITE* OF SOME EXHIBIT THERE!

BIZARRO NO. 1

TO BIZARRO'S SUPER-SURPRISE...

WATCH, *KRYPTO!* ME LIFT BIG WEIGHT JUST LIKE *DADDY SUPERMAN!*

WHY...UH...HIM MY *SON!* HIM WAS NOT LOST IN SPACE AFTER ALL! HIM ARRIVED ON EARTH!

7

293

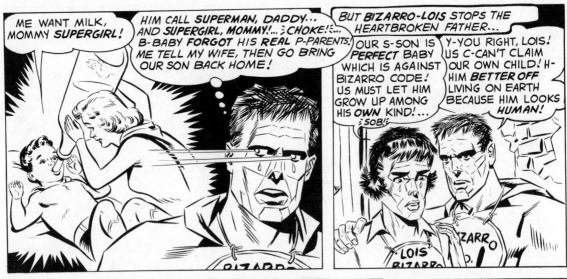

294

SUPERMAN

REG. U.S. PAT. OFF.

GO AWAY, *SUPERMAN!* YOU TOO, *SUPERGIRL!* ME NOW BE FOSTER MOTHER OF *BABY BIZARRO!* ME KEEP HIM AND RAISE HIM AS MY SON!

PART III
THE BIZARRO SUPERGIRL!

STRANGE INDEED WERE THE EVENTS THAT BROUGHT THE HUMAN-LIKE *BIZARRO-BABY* TO EARTH, ONLY TO SUDDENLY TURN INTO HIS TRUE FORM LIKE HIS PARENTS! BUT EVEN MORE AMAZING ARE THE FOLLOWING TWISTS OF FATE AS AN IMPERFECT DOUBLE OF *SUPERGIRL* IS CREATED, WHICH LATER LEADS TO *WAR* BETWEEN EARTH AND THE *BIZARRO WORLD!*

G-GREAT SCOTT! NOW THERE'S A *BIZARRO SUPERGIRL*, TOO! AND WE CAN'T GET THE *BIZARRO* CHILD AWAY FROM HER!

AS THE *BIZARRO BABY* WAKENS AND ROMPS WITH *KRYPTO* IN THE FORTRESS...

CHASE ME, *KRYPTO!*

I'LL FLY AHEAD OF THEM! THAT POOR CHILD MUSTN'T *SEE* HOW MY CHEMICAL EXPERIMENT TURNED HIM INTO AN UGLY FREAK, SO...

...I'LL HIDE THIS BIG MIRROR *SUPERMAN* HAS AMONG HIS TROPHIES!

MIRROR FROM WORLD OF GIANTS.

MEANWHILE, *BABY BIZARRO'S* CURIOSITY IS AROUSED BY THE ORIGINAL *DUPLICATOR RAY MACHINE,* INVENTED BY *LUTHOR* AND NOW KEPT AS A SOUVENIR BY *SUPERMAN...*

ME PUSH BUTTONS AND SEE WHAT HAPPENS!

RRRRRR

FLYING PAST, *SUPERGIRL* IS UNAWARE OF THE RAY STRIKING HER!

I HID THE BIG MIRROR! NOW I MUST FLY BACK TO THE MIDVALE ORPHANAGE! THE BATTERY THAT POWERS MY LINDA LEE ROBOT, WHICH TOOK MY PLACE THERE, IS RUNNING LOW AND MAY GO DEAD!

AFTER *SUPERGIRL* LEAVES, AN IMPERFECT DUPLICATE OF HER FORMS OUT OF THE MOLECULAR SMOKE!

ME GOT *SUPERGIRL'S* MEMORY SO ME KNOW THERE IS A *BIZARRO SUPERMAN!* THEN ME ARE THE... THE *BIZARRO SUPERGIRL!*

ME LIKE YOU! YOU LOOK LIKE PEOPLE ON WORLD ME CAME FROM!

LATER, *SUPERMAN* ARRIVES TO GET A DOUBLE SHOCK!

GREAT SCOTT! H-HOW DID THE BABY TURN INTO A...A *BIZARRO?* AND WHERE DID THIS *BIZARRO-SUPERGIRL* COME FROM? HMM...I'LL BET THE BABY TAMPERED WITH *LUTHOR'S* DUPLICATOR RAY AND AIMED IT AT THE REAL *SUPERGIRL* TO FORM THIS WEIRD IMITATION OF HER!

THEN, AS THE CHILD SEES HIS REFLECTION IN A SHINY GOLD TROPHY CUP...

FACE CHANGED... GOOD! NOW ME LOOK LIKE MY *REAL MOMMY* AND DADDY!

WHY...UH... THAT MEANS HIS PARENTS ARE *BIZARRO* AND *BIZARRO-LOIS!* I NEVER SUSPECTED IT WHILE THE BABY LOOKED *HUMAN!*

KNOWING THE STRANGE TRUTH, *SUPERMAN* OPENS THE DOOR OF HIS FORTRESS, AND...

BABY BIZARRO BELONGS AMONG HIS OWN KIND! AND YOU TOO, *BIZARRO SUPERGIRL!* FLY HIM TO THE *BIZARRO WORLD* AND...ER...*STAY* THERE!

HMM...ON *BIZARRO WORLD* HIS *REAL PARENTS* WOULD TAKE HIM BACK! ≶CHOKE≶... HE VERY CUTE... ME LOVE HIM!

298

As SUPERMAN and SUPERGIRL use their TELESCOPIC VISION to follow the flight of the BIZARRO army...

THAT FLYING BIZARRO SQUADRON HAS ENOUGH SUPER-POWER TO SPLIT THE EARTH IN HALF—JUST AS IT'S CLEAVING THAT FARAWAY ASTEROID IN ITS PATH! BUT WE'RE OUTNUMBERED A...A HUNDRED TO ONE, SUPERGIRL! WE CAN'T STOP THEM! YOU MUST GET BIZARRO-SUPERGIRL TO GIVE UP THE BABY!

BUT WHEN SUPERGIRL TRIES...

IT'S NO USE, SUPERMAN! BIZARRO-SUPERGIRL STILL WANTS THE BABY!

GIVING THE CHILD BACK COULD STOP THE BIZARRO ARMY FROM MAKING WAR ON EARTH! HMM... THERE MAY BE ANOTHER WAY! FOLLOW ME BACK TO MY FORTRESS, SUPERGIRL!

AT HIS FORTRESS, SUPERMAN DONS HIS LEADEN SUIT EQUIPPED WITH A SPECIAL TV UNIT!

AS YOU KNOW, SUPERGIRL, NO HOLES ARE NEEDED TO LET ELECTRONIC IMPULSES ENTER WITHIN THIS SEALED SUIT! I CAN SEE THE OUTSIDE WORLD! BUT I'LL HAVE TO FLY SLOWLY OR THE LEAD WILL MELT FROM AIR-FRICTION!

TV ANTENNAE

TV SCREEN

TV CAMERA

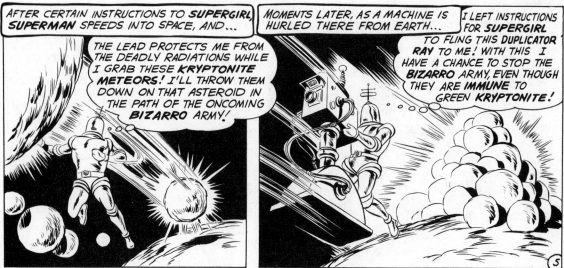

AFTER CERTAIN INSTRUCTIONS TO SUPERGIRL, SUPERMAN SPEEDS INTO SPACE, AND...

THE LEAD PROTECTS ME FROM THE DEADLY RADIATIONS WHILE I GRAB THESE KRYPTONITE METEORS! I'LL THROW THEM DOWN ON THAT ASTEROID IN THE PATH OF THE ONCOMING BIZARRO ARMY!

MOMENTS LATER, AS A MACHINE IS HURLED THERE FROM EARTH...

I LEFT INSTRUCTIONS FOR SUPERGIRL TO FLING THIS DUPLICATOR RAY TO ME! WITH THIS I HAVE A CHANCE TO STOP THE BIZARRO ARMY, EVEN THOUGH THEY ARE IMMUNE TO GREEN KRYPTONITE!

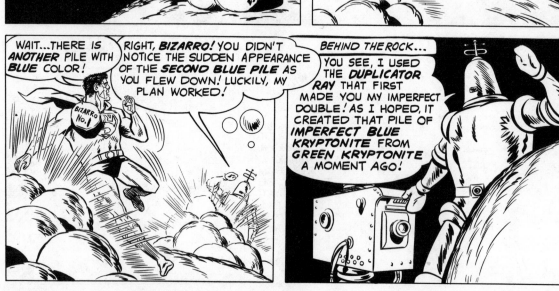

INSIDE THE HUT...

OHHH... ≷GASP!≷... ME TURNED WEAK...

CLEVER, *SUPERMAN!* SHE CAN'T HOLD ON TO *BABY BIZARRO* NOW! WE'LL FLY HIM BACK TO HIS PARENTS AS SOON AS HE RECOVERS FROM THE HARMFUL EFFECTS OF THE *BLUE KRYPTONITE* RAYS!

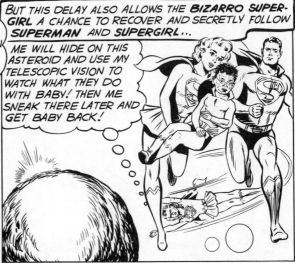

BUT THIS DELAY ALSO ALLOWS THE *BIZARRO SUPERGIRL* A CHANCE TO RECOVER AND SECRETLY FOLLOW *SUPERMAN* AND *SUPERGIRL*...

ME WILL HIDE ON THIS ASTEROID AND USE MY TELESCOPIC VISION TO WATCH WHAT THEY DO WITH BABY! THEN ME SNEAK THERE LATER AND GET BABY BACK!

PRESENTLY, AS *BABY BIZARRO* IS DELIVERED TO HIS OVERJOYED PARENTS...

MY BABY! AND HIM LOOK LIKE US NOW! OH, ME SO HAPPY HIM BACK!

YOU GOOD MAN, *SUPERMAN!* US CALL OFF WAR WITH EARTH! YOU EXPLAINED HOW IT WAS ONLY *BIZARRO SUPERGIRL* WHO CAUSED THE TROUBLE!

BEFORE LEAVING, AS *SUPERMAN* SHOWS *SUPERGIRL* MORE OF THE ODD *BIZARRO* WORLD...

I STILL FEEL GUILTY THAT MY CHEMICAL EXPERIMENT TURNED THAT HUMAN-LIKE BABY INTO AN UGLY *BIZARRO!*

IT'S ODD THAT *YOU* WEREN'T CHANGED TOO, *SUPERGIRL!* HMM... WHY IS THAT *BIZARRO* COUPLE LIVING SECRETLY HERE IN A WILDERNESS?

WHY, THEY HAVE A *HUMAN* CHILD TOO!

YES, OUR CHILD WAS BORN SOON AFTER LEADER *BIZARRO* AND HIS WIFE HAD THEIR BABY! US MOVED AWAY SO OUR FRIENDS NEVER SAW OUR DISGRACE OF HAVING *PERFECT* CHILD!

SUDDENLY...

L-LOOK! OUR BABY *CHANGING* TO *BIZARRO* FORM BY ITSELF! WONDERFUL! B-BUT HOW COULD THIS MAGIC HAPPEN!

HMMM! IT'S NOT MAGIC, BUT JUST A *LAW OF NATURE* WITH CERTAIN SPECIES OF LIFE! FOR INSTANCE...

⑦

...TADPOLES *METAMORPHOSE*, OR CHANGE, INTO FROGS! CATERPILLARS BECOME BUTTERFLIES! IN THE SAME WAY, YOUR HUMAN-LIKE BABIES AUTOMATICALLY *CHANGE* INTO *BIZARRO* BABIES AT A CERTAIN AGE!

SO YOU'RE INNOCENT, *SUPERGIRL!* BY PURE COINCIDENCE, *BABY BIZARRO'S NATURAL* CHANGE CAME AT THE SAME TIME YOU DID YOUR CHEMICAL EXPERIMENT!

WHAT A RELIEF TO KNOW I WASN'T RESPONSIBLE!

BUT ANOTHER WORRY HAUNTS *SUPERGIRL* ON THE WAY TO EARTH...

IF PEOPLE ON EARTH GLIMPSE THE *BIZARRO SUPERGIRL*, THEY'LL KNOW SHE'S THE IMPERFECT DOUBLE OF A *HUMAN SUPERGIRL!* IT'LL G-GIVE AWAY MY *SECRET EXISTENCE!*

BUT *SUPERGIRL* FINDS THE PROBLEM IS SOLVED AS THEY PASS THE ASTEROID ON WHICH HER PATHETIC DUPLICATE HAD PLANNED AN AMBUSH!

LOOK, *SUPERMAN!* SOMEHOW, *BIZARRO SUPERGIRL* BLUNDERED INTO HER OWN *DEATH-TRAP!* THE RADIATIONS OF THE *BIZARRO KRYPTONITE* TURNED HER BLUE AND SNUFFED OUT HER LIFE!

POOR CREATURE! IT'S BETTER THIS WAY!

LATER, AS *SUPERGIRL* RESUMES HER DAILY GUISE AS LINDA LEE...

THANK HEAVENS THERE ARE ONLY *ORDINARY* BABIES HERE IN THE NURSERY OF MIDVALE ORPHANAGE NOW!

AND CLARK (*SUPERMAN*) KENT IS BACK AT THE PLANET...

HOW STRANGE THAT THE "SECOND *SUPERBABY*" WHO APPEARED ON EARTH FOR A WHILE TURNED OUT TO BE A *BIZARRO SUPERBABY!*

The END.

⑧

SUPERMAN

I'M BACK IN THE PAST, YEARS BEFORE **SUPERMAN** CAME TO EARTH! I DON'T DARE SWITCH INTO MY ACTION COSTUME, BECAUSE HISTORY HAS NO RECORD OF **SUPERMAN'S** FIGHTING WITH AL CAPONE'S GANG!

BULLETS... KNIVES... NOTHING RUBS HIM OUT! **NOTHING** CAN HARM THAT FEDERAL AGENT!

IN THE ANNALS OF CRIME HISTORY, THERE IS AN UNSOLVED MYSTERY GOING BACK TO THE RACKET-RIDDEN 1920's BEFORE **FEDERAL AGENTS** FINALLY SMASHED THE GREATEST CRIMINAL RING OF THAT TIME! WHO WAS THE MAN THAT DEFIED THE MOST POWERFUL MOB? WHAT WAS THE SECRET OF HIS "CHARMED LIFE" AGAINST THE RUTHLESS KILLERS? YOU CAN GUESS THE ANSWER...BUT NOT ALL THE AMAZING RESULTS... WHEN,

SUPERMAN MEETS Al CAPONE!

JUNE 5 192

AT THE **DAILY PLANET** ONE DAY, EDITOR PERRY WHITE SHOWS REPORTER CLARK KENT A SCIENTIFIC REPORT...

LOOK, CLARK! AN ARCHEOLOGIST FOUND THE FOSSIL FOOTPRINT OF A NEW SPECIES OF DINOSAUR THAT HE CLAIMS MAY BE BIGGER THAN **TITANO**, THE SUPER-APE! IT WOULD MAKE A GOOD HEADLINE BUT...

...IS IT TRUE? AFTER **TITANO** BECAME A MENACE, **SUPERMAN** FLUNG HIM ACROSS THE TIME-BARRIER INTO PREHISTORIC TIMES! HE'S THE ONLY ONE WHO COULD CHECK ON THIS FOR US!

I...ER...THINK THAT CAN BE ARRANGED WITH **SUPERMAN**, PERRY!

303

IT CAN EASILY BE ARRANGED BY CLARK KENT, WHO IS **SUPERMAN** HIMSELF!

I'LL CHANGE OUT OF SIGHT AND DO PERRY A FAVOR! I CAN VISIT THE PAST BY FLYING FASTER THAN LIGHT!

PRESENTLY, AS **SUPERMAN** FLASHES ACROSS THE TIME-BARRIER INTO ANCIENT TIMES...

I'LL HAVE TO AVOID MEETING **TITANO** WHEN I ARRIVE! AT SIGHT OF ME HE ALWAYS GETS MAD AND TURNS ON HIS **KRYPTONITE VISION**!

REACHING HIS PRIMEVAL GOAL, **SUPERMAN** SEARCHES UNTIL...

AH, **TITANO** LEFT HIS IMPRINT IN THIS SOFT SOIL! I'LL MEMORIZE THE MEASUREMENTS FOR PERRY! THEN HE'LL KNOW WHICH ONE IS BIGGER-- **TITANO** OR THE **GIGANTOSAUR**!

BUT A MOMENT LATER...

GRR-RR

I'LL PACE OFF THE WIDTH OF THIS FOOTPRINT AND... **GREAT SCOTT!** THAT HUGE SHADOW... **TITANO** HIMSELF IS COMING BACK THIS WAY! HE ALREADY SEES ME!

ALARMED, **SUPERMAN** TRIES TO ESCAPE INTO THE FUTURE, BUT...

TITANO BRUSHED ME WITH HIS **KRYPTONITE VISION** BEFORE I COULD GET UP ENOUGH SPEED TO CRASH THROUGH THE TIME-BARRIER...⚡GASP!⚡ ALREADY I FEEL WEAK...

AS A RESULT OF BEING EXPOSED TO **TITANO'S KRYPTONITE** RADIATIONS, **SUPERMAN'S** FLIGHT INTO THE YEAR 1960 IS DETOURED...

MY SPEED ACROSS THE TIME-BARRIER IS SLOWING DOWN... ⚡GASP!⚡ I'M OFF COURSE! THAT'S NOT METROPOLIS...IT'S THE CITY OF CHICAGO DURING THE GREAT FIRE OF 1871!

2

I'LL DO IT, SIR... WAIT AND SEE!

THAT SHOESHINE BOY'S VOICE SOUNDS FAMILIAR... HOLY MACKEREL! IT'S PERRY WHITE AS A YOUNG MAN BEFORE HE BEGAN HIS NEWSPAPER CAREER! I'LL TAKE OFF MY GLASSES AND...

PERRY WHITE'S DELUXE SHOE SHINES

...SMEAR SOME SHOE-POLISH ACROSS MY CHEEK TO ALTER MY APPEARANCE! THEN PERRY OF 1960 WON'T RECALL HAVING SEEN AN ADULT CLARK KENT WHEN HE WAS YOUNG! OTHERWISE HE'D FIGURE OUT I'M SUPERMAN WHO CAN TRAVEL THROUGH TIME!

BUT WHILE CLARK'S "SCAR" FOOLS PERRY, IT ALSO FOOLS A SMALL-TIME CROOK...

HI, "TOUCH"! YOU DON'T FOOL ME! WHO ELSE COULD YOU BE WITH THAT SCAR BUT "TOUCH" VINCENT? YOU MUSTA JUST GOT OUT OF PRISON, EH? YOU REMEMBER ME--"SILKY" HALE!

HUH?

LISTEN, "TOUCH"! MR. BIG SAID TO WATCH FOR YOU AROUND TOWN! HE'LL LET YOU JOIN OUR MOB IF YOU'RE GOOD ENOUGH!

HMM...WHY NOT, FOR PERRY'S SAKE? HE'LL GET HIS CUB REPORTER JOB IF I HELP HIM GET A CRIME SCOOP! I'LL PLAY ALONG WITH THESE CROOKS!

LATER, ON A ROOFTOP...

ISN'T THIS PENTHOUSE SOMETHING, "TOUCH"?

I REMEMBER READING HOW THE GANGLAND CHIEFS OF THIS TIME LIVED IN LUXURY WITH FABULOUS PROFITS FROM THEIR RACKETS!

PRESENTLY, CLARK MEETS MR. BIG!

IT...IT'S AL CAPONE! GREATEST PUBLIC ENEMY IN CRIME HISTORY!

BOSS, HERE'S "TOUCH" VINCENT! HE CAN OPEN A SAFE EASIER THAN YOU CAN OPEN A SARDINE CAN! HE'S BETTER THAN JIMMY VALENTINE!

YEAH??

4

SHOW YOUR STUFF FIRST, VINCENT! SEE THAT SAFE? WE TOOK IT FROM A GUY WHO OWED US PROTECTION MONEY! THE DOUGH'S INSIDE, BUT HE RIGGED A BOMB INSIDE TO EXPLODE IT IF IT'S OPENED BY FORCE! *YOU* OPEN IT!

SECRETLY USING HIS SUPER-HEARING, CLARK SOLVES THE TRICKY TASK...

THIS IS A CINCH! ALL I HAVE TO DO TO OPEN THE SAFE IS LISTEN TO THE FAINT CLICK OF THE TUMBLERS AS I TWIRL THE DIAL! EACH CLICK STANDS FOR A DIFFERENT NUMBER OF THE COMBINATION!

CLICK!

AH! IT'S OPEN! THEY'LL THINK THE SENSITIVE FINGERS OF "TOUCH" VINCENT OPENED THE COMBINATION LOCK!

NOT BAD, VINCENT! BUT YOU GOTTA PASS ANOTHER TEST! I JUST GOT WORD THAT A RIVAL GANG GRABBED ONE OF MY BEER TRUCKS! YOU HIJACK IT BACK FROM THEM, SEE?

THEY'RE DRIVING MY TRUCK ALONG HIGHWAY 17-A TO THEIR OWN HIDEOUT! BRING THAT TRUCK BACK, SEE?

I'LL SAVE TIME BY OPERATING AS *SUPERMAN!*

SHORTLY...

LEAPING LENA! LOOK... IS THAT A...A *FLYING MAN?* OH, NO...IT CAN'T BE...IT MUST BE AN ILLUSION!

WHAT'S THE MATTER WITH HIM? WHY SHOULD THAT PILOT BE SO AMAZED AT SEEING ME? EVERYBODY KNOWS ABOUT *SUPERMAN!*

WAIT...I FORGOT! THIS IS IN THE TIME *BEFORE* I ARRIVED ON EARTH AS *SUPERBABY* OR GREW UP IN SMALLVILLE AS *SUPERBOY!* I'M COMPLETELY *UNKNOWN* TO THE WORLD OF THIS DECADE!

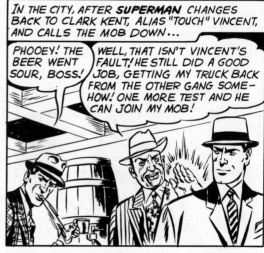

308

DESPERATE, THE RUTHLESS GANG LEADER TRIES ONCE MORE...

STAND BACK, MEN! I'LL SHOOT APART THAT HIGH-VOLTAGE POWER-LINE THAT RUNS ACROSS THE ROOF! ONE END WILL FALL IN THE SKYLIGHT AND GET HIM!

BUT LIVE WIRES ARE HARMLESS TO THE INDESTRUCTIBLE *MAN OF STEEL*...

I CAN'T BELIEVE IT! MORE JUICE WENT THROUGH HIM THAN HE'D GET IN 10 ELECTRIC CHAIRS...AND HE JUST GRINS!

I'LL LET HISTORY TAKE CARE OF AL CAPONE! *TREASURY AGENTS* WILL LATER ARREST HIM FOR INCOME TAX EVASION!

AS THE AWED MOBSTERS LET CLARK GO...

IS HE WEARING A NEW TYPE BULLETPROOF SUIT INVENTED BY THE LAW? WHATEVER IT IS...THAT *FED* IS...UH...*UNTOUCHABLE!*

HMM...SEEMS I'LL GO DOWN IN CRIME HISTORY AS AN UNSOLVED MYSTERY!

AFTER CHANGING BACK INTO HIS *SUPERMAN* COSTUME...

I LEFT THE SCOOP HERE AT YOUNG PERRY WHITE'S SHOE-SHINE STAND! HE CAN WIN HIS CUB REPORTER JOB AT THE CHICAGO JOURNAL WITH IT! NOW BACK ACROSS THE TIME-BARRIER TO 1960!

PERRY WHITE'S DELUXE SHOE SHINE

CLOSED

AT THE *PLANET* FINALLY, WHERE CLARK KENT HAS RESUMED HIS USUAL APPEARANCE...

I OWE MANY OF MY SCOOPS, LIKE THIS ONE ABOUT *TITANO*, TO *SUPERMAN*, CLARK! BUT WHEN I WAS A SHOESHINE BOY LONG AGO, IN CHICAGO, I'VE OFTEN WONDERED WHO IT WAS THAT...

DAILY PLANET
SUPERMAN PROVES TITANO LARGER THAN GIGANTOSAUR

...GAVE ME MY *FIRST* SCOOP, LONG BEFORE I CAME TO WORK FOR THE *DAILY PLANET!*

I GUESS *SUPERMAN* CAN'T...ER...TAKE CREDIT FOR THAT ONE, PERRY! I WONDER WHO...ER...WAS THAT FIRST *"UNTOUCHABLE"!*

CHICAGO JOURNAL
UNTOUCHABLE STRANGER FOILS CAPONE MOB!

The End.

310

SUPERMAN

REG. U.S. PAT. OFF.

LOOK, PAPA! EARTH TV SHOWS FRANKENSTEIN SCARING DOZEN PEOPLE!

BAH! THAT NOTHING, SON! ME SCARED WHOLE CITY OF *METROPOLIS* ONCE! ME, *BIZARRO NUMBER ONE*, AM *MOST FAMOUS MONSTER IN HISTORY!*

ARGHHHHH!

BIZARRO No. 1

WHO IS THE MOST FAMOUS MONSTER IN HISTORY... *THE WOLFMAN?*... *THE MUMMY?*... *THE BLACK OGRE?*... *THE ABOMINABLE SNOWMAN?*... ALL THESE UGLY CREATURES MUST BOW DOWN TO THEIR UNBEATABLE SUPERIOR, *BIZARRO,* WHO POSSESSES SUPER-POWERS JUST LIKE *SUPERMAN!* IN FACT, HE IS AN ARTIFICIAL *IMITATION* OF THE *MAN OF STEEL* THAT CAME OUT IMPERFECT! AND ONE DAY, WHEN THIS PATHETIC, GROTESQUE CREATURE VISITS EARTH, HE SEEKS TO WIN THE CROWN OF UGLINESS. THRILLS AWAIT YOU WHEN...

BIZARRO meets FRANKENSTEIN!

EARTH SPACEMEN EXPLORING THE STRANGE WONDERS OF THE OUTER UNIVERSE WOULD BE MOST STARTLED AT ONE PHENOMENON... A *SQUARE WORLD!*

ON THIS CUBE-SHAPED PLANET EXISTS A MAD IMITATION OF EARTHLY CIVILIZATION WHERE CITY SKYSCRAPERS LEAN CROOKEDLY AT ALL ANGLES! ON THIS WORLD, PERFECTION IS HATED AND EVERYTHING IS MIXED UP...

311

FOLLOWING A CRAZY CALENDAR, ALL EARTHLY HOLIDAYS ARE MISPLACED!

AMERICA CELEBRATING THANKSGIVING DAY! BUT US SHOOT OFF FIREWORKS!

DECEMBER 24 IS HALLOWEEN EVE HERE, NOT OCTOBER 31ST!

IS JULY 4TH! TIME TO GIVE OUT CHRISTMAS PRESENTS!

IT IS THE WORLD OF BIZARROS, WHERE ALL EARTHLY CUSTOMS ARE BACKWARDS... INCLUDING THE USE OF ALARM CLOCKS!

HO HUM! ALARM CLOCK WENT OFF! IS TIME FOR BED!

DUMB EARTH PEOPLE USE IT TO WAKE UP! HA, HA!

BRRINNNGG!

ORIGINALLY CREATED BY A DEFECTIVE DUPLICATOR RAY, THESE ARTIFICIAL CREATURES ARE IMPERFECT IMITATIONS OF SUPERMAN AND LOIS LANE! LEAVING EARTH, BIZARRO #1 AND LOIS-BIZARRO #1 SETTLED ON THEIR SQUARE WORLD AND DUPLICATED MANY MORE BIZARRO CITIZENS! ALL ANIMAL, VEGETABLE AND MINERAL OBJECTS OF EARTH CAME OUT IMPERFECT WHEN IMITATED... EXCEPT FOR THE SUPERMAN-TYPE UNIFORM WHICH WAS MADE ORIGINALLY FROM SYNTHETIC FIBER OF KRYPTON!

LET US LOOK IN ON THE NUMBER ONE BIZARRO FAMILY AS THEY TUNE IN TV FOR THE LATE LATE SHOW FROM EARTH...

US WATCH EARLY EARLY SHOW!

BIZARRO NO 1

LOIS BIZARRO NO 1

CHARLIE CHAPLIN IN A MOVIE CLASSIC

BUT A COMEDY IS LIKE A SHOCK THEATER PROGRAM TO THEM!

OH, ME SCARED, MOMMY!

THE CHILDREN WILL HAVE BAD DREAMS IF THEY WATCH THAT, BIZARRO! TUNE IN A LAUGH PROGRAM!

CLEVERLY, **SUPERMAN** HAS MADE EVERYONE'S HAIR STAND ON END BY USING ONE OF THE MACHINE PROPS ON THE **FRANKENSTEIN** LABORATORY SET...

I GAVE THIS STATIC MACHINE A SUPER-SPIN! IT CREATED A HARMLESS STATIC VOLTAGE IN THE FLOOR UNDER THE ACTORS! WHEN HUMAN HAIR GAINS AN ELECTRICAL CHARGE, IT ALWAYS BECOMES BRISTLY AND STANDS ON END!

I ALSO TURNED ON THIS **SOUND EFFECTS** RECORD! **BIZARRO** WOULD HAVE REALIZED IT WAS ONLY AN **ADVERTISEMENT** IF HE HAD HEARD THE **ENTIRE** MESSAGE...

HELP! HELP! RUN FOR YOUR LIVES! BEWARE THE MONSTER! YES, EVERYBODY WILL SCREAM LIKE THIS WHEN THEY SEE THE NEW FRANKENSTEIN MOVIE!

SOON, AS THE **FRANKENSTEIN** ACTOR RETURNS FROM THE DOCTOR'S OFFICE, **SUPERMAN** REVEALS HIMSELF AND EXPLAINS...

FOLKS! TO AVOID PANIC, I LET YOU THINK I WAS DOING A "PUBLICITY STUNT"! BUT IT WAS THE **REAL BIZARRO** WHO THREATENED YOU! HE WAS JEALOUS OF "FRANKENSTEIN" HERE!

WHAT!?

TH-THEN WE KISSED THE REAL **BIZARRO**, THINKING IT WAS **SUPERMAN!** OHHHHH!

DATE IS DECEMBER 24, HALLOWEEN EVE! ME BROUGHT SOUVENIR FROM EARTH TO GIVE KIDS A GOOD SCARE!

YIPES! LOOK... IS IT WITCH?... GOBLIN?... OGRE?

AS **SUPERMAN** OBSERVES WITH HIS TELESCOPIC VISION AND READS THEIR LIPS...

NO... IS **WORSE!**... IT'S **SUPERMAN!** HELP!

YOU... ER... LIKE THAT UP THERE, **I'M** THE WORLD'S WORST MONSTER! EVEN MY MARIONETTE SCARES **BIZARRO** KIDS!

HOW DO

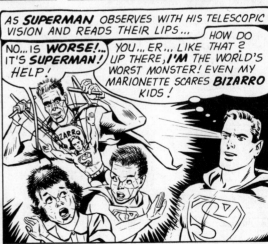

WATCH FOR MORE STORIES ABOUT THE TWISTED CREATURES ON THE MAD WORLD OF **BIZARROS!** (END)

319

"SHORTLY, IN THE STORE'S BASEMENT, I REMOVED MY OUTER GARMENTS, REVEALING MY *SUPERBOY* COSTUME UNDERNEATH, THEN I FLEW INTO A SECRET TUNNEL..."

CAREFUL, SON!

÷CHOKE÷...THIS IS A PROUD MOMENT! GOOD LUCK, BOY!

"MOMENTS LATER, I EMERGED THROUGH THE TUNNEL'S EXIT, IN A DISTANT WOODS."

IT'S A GOOD THING I HAD BUILT *TWO* SECRET TUNNELS-- ONE LEADING FROM THE STORE, AND ONE FROM MY HOME--

--SO PEOPLE WON'T SEE ME ENTERING AND LEAVING AND GUESS THAT CLARK KENT AND *SUPERBOY* ARE ONE AND THE SAME PERSON!

"MEANWHILE, AT THE SCENE OF THE EMERGENCY I HAD SIGHTED WITH MY SUPER-VISION..."

ROBBERS IN DIVING-SUITS! I DON'T GET IT!

THERE MUST BE A METHOD IN THEIR MADNESS!

"THE METHOD WAS SOON DIABOLICALLY CLEAR..."

THEY MUST BE THE ROBBERS REPORTED ON THE RADIO!

AND THEY'RE JUMPING INTO THE MURKY WATER, FOR A GETAWAY! HOW DEVILISHLY CLEVER!

HARBOR POLICE

"BUT THEN, AN EVEN MORE ASTOUNDING SIGHT ARRIVED...*ME!*

MY EYES MUST BE PLAYING TRICKS! A F-FLYING BOY IN A STRANGE COSTUME...! IS HE PART OF THAT GANG!

I'M *SUPERBOY,* FOE OF ALL CRIMINALS-- WATCH.!!

3

327

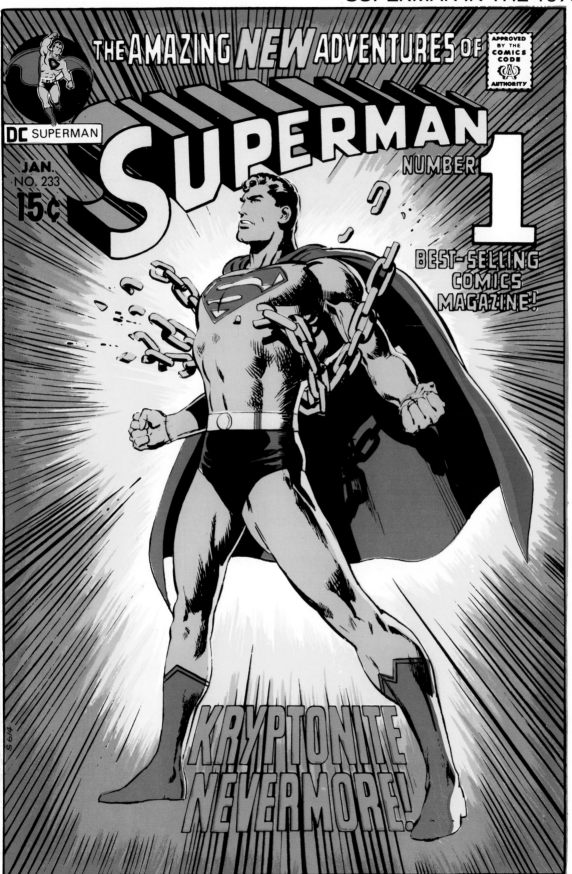

I'M GIVING YOU THIS *ROLLING NEWSROOM*...A SOUPED-UP MOBILE TV STUDIO...TO HELP YOU COVER HOT NEWS STORIES WHENEVER AND WHEREVER THEY BREAK!

WOW! NOW THERE'S A FREAKY SET OF WHEELS!

WCBS GALAXY BROADCASTING SYSTEM

YOU CAN TRANSMIT ANY SCOOP, LIVE, TO OUR ENTIRE TV NETWORK. TELEPHOTO LENSES, REMOTE PICK-UP MICROPHONES, RADAR... THERE'S ENOUGH ADVANCED EQUIP-MENT TO MAKE YOU A *SUPER-REPORTER!*

NATURALLY!

AFTER EDGE LEAVES...

ME, A *TV REPORTER!* I'LL GET AROUND EASIER NOW, BUT I'LL STILL MISS THE *PLANET!*

...I'LL MISS THE *THUNDER* OF THOSE PRESSES...

...THE *SMELL* OF PRINTERS' INK!

BUT TIMES CHANGE...AND EVEN *SUPERMAN* HAS TO CHANGE ALONG WITH THEM!

WHAT I NEED IS A *BIG STORY* TO GET ME OFF THE LAUNCHING PAD!

TOMORROW SEASIDE FOLK ROCK FESTIVAL
STARS OF THE WORLD OF ROCK
THE DING-A-LINGS
THE SODA POPS
PORKY and the HAMLETS
THE ASTRONAUTS

HEY, *THERE'S* AN ANGLE! THOSE ROCK FESTIVALS ARE THE BIG THING NOW! A LIVE TELECAST OF THIS EVENT WOULD BE TERRIFIC FOR A STARTER!

GALA

AND SO, NEXT DAY AT THE FESTIVAL SITE...

YES, FOLKS, WOODSTOCK SET THE PACE! OUR NATION'S YOUTH IS FLOCKING TO ROCK FESTIVALS LIKE *THIS* ONE AT *SEASIDE!* JEEPS... JALOPIES, THEY'RE USING *EVERYTHING* BUT POGO STICKS TO GET HERE!

AND THIS IS *CY HORKIN*, PRODUCER OF ROCK FESTS ACROSS THE COUNTRY. CY WAS A SCIENCE PROFESSOR AT CENTRAL UNIVERSITY UNTIL HE LEFT THREE YEARS AGO--

--BECAUSE OF A FACULTY DISPUTE!

ROCK MUSIC IS MY BAG NOW! IT BRINGS KIDS TOGETHER, TURNS THEM ON! DIG ALL THOSE BEAUTIFUL FANS WHO TRAVELED *THOUSANDS OF MILES* TO MAKE THIS SCENE!

YOU MUST BE PROUD, CY!

BY THE WAY, KENT, YOU *CAN'T* BROADCAST THE MUSIC! I SOLD THE MUSIC RIGHTS TO A RECORD COMPANY!

OKAY, I'LL JUST TELE-CAST THE PICTURES AND MY COMMENTARY FROM *INSIDE* MY SOUND-PROOF TRUCK!

SOON, THE BASH IS GOING FULL BLAST...

PIN-UP BABY, YOU BLOW MY MIND!

PIN-UP BABY, GONNA LEAVE YOU BEHIND!

4

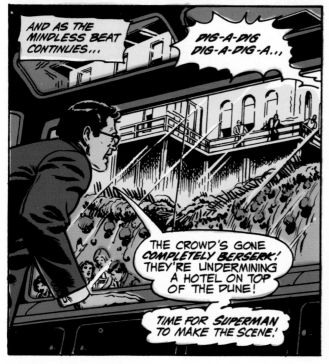

WOW! SUPERMAN AIRLIFTED OUR HOTEL JUST IN TIME!

NOT A BAD *SUPER-FEAT,* IF I DO SAY SO MYSELF... AND THE TV AUDIENCE IS FOLLOWING MY ACTION ON THE AUTOMATED CAMERA!

BUT HOW DO I TURN OFF THOSE *KOOKS* BELOW?

DIG-A-DIG-A-DIG-A...

ABRUPTLY, AS THE MUSIC ENDS...

HUH? WHAT *HAPPENED?* WHY WERE WE DIGGING HERE?

THERE WAS SOMETHING ABOUT THAT *MUSIC...*

MAN, I COULD HAVE DUG A HOLE TO *CHINA!*

MEANWHILE, AFTER *SUPERMAN* RETURNS AND SWITCHES TO CLARK...

WHAT CAUSED THE WEIRD EFFECT OF THAT MUSIC ON YOUR AUDIENCE, CY? IT WOULD'VE BEEN A DISASTER IF *SUPERMAN* HADN'T SHOWN UP!

GUESS THAT TUNE CAME ON TOO STRONG! CALL IT *ROCK POWER!* HA-HA!

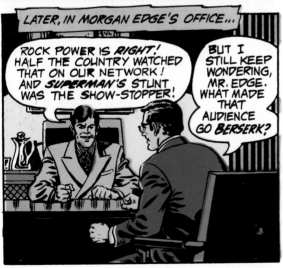

LATER, IN MORGAN EDGE'S OFFICE...

ROCK POWER IS *RIGHT!* HALF THE COUNTRY WATCHED THAT ON OUR NETWORK! AND *SUPERMAN'S* STUNT WAS THE SHOW-STOPPER!

BUT I STILL KEEP WONDERING, MR. EDGE. WHAT MADE THAT AUDIENCE GO *BERSERK?*

FORGET IT, KENT! STAY WITH THOSE ROCK FESTIVALS ON YOUR NEWSCASTS! THEY'RE *SWEEPING* THE COUNTRY BY *STORM!*

WHATEVER YOU SAY... HORKIN IS PUTTING ON ANOTHER JAMBOREE AT *STONE MOUNTAIN* NEXT WEEK! I'LL COVER IT!

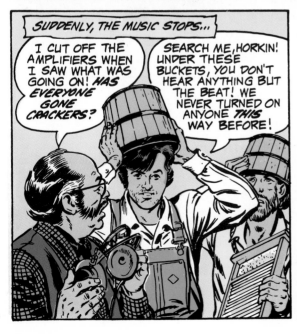

339

LATER, AFTER *SUPERMAN* RESUMES HIS ROLE OF CLARK...

THAT'S *TWICE* I'VE SEEN YOUR AUDIENCE FLIP THAT WAY, CY! HOW DO YOU EXPLAIN IT?

BECAUSE THAT *ROCK BEAT* HITS THEM WHERE THEY *LIVE*, KENT! MAYBE THAT'S WHY MY FESTS ARE SO POPULAR!

HORKIN COULD BE RIGHT, FOLKS! FANS FLOCK TO HIS FESTIVALS BECAUSE THE MUSIC TURNS THEM ON!

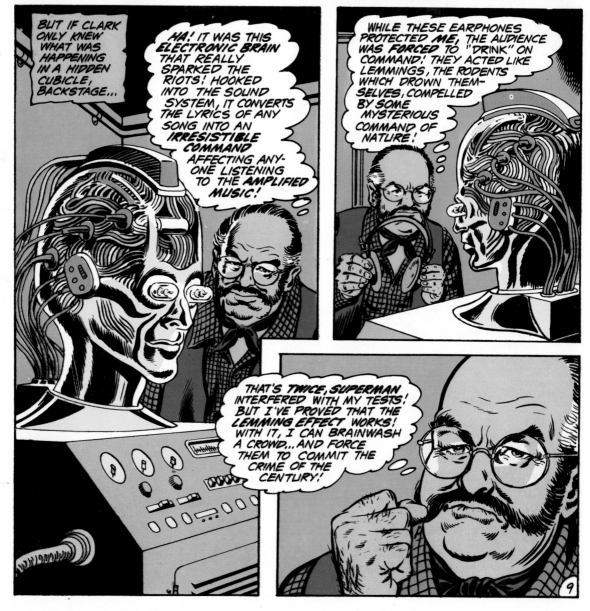

BUT IF CLARK ONLY KNEW WHAT WAS HAPPENING IN A HIDDEN CUBICLE, BACKSTAGE...

HA! IT WAS THIS *ELECTRONIC BRAIN* THAT REALLY SPARKED THE *RIOTS!* HOOKED INTO THE SOUND SYSTEM, IT CONVERTS THE LYRICS OF ANY SONG INTO AN *IRRESISTIBLE COMMAND* AFFECTING ANY-ONE LISTENING TO THE *AMPLIFIED* MUSIC!

WHILE THESE EARPHONES PROTECTED *ME*, THE AUDIENCE WAS *FORCED* TO "DRINK" ON COMMAND! THEY ACTED LIKE LEMMINGS, THE RODENTS WHICH DROWN THEM-SELVES, COMPELLED BY SOME *MYSTERIOUS* COMMAND OF NATURE!

THAT'S *TWICE, SUPERMAN* INTERFERED WITH MY TESTS! BUT I'VE PROVED THAT THE *LEMMING EFFECT* WORKS! WITH IT, I CAN BRAINWASH A CROWD...AND FORCE THEM TO COMMIT THE *CRIME OF THE CENTURY!*

DAYS LATER, IN HIS ARCTIC FORTRESS...

CY HORKIN WOULDN'T LET CLARK BROADCAST THE MUSIC...BUT I TAPED SOME OF IT SECRETLY FOR ANALYSIS!

HM! MY SONIC ANALYZERS GIVE NO CLUE TO THE AUDIENCE'S WEIRD REACTION!

DRINK, BABY! DRINK IT DOWN!

SUDDENLY...

OH, NO! THAT TAPE RECORDER MUST HAVE BEEN DEFECTIVE! IT SHORT-CIRCUITED, AND RUINED THE TAPE!

FF FZZZZ AAAPP

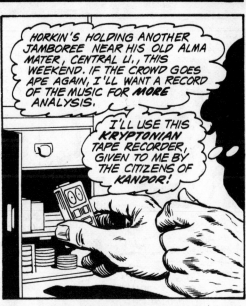

HORKIN'S HOLDING ANOTHER JAMBOREE NEAR HIS OLD ALMA MATER, CENTRAL U., THIS WEEKEND. IF THE CROWD GOES APE AGAIN, I'LL WANT A RECORD OF THE MUSIC FOR MORE ANALYSIS.

I'LL USE THIS KRYPTONIAN TAPE RECORDER, GIVEN TO ME BY THE CITIZENS OF KANDOR!

KANDOR... ONCE A MIGHTY CITY OF MY NATIVE PLANET KRYPTON... BEFORE IT WAS DESTROYED! KANDOR WAS SHRUNKEN INTO THAT BOTTLE BY THE EVIL COMPUTER, BRAINIAC!

SOME DAY, I'LL FIND A WAY TO ENLARGE THE CITY AND MY KINSMEN TO NORMAL SIZE!

BUT, AS EARTH'S GUARDIAN, I HAVE OTHER PROBLEMS RIGHT NOW... LIKE SOLVING THE PUZZLE OF THOSE MOBS WHO GO HAYWIRE AT HORKIN'S PERFORMANCES!

10

343

SUPERMAN... SMASHING THOSE BUILDINGS LIKE A *HUMAN STEAMROLLER!* MY BRAIN-CONTROL CIRCUITS ARE *MORE POWERFUL* THAN I DREAMED!

HEY! WHAT'S HAPPENING?

HE'S TURNED *BACK!* HEADING *THIS* WAY! AND THOSE IDIOTS ARE FOLLOWING HIM LIKE THE PIED PIPER!

THEN, LIKE A HURRICANE OF HAVOC...

♪♩♫ BREAK IT UP! ♬ TEAR IT DOWN! ♫ WIPE IT OUT! ♩♪♩

CRRAAASH

KAPOWWW

KRRUMMP

NO! NOT THE BRAIN! THE *LEMMING EFFECT* ISN'T SUPPOSED TO WORK THIS WAY!

AND AS THE CIRCUITS ARE SEVERED...

SUPERMAN! WHAT HAPPENED? WHAT MADE US START THAT SMASHING SPREE... AND WHY DID *YOU* LEAD US?

THIS ELECTRONIC BRAIN-CONTROL IS THE ANSWER! HORKIN, HERE, WILL EXPLAIN... *OR ELSE!*

AFTER HORKIN REVEALS HIS *DIABOLICAL* SCHEME...

UNDER THE *LEMMING EFFECT*, YOU'D HAVE DESTROYED THE UNIVERSITY I *HATED* -- IF THIS SUPER-FINK HADN'T INTERFERED!

WE GET IT, *SUPERMAN!* IT'S ALL STARTING TO ADD UP!

13

345

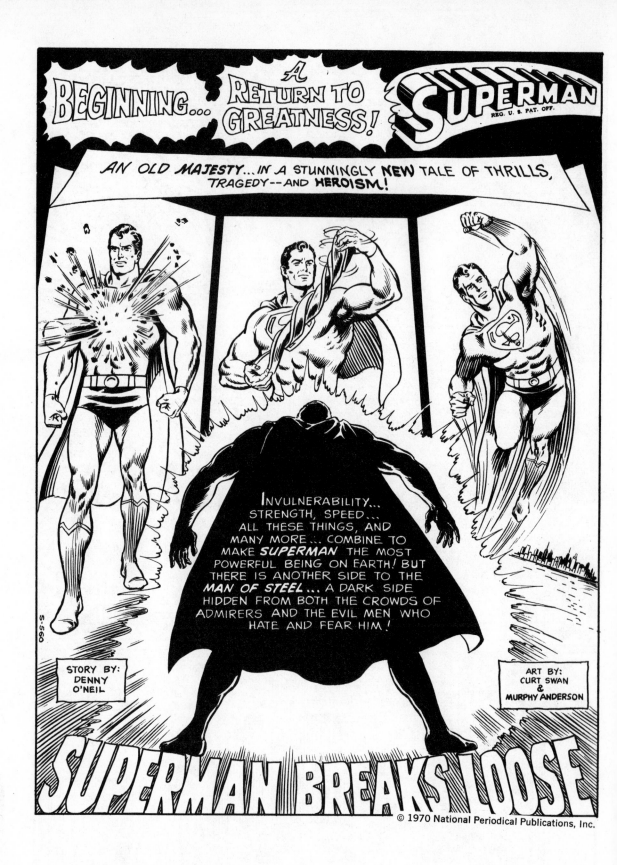

AT AN ISOLATED PROVING GROUND, SOMEWHERE IN THE WESTERN UNITED STATES...

I'M RUNNING A *RISK* BEING HERE! IF ANYTHING GOES WRONG WITH PROFESSOR BOLDEN'S EXPERIMENT...

...IT COULD BE *FATAL* TO ME! STILL, THE WORK'S *IMPORTANT!*

THE PROFESSOR'S *KRYPTONITE-ENGINE* COULD SUPPLY CHEAP ELECTRICITY FOR VIRTUALLY *EVERY* UNDERDEVELOPED AREA--

LOOKS LIKE THE PROF'S READY TO BEGIN!

A SWITCH IS THROWN... POWER PULSES ALONG CABLES TO ACTIVATE A BIZARRE DEVICE...

OFF ⟶ FULL

SUDDENLY...

SOUND THE *EMERGENCY ALARM*--! THE ENGINE'S OUT OF *CONTROL!*

JUST AS BOLDEN FEARED... HE COULDN'T *CONTROL* THE *KRYPTONITE* CHAIN REACTION!

I *PREPARED* FOR A PROBLEM LIKE THIS--

--BY MAKING A LEAD-COATED *SHIELD* TO FIT OVER THE ENERGY UNIT!

HOPE I CAN GET THERE IN *TIME!*

2

K-RASSH!

GOT TO KEEP THE SHIELD IN FRONT OF MY BODY!

ONE DOSE OF THAT RADIATION AND I'M *COOKED* --LITERALLY!

SSSS

HOWEVER, AS THE *MAN OF STEEL* APPROACHES THE SEETHING, GLOWING PILE...

KA-VLOCMP

THE BLAST SNATCHED THE SHIELD FROM MY GRASP... I TOOK A FACE FULL OF *K*--

...COULD BE *FATAL*--

LIKE A STONE, *SUPERMAN* DROPS TO THE SAND, AND LIES STILL...

SEVERAL MINUTES LATER...

DOCTOR... YOU'VE GOT TO DO SOMETHING FOR HIM!

SURE... BUT *WHAT?* I HAVE NO *IDEA* HOW THE EXPLOSION AFFECTED HIS BODY...

N-NOT SERIOUSLY, IT SEEMS...

3

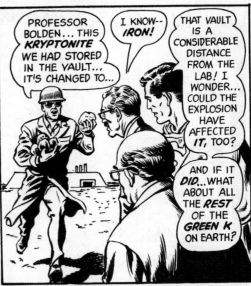

351

THE ROCKET WILL PROCEED STRAIGHT UP THROUGH THE STRATOSPHERE AND DESCEND IMMEDIATELY! EXPERTS SAY THE CROSS-COUNTRY TRIP WILL TAKE LESS THAN TEN MINUTES...

HUH-UH! MY *X-RAY VISION* REVEALS SOMEONE HIDING BEHIND THAT BLOCKHOUSE-- A SUSPICIOUS LOOKING GUY WITH A *WALKIE-TALKIE!*

WE'LL BE BACK AFTER THESE IMPORTANT MESSAGES!

THOSE COMMERCIALS WILL TAKE ABOUT *THREE MINUTES,* COUNTING STATION-BREAKS...

-- WHICH *MAY* BE ENOUGH TIME FOR ME TO LEARN WHAT'S HAPPENING...

...AS *SUPERMAN!*

I NEVER IMAGINED I'D BE *GRATEFUL* FOR COMMERCIALS...!

THEN, A FEW DOZEN YARDS AWAY...

YOU GOT HER, BOSS! THAT OVERGROWN ROMAN CANDLE IS SET TO LIFT OFF...

SOUNDS LIKE AN INTERESTING CONVERSATION--

7

SUPERMAN!?

HOW ABOUT LETTING *ME* IN ON IT?

SURE, *SUPEY*... WE'RE PLANNIN' TO HEIST THE ROCKET--

--IT AIN'T CARRYIN' NO *MONEY*, BUT WE FIGURE SOME FOREIGN GOVERNMENTS'LL PAY PLENTY FOR THE GADGET *ITSELF*, SO'S THEY CAN BUILD THEIR OWN!

I DON'T MIND TELLIN' YA... 'CAUSE YA AIN'T GONNA *LIVE* LONG ENOUGH TO DO ANYTHING ABOUT IT!

WHAT I GOT HERE IS THE STUFF AS WILL *ZAP* YA--*PERMANENT!*

--WHAT YA CALL *KRYPTONITE!*

EITHER YOU HAVEN'T SEEN A *PAPER*-- OR YOU CAN'T *READ!*

LOOKS *GOOD!* MIND IF I TRY SOME?

MMMM... NOT BAD! A TRIFLE *STALE*...

...AND IT COULD USE A BIT OF *SALT*...

...BUT ALL IN ALL, A NICE LITTLE SNACK!

AND BY THE WAY...

...YOU'RE UNDER ARREST!

TAPP!

THAT LOVE-TAP WILL KEEP HIM ON ICE...

I'LL ALERT THE POLICE TO THIS LOCATION AFTER I FINISH MY REPORTING STINT.

THE THREE MINUTES ARE ALMOST *UP!* I'LL HAVE TO GET A MOVE ON!

EXACTLY FOUR SECONDS LATER...

CLARK KENT FOR *WGBS-TV* AGAIN! THE MAIL ROCKET IS IN FINAL COUNTDOWN...

LIFT-OFF!

WE TAKE YOU NOW TO *LOS ANGELES* WHERE - - -

THE SMOKE AND DUST RAISED BY THE ROCKET WILL HIDE ME FROM THE ONLOOKERS...

SO I CAN SWITCH CLOTHES WITHOUT DUCKING INTO A *PHONE BOOTH* OR SOMETHING!

357

THE MAIL-ROCKET IS SAFE AND SOUND! THE MEN ON THE GROUND PROBABLY DON'T REALIZE IT WAS EVER IN *DANGER!*

STILL BOTHERS ME ABOUT THAT TEMPORARY LOSS OF *HEAT VISION...*

IT'S HARD TO WORRY, THOUGH...NOT WHEN I KNOW I'M SAFE FROM *GREEN K!*

THERE'S THE OUTLAW PLANE BELOW...EXACTLY WHERE I *AIMED* IT!

NEXT STOP, THE *METROPOLIS AIRFIELD...* AND THEN *JAIL!*

CURIOUS COINCIDENCE... I'M NOW DIRECTLY OVER THE SPOT WHERE I LANDED YESTERDAY, AFTER THE PROF'S GIMMICK EXPLODED!

HUH--? SUDDENLY FEEL *...DIZZY!--* EXHAUSTED!

... LIKE THE STRENGTH IS BEING... *DRAWN* FROM MY LIMBS!

...A COMPLETELY *DIFFERENT* SORT OF WEAKNESS... EVEN *WORSE* THAN THE EFFECTS OF *KRYPTONITE!*

359

EPILOGUE

Even as Clark ponders new complications, a blazing sun beats upon the desert...upon a figure in the sand...

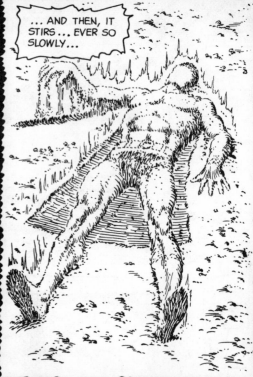

...and then, it stirs...ever so slowly...

It is a *THING* created from soil and rock and a burst of raw energy...cast in the mold of *SUPERMAN*...

15

...and it *LIVES!* Like some nightmare creature, it plods toward the distant mountains...

...and toward the villages and towns and cities beyond...

...moving slowly, relentlessly to a terrible destiny...

END

NEXT ISSUE!-- EXPLOSIVE ACTION AS SUPERMAN SHOWS "HOW TO TAME A WILD VOLCANO!"

SUDDENLY...

SOME INCREDIBLE FORCE...LIFTING ME...SPINNING ME LIKE A FEATHER IN A WHIRLWIND...

I'M BLACKING OUT!

AS *SUPERMAN* COMES TO...

NO, SUPERMAN! THIS IS NOT A HOAX...NOT AN ILLUSION...NOT A MASQUERADE! THESE ARE THE *GENUINE* HEROES OF HISTORY, *IN THE FLESH!* BUT EVERYONE KNOWS THEY DIED LONG AGO, SO HOW CAN YOU MEET THEM *FACE TO FACE?* THERE'S ONLY *ONE* ANSWER...

"SUPERMAN, YOU'RE DEAD...DE

365

IN THE NEXT MOMENT...

THE WALL WEAKENED! *I'M BREAKING THROUGH!*

ULP! IT WAS A MISTAKE TO BRING *SUPERMAN* OUT OF THE PAST! HIS SUPER-HUMAN POWERS ARE *IMPOSSIBLE* TO CONTROL!

ALL RIGHT, FRIEND, WHAT'S THE PITCH?

WELCOME TO THE *24TH* CENTURY HISTORICAL FOUNDATION! OUR CHRONO-SELECTOR BROUGHT YOU HERE WITH THE OTHER GREAT HEROES BECAUSE YOU WERE THE *LAST* MIGHTY *SUPERMAN* OF YOUR ERA!

THE *LAST* SUPERMAN?? IN MY ERA, I AM THE *ONE* AND ONLY MAN OF STEEL!

THE MEMORY BLACKOUT EFFECT! POOR FELLOW!...SOME OF YOUR MEMORY CELLS WERE ERASED!

PUT ON A CEREBRO-HELMET! A HISTORY TAPE RECORDS THE TRAGIC EVENTS IN YOUR PAST WHICH YOUR BRAIN WAS PRO-GRAMMED TO *FORGET!*

THIS I'VE GOT TO SEE!

"BACK IN THE MIDDLE OF THE 20TH CENTURY, AN INFANT NAMED KAL-EL WAS ROCKETED TO EARTH JUST AS HIS NATIVE PLANET, KRYPTON, EXPLODED!"

I'LL NEVER FORGET *THAT* GHASTLY DAY!

366

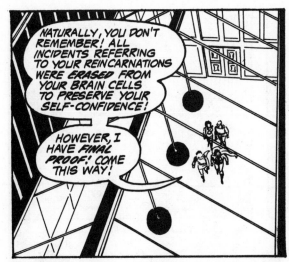

NATURALLY, YOU DON'T REMEMBER! ALL INCIDENTS REFERRING TO YOUR REINCARNATIONS WERE ERASED FROM YOUR BRAIN CELLS TO PRESERVE YOUR SELF-CONFIDENCE!

HOWEVER, I HAVE FINAL PROOF! COME THIS WAY!

OUR HISTORICAL FOUNDATION WAS BUILT ON THE SITE OF THE OLD RESEARCH INSTITUTE WHICH RECONSTRUCTED YOUR BODY TWICE! THIS CRYPT WAS YOUR FINAL RESTING PLACE!

AND IN THE MACABRE DEPTHS OF THE MAUSOLEUM....

THESE ARE THE REMAINS OF SUPERMAN I!

SUPERMAN I

SUPERMAN II

AND IN THIS JAR, SUPERMAN II IS PRESERVED FOREVER!

AND NOW, THE PROOF YOU'VE BEEN ASKING FOR! DO YOU WANT TO SEE IT?

SUPERMAN III

NO! NO! NO!... I-I BELIEVE YOU! HOW COULD I BEAR TO LOOK AT MY OWN DEAD BODY!?

BUT YOU DIED A SUPER-HERO! SEE, CENTURIES AFTERWARD, WE HONOR YOUR MEMORY WITH THIS MEDAL-- GRANTED ONLY FOR THE GREATEST COURAGE!

9

369

WEAR IT! YOU EARNED IT A THOUSAND TIMES OVER ON YOUR *FINAL MISSION!*

HOW IRONIC! ACCEPTING A POSTHUMOUS REWARD... FOR THE FEAT WHICH KILLED ME!

AS THEY LEAVE THE CRYPT, SUDDENLY...

BLEEP! BLEEP!

THAT SIGNAL...IT'S A VISI-CAST NEWS BULLETIN!

ATTENTION ALL RESCUE SERVICES! THIS IS AN *EMERGENCY ALERT!*

AN ARCHAEOLOGICAL EXPEDITION SEEKING A LOST CIVILIZATION UNDER THE GREENLAND ICE-CAP HAS BEEN BURIED IN AN ICE-QUAKE! FIFTY MEN ARE TRAPPED!

THEY DON'T KNOW IT, BUT THEY'RE PAGING *SUPERMAN!*

DON'T WORRY! I'LL SAVE THEM!... UP...UP AND AWAY!

SUPERMAN'S LEGENDARY CALL TO ACTION! IT HASN'T BEEN HEARD IN *CENTURIES!*

SPLIT-SECONDS LATER, A MILE BENEATH THE ICE-CAP...

NO...IT'S A SUPER-BEING... BORING THROUGH THE ICE TO RESCUE US...A *SUPERMAN!*

WH-WHAT IS IT... ANOTHER QUAKE?

BUT *SUPERMAN* DIED CENTURIES AGO!

WHAMMMO

KRRRUNNNCHH

KAPPOWWW

10

SOON, BACK AT THE *HISTORICAL FOUNDATION*...

HE NOT ONLY *RESCUED* THE EXPEDITION, BUT *UNCOVERED* THE *LOST CIVILIZATION!*

NOW WE *KNOW* WHAT IT MEANS TO HAVE A *SUPERMAN* AS EARTH'S *GUARDIAN!*

PRESENTLY...

SUPERMAN... HOW CAN WE *THANK* YOU?

BY ANSWERING *ONE* QUESTION!... FIRST TELL ME IF I HAVE IT FIGURED *RIGHT!*

LINCOLN IS HEADED FOR THE THEATER WHERE HE'LL BE *ASSASSINATED!* CUSTER IS BOUND FOR HIS FAMOUS *"LAST STAND"*! AND WASHINGTON IS ABOUT TO DIE OF *PNEUMONIA!*

CORRECT! WE SELECTED EACH HERO AT THE *END* OF HIS *CAREER!*

THEN WHAT ABOUT *ME?* TELL ME... *HOW* AM I SUPPOSED TO *DIE?*

IF YOU MUST KNOW... ACCORDING TO HISTORY, YOU WILL PERISH WHEN YOU SAVE THE EARTH FROM A *CATASTROPHIC EXPLOSION* CAUSED BY A NEW FORM OF *ENERGY!*

SUDDENLY...

THE *ALARM!* TIME'S *UP!* YOU MUST GO BACK INTO THE *FORCE-FIELD!* YOU AND THE OTHERS MUST BE RETURNED INTO THE *PAST!*

BEEP BEEP BEEP

NO! WHY SHOULD I GO BACK *TO DIE?* I'M STAYING *HERE!*

11

371

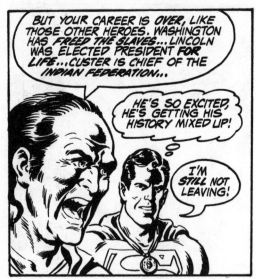

BUT YOUR CAREER IS *OVER*, LIKE THOSE OTHER HEROES. WASHINGTON HAS *FREED THE SLAVES*... LINCOLN WAS ELECTED PRESIDENT *FOR LIFE*... CUSTER IS CHIEF OF THE *INDIAN FEDERATION*...

HE'S SO EXCITED, HE'S GETTING HIS HISTORY MIXED UP!

I'M *STILL NOT* LEAVING!

LISTEN!... THE SECOND AND *FINAL* WARNING!

HOW WOOOO OOOWWWW OO EEEEE EEEEE

BY THE NATURAL LAWS OF TIME AND SPACE, YOU *MUST* RETURN TO YOUR PLACE IN THE PAST... *OR OUR UNIVERSE WILL BE DESTROYED!*

WHILE YOU AND THE OTHERS ARE HERE, THE TIME-FLOW HAS STOPPED COMPLETELY IN YOUR ERA! BACK THERE, HISTORY CAN'T GO ON WITHOUT YOU! IT'S DAMMED UP LIKE A RAGING RIVER!

THE FEEDBACK OF SPATIO-TEMPORAL FORCES IS BUILDING UP TO *CATASTROPHE!* IF THE PAST HAS CEASED, THERE CAN BE NO PRESENT! ALREADY OUR WORLD'S BEGINNING TO *DISSOLVE INTO PURE ENERGY!*

GO BACK... OR *BILLIONS* WILL DIE!

THE BLOOD OF COUNTLESS PEOPLE WOULD BE ON MY HANDS! I MUST RETURN... *THOUGH IT MEANS MY LIFE!*

HE'S LEAVING... THERE'S STILL TIME TO ACTIVATE THE RETRO-CIRCUIT!

12

AS SUPERMAN SMASHES THROUGH THE FORCE-FIELD....

SUPERMAN!... STRANGE FORCES ARE CARRYING US AWAY! WHAT'S HAPPENINNNNNG?

HOW CAN I TELL THEM? THOSE POOR DEVILS ARE HEADED BACK TO THE PAST.... TO DIE!

AND SO AM I!

THEN, HURTLING THROUGH THE VORTEX OF TIME....

RRROOOAAARR

≡GASP!≡ I'M BACK IN MY OWN ERA....IN THE MIDST OF MY LAST MISSION... IT'S AS IF TIME STOOD STILL BACK HERE WHILE I WAS IN THE FUTURE!

RRRROOOOAAARRR

I REMEMBER WHAT I WAS TO DO! THE NEW FORM OF ENERGY FROM THIS SOLAR FURNACE IS STARTING A CHAIN REACTION WHICH MIGHT IGNITE EARTH'S ATMOSPHERE! THERE'S ONLY ONE WAY TO STOP IT!

I'LL CARRY THIS SOLAR SUPER-TORCH INTO DEEP SPACE.... WHERE IT WILL BE HARMLESS! THIS WEIRD ENERGY WILL PROBABLY DESTROY MY ARTIFICIAL, UNSTABLE PROTOPLASM!

THIS IS THE MISSION THAT'S SUPPOSED TO KILL ME!

13

BUT ON HIS RETURN TO EARTH...

I DON'T UNDERSTAND! I'M STILL ALIVE! BUT THIS MISSION WAS *SUPPOSED* TO MEAN MY DEATH! THE RECORDS OF THE 24TH CENTURY *PROVED* IT! I EVEN SAW MY OWN *TOMB!*

MY DEATH MADE ME A HERO IN THE FUTURE. THIS MEDALLION *PROVES* IT!

HOLD IT! MY MICROSCOPIC VISION INDICATES THERE'S *NO METAL LIKE THIS ON EARTH!*

AND THAT TWISTED HISTORY THEY WERE SPOUTING... ABOUT WASHINGTON FREEING THE SLAVES... AND LINCOLN ELECTED PRESIDENT FOR LIFE...

THERE'S ONLY *ONE WAY* IT ADDS UP!

YES, I WAS IN THE FUTURE-- THE FUTURE OF A *PARALLEL WORLD...* A WORLD LIKE OUR OWN, BUT IN *ANOTHER DIMENSION.'*

"*IT'S LIKE AN IMAGE OF OUR UNIVERSE, SEEN IN A WARPED MIRROR. EACH HERO OF OUR WORLD HAS A DUPLICATE IN THE PARALLEL EXISTENCE. BUT THEIR LIVES AND FATES DIFFER.'*"

14

"THAT EXPERIMENTAL CHRONO-SELECTOR WARPED THE FORCES OF TIME AND SPACE SO BADLY, IT TORE AN OPENING IN *OUR* WORLD AND ACCIDENTALLY PULLED ME INTO *THEIR* FUTURE INSTEAD OF THEIR SUPERMAN III!"

LATER, AS *SUPERMAN* SWITCHES TO CLARK...

WASHINGTON... AND THE OTHERS I MET... WERE THEY FROM *OUR* HISTORY, OR FROM THE HISTORY OF THAT *TWIN EARTH?* I'LL *NEVER* KNOW!

WHATEVER THE ANSWER, IT'S *GREAT* TO BE ALIVE AND WELL.... BACK IN...

...MY OWN ERA.... IN MY OWN WORLD!

BUT SOMEWHERE, IN ANOTHER CORNER OF TIME AND SPACE, MY DOUBLE, SUPERMAN III, LIES DEAD-- A HERO ENSHRINED FOREVER!

The End

375

BUT, DARLING, *SUPERMAN* TAUGHT *SUPERGIRL* EVERYTHING SHE KNOWS. FACE IT, MEN ARE NATURALLY *SUPERIOR!*

HOW DID I EVER FALL IN LOVE WITH SUCH AN EGOTISTIC BLOWHARD? I SUPPOSE *YOU'RE* SUPERIOR, TOO... WELL, HERE'S A CHALLENGE!

...BEFORE WE GRADUATE, WE MUST PASS OUR FINAL EXAMS BY PERFORMING SOME SUPERIOR ACHIEVEMENT IN OUR FIELDS. I BET *I* GET A *HIGHER MARK* THAN *YOU* IN THE FINALS!

IT'S A DEAL! BUT YOU HAVEN'T GOT A CHANCE!

ANNUAL SUPER-SCHOLARSHIP TROPHY

AFTER ALL, EVEN AS A STUDENT ELECTRONICON, I EARNED THESE AWARDS FOR MY ELECTRONIC INVENTIONS!

MERE PUSHBUTTON GADGETS! HOW ABOUT THIS UNDERGRADUATE ARCHAEOLOGY AWARD I WON FOR DECIPH-ERING A PREHISTORIC MANUSCRIPT?

ARCHAEOLOGY! WHAT USE IS *THAT* IN A BOTTLED CITY? YLLURA SHOULD *FORGET* HER CAREER AND MARRY ARVOR! HE'S A *GENIUS!*

TYPICAL MASCULINE ARROGANCE! SHE'LL OUTCLASS HIM IN THE FINALS AND WIN THE TROPHY! WAIT AND SEE!

A FEW DAYS LATER...

...AND SO, STUDENTS, YOUR FINAL EXAM WILL BE TO PERFORM AN ORIGINAL EXPLORATION INTO KANDOR'S PAST...GOOD LUCK!

I HAVE MY PROJECT ALL PICKED OUT. IT CAN'T MISS!

MEANWHILE, IN THE HEART OF THE CITY...

IS IT A BIRD?

IS IT AN AIRCRAFT?

IT *CAN'T* BE *SUPERMAN!* HE HAS NO POWERS IN KANDOR!

IT'S *ARVOR!*... TAKING HIS FINAL EXAM! HE'S DEMONSTRATING HIS LATEST INVENTION!

BUT ANTI-GRAVITY FLIGHT IS NOTHING NEW HERE IN KANDOR!

HA-HA! THEY DON'T REALIZE I'M TESTING AN ELECTRONIC *INFRA-SCOPE,* WHICH GIVES ME MENTAL VISION, ALLOWING ME TO FLY BLINDFOLDED PAST UNSEEN OBJECTS LIKE THE BATS IN EARTH'S CAVERNS!

MY *INFRA-SCOPE* IS A *SUCCESS!* I CAN SEE THE WHOLE COUNTRYSIDE JUST AS IF I HAD THE *X-RAY VISION* OF MY HERO, *SUPERMAN!*

BUT, SUDDENLY, BEYOND THE OUTSKIRTS OF THE CITY...

BZZZT
BZZZT
BZZZT
BZZZT

OH, NO! THE POWER-PACK ON MY ANTI-GRAV BELT IS *DEFECTIVE!* I'M FALLING... PLUNGING INTO THAT LAKE BELOW!

4

THEN, AS IF EMERGING FROM SOME EERIE, SATANIC WORLD...

YYY...IIEEEE... IIIIEEEEEE!

AT THAT MOMENT, NOT FAR AWAY...

YYY...IIIEEEEEE!

SOMEONE SCREAMING IN TERROR-- COMING FROM *THAT* TUNNEL OPENING!

EEEEEEEEEEEE

SOUNDS LIKE A GIRL... IN MORTAL FEAR! BUT *HOW* DO I *FIND* HER IN THIS MAZE OF PASSAGES?

AT LAST, AFTER FOLLOWING THE SCREAMS...

YLLURA!

ARVOR... *RUN!* SAVE YOURSELF BEFORE THIS MONSTER KILLS US *BOTH!*

SEIZING A STONE, ARVOR HURLS IT, BUT...

KRUNNCCHH

I WAS *AIMING* AT THAT CARVED STONE IMAGE... WITH THE GLOWING EYES!

IT'S *HOPELESS!* THE ROCK WENT RIGHT *THROUGH* THAT DEMON!

6

THAT HORRIBLE THING--IT'S *VANISHING!*

NATURALLY! IT WAS BEING PROJECTED BY AN INGENIOUS OPTICAL SYSTEM PLANTED BEHIND THE EYES OF THAT CARVING WHICH I SMASHED!

THESE TUNNELS WERE *SACRED* TO THE ANCIENT DEMON-WORSHIPPING *TORGS.* THEY USED THOSE GHASTLY BOOBY TRAPS TO FRIGHTEN INTRUDERS TO DEATH! BUT *YOU* SAVED ME!

I FOUND YOU BY ACCIDENT! YOU SEE--

BUT BEFORE ARVOR CAN EXPLAIN HIS PRESENCE...

THE *TUNNEL*... IT'S GROWING *DARK!* THAT WEIRD LUMINOUS LIGHT IS *FADING!*

I THINK I KNOW WHY! I MUST HAVE SHORT-CIRCUITED SOME ENERGY SUPPLY WHEN I SMASHED THAT GARGOYLE!

AND AS THE LAST RAYS OF LIGHT VANISH...

ARVOR, WE'RE TRAPPED... LOST IN THIS AWFUL DARKNESS!

MY POOR DARLING! I SAVED YOU FROM ONE HIDEOUS FATE... ONLY TO HAVE YOU SUFFER ANOTHER!

DON'T BLAME *YOURSELF,* ARVOR. IF WE *MUST* DIE HERE...AT LEAST WE'LL BE WITH EACH OTHER... *TO THE END!*

SUDDENLY, IN THE MIDST OF THE EMBRACE...

ARVOR! I JUST REMEMBERED! THE *INFRA-SCOPE,* WHICH YOU TOLD ME ABOUT--IT GIVES YOU MENTAL VISION! IT COULD GUIDE US OUT OF HERE!

WHY DIDN'T *I* THINK OF THAT?

SHORTLY...

ARVOR, ARE YOU SURE WE'RE NOT WANDERING IN CIRCLES?

NOT A CHANCE! MY MIND SEES THE TUNNEL AS IF IT WERE IN BROAD DAYLIGHT!

AT LAST!

WE MADE IT! SUPERMAN'S X-RAY VISION COULDN'T HAVE DONE BETTER!

YOU MEAN SUPERGIRL, DON'T YOU, DARLING?

SUPERGIRL OR SUPERMAN... IT DOESN'T MATTER! AFTER ALL, THEY WORK BEST TOGETHER!

AND SO DO WE!

DAYS LATER, AT KANDOR UNIVERSITY--

SUPERMAN AND SUPERGIRL! THEY USED THEIR SHRINKING RAY TO REDUCE THEMSELVES TEMPORARILY SO THEY COULD ATTEND OUR GRADUATION!

AND THEY HAVE TO USE PARACHUTES TO DROP INTO OUR WORLD BECAUSE THEY HAVE NO POWERS, HERE IN KANDOR!

LATER, AT THE CEREMONY...

WE THEREFORE PRESENT THIS SUPER-TROPHY TO YLLURA AND ARVOR ...THEY PROVED THAT THE FINEST SCIENTIFIC ACHIEVEMENTS ARE NOT DUE TO RIVALRY... BUT TEAMWORK!

The End

BIBLIOGRAPHY

Comic-Book Appearances of Superman

Action Comics
  Vol. #1 (June 1938)
Action Comics—Special Editions for the U.S. Navy
  1944–1945
Adventure Comics (as Superboy)
  Vol. 103 (April 1946); Vol. 345 (June 1966)—solo appearance
  Vol. 346 (July 1966); Vol. 380 (May 1969)—as member of Legion of Super-
    Heroes
  Vol. 381 (June 1969)—guest shots with Supergirl
All Star Comics
  Vol. #7 (Oct.—Nov. 1941)—cameo
  Vol. #36 (Aug.—Sept. 1947—guest star
The Brave and the Bold
  Vol. #28 (March 1960); Vol. #30 (July 1960)
D.C. 100 Page Super Spectacular
  Vol. #6 (1971)
80 Page Giant (as Superboy)
  Vol. #10 (May 1965)
80 Page Giant (as Superman)
  Superman Issues—Vol. #1 (August 1964)
                   Vol. #6 (Jan. 1965)
                   Vol. #11 (June 1965)
  Jimmy Olsen Issues—Vol. #2 (Sept. 1964)
                      Vol. #13 (Aug. 1965)
  Lois Lane Issues—Vol. #3 (Sept. 1964)
                    Vol. #14 (Sept. 1965)
  With Batman and Robin—Vol. #15 (Oct. 1965)
The Forever People (as guest star)
  Vol. #1 (March 1971)
Giant Superboy Annual (as Superboy)
  Vol. #1 (1964)
Giant Superman Annual
  Vol. #1 (1960); Vol. #8 (Winter 1963–1964)
Jerry Lewis Comics (guest star)
  Vol. #105 (April 1968)
Jimmy Olsen
  Vol. #1 (Sept.—Oct. 1954)
Justice League of America
  Vol. #1 (Oct.—Nov. 1960)
Lois Lane
  Vol. #1 (March—April 1958)
More Fun (as Superboy)
  Vol. #101 (Jan.—Feb. 1945); Vol. #107 (Jan.—Feb. 1946)
Mystery in Space
  Vol. #75 (May 1962)

Showcase
   Vol. #9 (July—Aug. 1957)
   Vol. #10 (Sept.—Oct. 1957)
Superboy Comics (as Superboy)
   Vol. #1 (March 1949)
Superman at the Gilbert Hall of Science
   1948
Superman Comics
   Vol. #1 (Summer 1939)
Superman Three-D
   1953
Superman Miniature
   Three issues—1955
Superman Workbook n.d.
World's Fair Comics
   Vol. #1 (1939)
   Vol. #2 (1940)
World's Finest
   Vol. #1 (World's Best) (Summer 1941); Vol. #70 (May—June 1954)—solo
   Vol. #71 (July—Aug. 1954); Vol. #196 (Sept. 1970)—With Batman and
   Robin
   Vol. #198 (Nov. 1970)

Other Media in Which Superman Has Appeared

"Adventures of Superman"
   Serialized radio program
   1940
"Adventures of Superman"
   Television program
   1954
Animated Cartoons for Television: 1960s
Atom Man vs Superman
   Columbia movie serial
   1948
It's a Bird . . . It's a Plane . . . It's Superman
   Broadway musical
   1966
Paramount Animated Movie Cartoons
   1941–1943
Superman
   A novel by George Lowther
   Random House, 1942
Superman
   Columbia movie serial
   1948
Superman and the Mole Men
   A feature film
   1952
Syndicated Newspaper Strip
   1939